Sounds Interesting

How do you pronounce *omega, tortoise* and *sloth*? –
charted and *chartered* sound the same? How do people ₁
names *Charon, Punjab* and *Sexwale*?

In this engaging book, John Wells, a world-renowned phonetician and
phonologist, explores these questions and others. Each chapter consists of
carefully selected entries from Wells's acclaimed phonetics blog, on
which he regularly posted on a range of current and widely researched
topics such as pronunciation, teaching, intonation, spelling and accents.

Based on sound scholarship and full of fascinating facts about the
pronunciation of Welsh, Swedish, Czech, Zulu, Icelandic and other
languages, this book will appeal to scholars and students in phonetics
and phonology, as well as general readers wanting to know more about
language.

Anyone interested in why a poster in Antigua invited cruise ship
visitors to enjoy a game of porker, or what hymns can tell us about
pronunciation, should read this book.

J.C. WELLS is Emeritus Professor of Phonetics at University College
London and a Fellow of the British Academy. His interests centre on
the phonetic and phonological description of languages but also extend to
lexicography and language teaching.

Sounds Interesting
Observations on English
and General Phonetics

J.C. WELLS

Emeritus Professor of Phonetics, University College London

Illustrations by Lhinton Davidson

CAMBRIDGE
UNIVERSITY PRESS

University Printing House, Cambridge CB2 8BS, United Kingdom

Cambridge University Press is part of the University of Cambridge.

It furthers the University's mission by disseminating knowledge in the pursuit of
education, learning and research at the highest international levels of excellence.

www.cambridge.org
Information on this title: www.cambridge.org/9781107427105

First published 2014

Printed in the United Kingdom by Clays, St Ives plc

A catalogue record for this publication is available from the British Library

Library of Congress Cataloguing in Publication data
Wells, J. C. (John Christopher) author.
Sounds interesting : observations on English and general phonetics / J.C. Wells.
    pages   cm
ISBN 978-1-107-07470-5 (Hardback) – ISBN 978-1-107-42710-5 (Paper back)
1.   English language–Phonetics.   2.   English language–Pronunciation.   3.   English language–
Phonology.   I.   Title.
PE1135.W36 2014
414–dc23   2014022387

ISBN 978-1-107-07470-5 Hardback
ISBN 978-1-107-42710-5 Paperback

Contents

Preface   xi

1 How do you say...?   1
   1.1   sloth   1
   1.2   nucular snitchel   2
   1.3   artisanal   3
   1.4   *C. diff.*   3
   1.5   shih tzu   4
   1.6   omega   5
   1.7   plethora   5
   1.8   diocese   6
   1.9   West Indian islands   7
   1.10   place names   8
   1.11   Madejski   9
   1.12   Charon   9
   1.13   Judea   11
   1.14   Chagos   11
   1.15   proceed and precede   12
   1.16   hypernymy and thrombosis   12
   1.17   amiodarone   13
   1.18   French, German or Welsh?   13
   1.19   Loony what?   14
   1.20   Richter   15
   1.21   Punjab and feng shui   15
   1.22   ylang-ylang   16
   1.23   Mbabane   17
   1.24   brand names   18
   1.25   Sexwale   19
   1.26   tortoise   20
   1.27   continental and English values   21
   1.28   my liege, we are besieged   21
   1.29   Rothersthorpe   22
   1.30   Campbell   23
   1.31   malapropisms   24
   1.32   ho, ho, ho   24
   1.33   d'oh, doh... duh   25
   1.34   ring in the old ear   25
   1.35   /Who did you say were all liars?   26
   1.36   anglicized Welsh place names   27

1.37	Jersey *h*	28
1.38	Friern Barnet	28
1.39	veterinary	29
1.40	Marcel Berlins and Sarkozy	29
1.41	repertory	30
1.42	Penwortham	30
1.43	hello?	31
1.44	Lucida	32
1.45	phonetic numerals	33
1.46	Llantwit Major	34
1.47	apostasy	34
1.48	pwn	35
1.49	Entwistle	36
1.50	Chinese into English	36
1.51	inter(n)ment	37

2	**English phonetics: theory and practice**	**38**
2.1	assimilation	38
2.2	internal intrusive r	38
2.3	royal toil	39
2.4	*wronger*	40
2.5	compression	40
2.6	compression in hymnody	41
2.7	GOAT compression	43
2.8	analogical decompression	44
2.9	compression anomalies	45
2.10	oh, oh!	45
2.11	stressing schwa	46
2.12	Latin stress in English	47
2.13	gemination and degemination	48
2.14	reductions in casual speech	50
2.15	abject haplologies	51
2.16	the happY vowel	52
2.17	crazes and crazies	53
2.18	banded or bandied?	54
2.19	the status of schwa	54
2.20	charted and chartered	55
2.21	singing strongly	56
2.22	happY prefixes	56
2.23	happY endings	57
2.24	some	58
2.25	the symbol for STRUT	60
2.26	the Teutonic Rule	60
2.27	problems with lexical stress	62
2.28	twenty-twenny	63
2.29	phantom r	64
2.30	Nadsat is non-rhotic!	65
2.31	non-rhotic loanwords	66
2.32	Gordon Brown	67

2.33	an albatross on the balcony	68
2.34	changes in English vowels	68
2.35	Christmas puzzles	69
2.36	data processing under stress	70
2.37	a cab, innit?	70
2.38	instances and incidences	71
2.39	settee	72
2.40	imma	73
2.41	terraced attacks	74
2.42	synthetic homographs	75
2.43	mine and my	75
2.44	um... er...	76
2.45	thou hast, he hath	77
2.46	rhotic	78
2.47	progressive assimilation	79
2.48	homographs	80

3	**Teaching and examining**	**82**
3.1	deceptive strings	82
3.2	practical tests	82
3.3	faulty abbreviations	83
3.4	exotic sounds	83
3.5	the Swedish sj-sound	84
3.6	pausing a problem	85
3.7	volcano	86
3.8	suddenly in Sydney	87
3.9	perceptions of /æ/	87
3.10	misled by spelling	88
3.11	unaspirated /p t k/	88
3.12	Yokohama and the like	89
3.13	struggling to teach phonetics	91
3.14	accents and actors	92
3.15	minimal pairs in action	94
3.16	a French user of English	95
3.17	Taiwan English	95
3.18	the IPA Certificate	96
3.19	dead letters	97
3.20	alveolopalatals	98
3.21	BrE or AmE for TEFL?	99
3.22	spot the mistake	101
3.23	excuse my excuse	101
3.24	miscellanea	102

4	**Intonation**	**103**
4.1	introduction	103
4.2	intonation notation	104
4.3	idiomatic intonation	105
4.4	systems	106
4.5	politeness	107

4.6	fall-rise or fall plus rise?	108
4.7	empty things	109
4.8	counterpresuppositional insists	110
4.9	that's funny	112
4.10	where? wohin?	113
4.11	examining intonation	114
4.12	the importance of being accented	115
4.13	accented *be*	116
4.14	O lift: your voice	117
4.15	stating the bleeding obvious	118
4.16	chunking	119
4.17	des accents enfantins	119
4.18	intonation idioms in the Germanic languages	120
4.19	compound stress in English and German	122
4.20	accenting phrasal verbs	123
4.21	train times	125
4.22	the rule of three	126
4.23	are you asking me or telling me?	126
4.24	accent on a VP subordinator	127
4.25	on the train	129
4.26	idiomatic nucleus on a pronoun	130
4.27	not a drop	131
4.28	a little while	132
4.29	international intonation	133
5	**Symbol shapes, fonts and spelling**	**136**
5.1	labiodental flap	136
5.2	similar symbols	137
5.3	clicks	138
5.4	IPA capitals	139
5.5	dashes	139
5.6	linguolabial trill	140
5.7	the symbol ʐ	140
5.8	scenes from IPA history	141
5.9	affricates	143
5.10	orthographic schwa	143
5.11	placing the suprasegmental symbols	144
5.12	why Hawai'i?	145
5.13	funny letters	146
5.14	anomalous *g*	147
5.15	the spelling *wor*	148
5.16	practicing (sic) wot I preach	148
5.17	why *ph*?	149
5.18	yogh and ezh	150
5.19	bevy, bevvy	151
5.20	low and long	151
5.21	palatoalveolars and the like	152
5.22	IPA reforms, 1976	153
5.23	Ortuguese	154

5.24   Panglish, or unintelligibility?   154
5.25   definitely   155
5.26   lexicographers and spelling   156
5.27   respelling   157
5.28   pea's, plea's   158
5.29   sibilant genitives   158
5.30   greengrocers' spellings   160
5.31   O tempora! O mores!   161
5.32   the cost of spelling   161
5.33   capital eszett   163
5.34   Jumieka   164
5.35   fame at last!   165

6   **English accents**   167
  6.1   po(r)ker   167
  6.2   holey ground   167
  6.3   hair lair!   168
  6.4   minor royalty   168
  6.5   Prince Harry   169
  6.6   fricative *t*   169
  6.7   hypercorrection   170
  6.8   Montserrat Creole   170
  6.9   television newsreaders' RP   171
  6.10   accents change over time shock horror   172
  6.11   bad sociophonetics   173
  6.12   *The Book of Dave*   174
  6.13   character, calendar   176
  6.14   Grand Turk   176
  6.15   popular phonetics   177
  6.16   changing London speech   178
  6.17   American T voicing and *sentence*   179
  6.18   sexy accents   180
  6.19   Maori names   181
  6.20   rich man, poor man   183

7   **Phonetics around the world**   184
  7.1   Scottish Gaelic   184
  7.2   tangnefedd a thragwyddoldeb   184
  7.3   Welsh letter names   186
  7.4   Welsh *ll*   187
  7.5   *c* what I mean   188
  7.6   Leewards, ABCs and Virgins   189
  7.7   clicks demonstrated   190
  7.8   an impossible sound   191
  7.9   fricative trill, trill fricative   192
  7.10   all the speech sounds in the world   192
  7.11   WALS   193
  7.12   IPA in a logo   194
  7.13   frozen in Italian   194

7.14   ugh!   195
7.15   Icelandic   196
7.16   wie war das?   196
7.17   simplicity   197
7.18   Calon lân   198
7.19   Ystrad Mynach   200

Postscript   201
Index of words   203
General index   205

Preface

After my retirement in 2006 I started to write a phonetic blog discussing everything to do with phonetics, seen from my personal and professional perspective. I did this partly to keep my mind active after retirement; in a sense the interaction with a web-based readership served to replace the daily dialogue with colleagues and students that I enjoyed while employed as professor at UCL. Now I'm delighted to be able to share this compilation from it with a wider audience.

I've assumed that the reader is familiar with basic phonetic notions and with the International Phonetic Alphabet: see the *IPA Handbook* (Cambridge University Press 1999) and the IPA chart (www.langsci.ucl.ac.uk/ipa/ipachart.html). If you want to brush up on this, there are plenty of textbooks available. Try *Practical Phonetics and Phonology* by Beverley Collins and Inger M. Mees (Routledge 2013, third edition). Wikipedia is also a useful and generally reliable resource. You may wish to refer to my own works: *Accents of English* (Cambridge University Press 1982, three volumes), *Longman Pronunciation Dictionary* (Pearson Education 2008, third edition – referenced below as LPD) and *English Intonation: an Introduction* (Cambridge University Press 2006).

In this book I put phonetic symbols in **bold**, without slashes or brackets unless it is relevant at that point to distinguish phonemes (in slashes //) from allophones or general-phonetic sound-types (in square brackets []). To indicate letters as opposed to sounds, I use italics. The prosodic conventions I use are a vertical stroke (|) to show an intonation phrase boundary, underlining to show the location of the nuclear (tonic) syllable, and the marks \, / and V to show a fall, a rise and a fall-rise respectively: see fuller discussion in 4.1–2 below.

Words written in capitals, e.g. DRESS, are keywords standing for the entire lexical set of words containing the vowel in question: see my *Accents of English*, chapter 2.2, or the Wikipedia article on 'lexical set'. Occasionally I use an asterisk (*) to denote an unacceptable form, as is usual in linguistic work.

I will be delighted if this modest collection of observations inspires a few readers to further explore traditional general phonetics for themselves and to make their own observations on how both English and other languages are pronounced. Linguistic diversity is fascinating, and pronunciation never stands still.

John Wells
London, February 2014

1 How do you say...?

The pronunciation of English words, including proper names

1.1 sloth

I saw an American TV programme recently based on the theme of the seven deadly sins. One of them is *sloth*, which the presenter pronounced **slɔːθ**, to rhyme with *cloth*. But this is not my pronunciation: I call it **sləʊθ**, to rhyme with *both* and *growth*.

The literal meaning of the name of both the deadly sin and the slow-moving animal named after it is 'slowness'. The word is cognate with the adjective *slow*: as *warm* is to *warmth*, so *slow* is to *sloth*. There are some abstract nouns in -*th* that involve a vowel change when compared with the adjective they are based on: *deep – depth*, *wide – width*. But historically *sloth* was not one of them. Indeed, in earlier times it was sometimes spelt *slowth* or *sloath*. So the form rhyming with *cloth* must have originated as a spelling pronunciation based on the now current spelling, which according to the OED was first used in the sixteenth century. British dictionaries generally give only the pronunciation rhyming with *growth*. But in American English (AmE) the pronunciation rhyming with *cloth* appears to predominate.

1.2   nucular snitchel

The pronunciation of *nuclear* as if it were spelt *nucular* is well known and widely condemned as a mispronunciation. President Bush, for example, normally said ˈnuːkjələ instead of the standard AmE ˈnuːkliə. This (mis)pronunciation presumably arose through the influence of the large number of familiar words ending in -kjələ (British English [BrE] -kjʊlə or -kjələ), among them *circular, particular, spectacular, molecular, secular, perpendicular, jocular.*

Two other mispronunciations that one hears from time to time are *percolator* as ˈpɜːkjəleɪtə instead of ˈpɜːkəleɪtə and *escalator* as ˈeskjəleɪtə instead of ˈeskəleɪtə. In these, a yod has been inserted between k and əl under the influence of words such as *speculator* and perhaps even our own technical term *articulator*. And then we have *prenuptial* and *nuptials* pronounced -tʃuəl, as if spelt *prenuptual, nuptuals.* I have also heard people referring to a *defibrillator* as if it were spelt *defribulator.*

But my all-time favourite of this type of thing has to be the Wiener *schnitzel* masquerading as a ˈsnɪtʃəl, thereby solving at a stroke what are from the English point of view two phonotactic problems in the German-style pronunciation: initial ʃn- and morpheme-internal -ts-.

Dictionaries perform various roles. The main users of pronunciation dictionaries such as LPD are teachers or students of English as a foreign language (EFL) who wish to know how to pronounce a word whose written form they perhaps know well but about whose pronunciation they are uncertain. A second group of users are native speakers who want to have their ignorance remedied or their prejudices confirmed or disconfirmed by a lexicographer they consider authoritative.

The lexicographer, though (me, for instance), if he is trained in linguistics, will always be acutely conscious that there is no absolute standard of correctness in language, particularly in a language with such a wide speakership and inadequate orthography as English.

That is why I have always striven to make LPD play a further role: that of documenting the current actual state of the language. That is why I felt it essential to include widespread though 'incorrect' pronunciations.

However, if I had merely listed these variants along with all the other variants that warrant inclusion, I would be failing in my duty, because I would be ignoring the attitude of careful, educated, literary-inclined, speech-conscious users towards them. That's why I use a special warning mark: the exclamation mark enclosed in a triangle.

Not to include such variants would be to fail to document the language properly – a charge that I think could reasonably be levelled against certain other pronunciation dictionaries. To include them but without a distinguishing mark would be to fail to indicate the attitude of other speakers towards them.

1.3   artisanal

How do you pronounce *artisanal*? That was a question a correspondent asked me. At the time I had to reply that I did not know the word: it wasn't part of my vocabulary and I'd never heard anyone say it. However, despite the fact that *artisan* is ˌɑːtɪˈzæn, I thought the regular stress effect of the suffix *-al* ought to yield ɑːˈtɪzənəl. Adjectives in *-al*, of three or more syllables, have penultimate stress if the penultimate vowel is long (*archetypal*, *primeval*, *universal*) or followed by a consonant cluster (*dialectal*, *incidental*), but otherwise have antepenultimate stress (*personal*, *industrial*, *medicinal*). (There are one or two exceptions in which the penultimate vowel lengthens on adding *-al*, as *adjectival* -ˈtaɪvəl.)

The word *artisanal* was not in the OED until added in 2008. It seems to have come into use quite recently as a kind of antonym of *industrial*, referring to small-scale production methods, agricultural or other.

Some would have us believe that it is ˈɑːtɪzənəl or ˌɑːtɪˈzænəl. I don't think so. That looks like someone's guess – someone who hasn't fully absorbed the English stress rules.

Early one morning I was jolted out of my half-sleep by hearing someone on my bedside radio, on the farming programme, use the word not once but twice. I can't remember what they were talking about, but my semi-conscious mind did note that the pronunciation used was indeed ɑːˈtɪzənəl. Result! And the OED now agrees.

1.4   C. diff.

The bacterium *Clostridium difficile* has been in the news recently. It is a cause of diarrhoea, usually acquired in hospital. Like all organisms it has a Latin binomial name, the first part referring to the genus and the second to the species. There's no difficulty about how to say the generic name: clearly, klɒˈstrɪdiəm. This can also be abbreviated to *C.*, and in this form is often pronounced just as siː.

It's the specific name that raises the interesting question. Apparently this species of Clostridium is called *difficile* because when it was first discovered it was difficult to grow in the laboratory. In Latin, *difficile* is the neuter singular nominative of the adjective *difficilis* 'difficult' – neuter because it agrees in gender with the neuter *Clostridium*. (With a masculine or feminine noun it would be *difficilis*.) In accordance with the usual rules for pronouncing Latin words in English, you would expect it to be dɪˈfɪsɪleɪ or perhaps dɪˈfɪkɪleɪ.

But it so happens that *difficile* is also the French word for 'difficult'. And in French it is pronounced difisil, anglicized as ˌdɪfɪˈsiːl. Because doctors and other health care professionals these days are much more likely to know French than to know Latin, it is perhaps not surprising that the bacterium is generally known in English as **klɒˈstrɪdiəm ˌdɪfɪˈsiːl**.

Or *C. diff.* **ˌsiː ˈdɪf** for short.

Here's a dreadful pun: *I went to the zoo the other day, and all they had was a dog. It was a shih tzu.* Apologies for the indelicacy.

This breed of dog can be spelt either *shih tzu* or *shi tzu*. Either way, it is an old (Wade–Giles) romanization of the Chinese word for 'lion', which in Hanyu Pinyin would be written *shizi*, or with tones *shīzi*. (See http://en.wikipedia.org/wiki/Wade–Giles and http://en.wikipedia.org/wiki/Hanyu_Pinyin for further details.) In Chinese characters it is 狮子 (simplified), 獅子 (traditional). The Chinese pronunciation is **ʂiˡ dʐɯˡ**, said on a high level pitch (the first syllable has tone 1, the second is toneless).

This word is in LPD, where I gave its English pronunciation as **ˌʃɪt ˈtsuː**. On reflection, having heard dog fanciers talking about the breed, I think that the second syllable ought rather to be shown as **ˈzuː** or **ˈsuː**. (In English we can't really manage **ts** in syllable-initial position, so we transfer the plosive into the preceding syllable. The spelling *tz* normally corresponds to the pronunciation **ts**, as in *quartz*; but the presence of *z* in the spelling tends to lead people to use **z** when the plosive and fricative are separated, as here.)

Given that, the pun reduces to **ˌʃɪt ˈzuː** vs. – what? Well, actually **ˈʃɪt ˌzuː**. What stops the pun being perfect is intonation: the fact that in the latent version *zoo* has already been mentioned, so that on the second mention it will be deaccented, throwing the nucleus onto *shit*. The dog is a *shih tzu*, but the rubbishy zoo is in this context a *shit zoo*.

I must thank Kwan-hin Cheung for the choice of symbols in the transcription of Chinese here. In 1992 he published the following paper in Chinese: '北京話 '知' '資'二韻國際音標寫法商榷 [IPA transcription of the so-called 'apical vowels' in Pekinese]', *Research on Chinese Linguistics in Hong Kong* (ed. T. Lee) (Linguistic Society of Hong Kong 1992, pp. 37–46). He comments, 'The collection itself was published bilingually, with a majority of papers in English. This paper predates John Laver's discussion on apical vowels in his *Phonetic Description of Voice Quality* (Cambridge University Press 1994, pp. 319–20).'

In his article Cheung mentions the symbols [ɿ] and [ʮ], which 'linguists within Chinese communities ... often regard ... as the IPA symbols for the two sounds', although in fact 'not only are they not official IPA symbols but they are hardly internationally known'. He would represent *shi* in IPA as [ʂ͡ɨ] and *si* as [s͡ɯ]. The slur marks reflect the fact that friction may extend into the vowel.

1.6   omega

'This food contains valuable omega-3 fatty acids,' says the nutrition expert on The Food Programme on BBC Radio 4. But he pronounces it əʊˈmiːgə.

I've got this pronunciation of *omega* in LPD as an AmE variant, along with -ˈmeɪgə and -ˈmegə. But at the time I drafted the first edition of LPD, back in the late 1980s, I clearly assumed that the only British pronunciation was ˈəʊmɪgə (or -məgə).

Not any more! The traditional BrE pronunciation of the name of the last letter in the Greek alphabet is indeed ˈəʊmɪgə. Studying classical Greek from the age of twelve on until I got my BA in Classics at age twenty-one I do not think I ever heard any other way of pronouncing it. Yet given that the classical Greek name was just ὦ (ō), this could be seen as a little surprising. Why don't we simply call the Greek letter əʊ? The name *omega* dates from the Byzantine period. By then the distinction between classical short ŏ and long ō had been lost, and the two letters o (ŏ) and ω (ō) had to be distinguished by special names: 'small o' *o micron* and 'big o' *o mega*.

Modern Welsh does something similar with the letters *i* and *u*. In southern Welsh they stand for the same vowel sound (*ci* 'dog' rhymes exactly with *tu* 'side'), so when I was learning Welsh I was taught to call the first one *i dot* and the second *u bedol* (i horseshoe).

OK, the medieval name of the Greek letter was ὦ μέγα (ō mega). That still doesn't explain why in English we traditionally stress it on the first syllable. Indeed, given that the element *mega* is in implicit contrast with *micron*, you might think that the syllable -*meg*- would bear fossilized contrastive stress. As usual, the reason that it doesn't is to be found in Latin. Most Greek words in English have passed to us via Latin, and on the way have become subject to the Latin stress rule (see also 1.3 above and 2.12 below). The Latin rule says look at the penultimate syllable: if it is light (= short vowel, not more than one following consonant), then stress the antepenultimate. In the *mega* element the *e* is indeed short (cf. *megabyte*, *mega store*, *megalomaniac*) and it is followed by the single consonant *g*. So stress goes onto the preceding syllable. The *e* itself undergoes vowel reduction. Hey presto: ˈəʊmɪgə.

1.7   plethora

How do you pronounce *plethora*?

Not everyone has this word in their vocabulary. The OED defines it as first having a medical meaning – a morbid condition – and then a figurative one, 'over-fullness in any respect, superabundance; any unhealthy repletion or excess'. *The Longman Dictionary of Contemporary English* (Longman 2009, fifth edition; hereafter LDOCE), more in tune with current usage, defines it as 'a very large number of something, usually more than you need: *a plethora of suggestions*'.

I pronounce it ˈpleθərə. That's also what's recommended by every dictionary I have to hand, and what I usually hear. I have also, however, heard plɪˈθɔːrə, which you will find in LPD and some other dictionaries as an alternative.

Ha!, I thought to myself, this must be another of those words like *omega*, a Greek/Latin word with a short penultimate vowel followed by a single consonant: the Latin stress rule (see 2.12 below) therefore gives us antepenultimate stress. People ignorant of the quantity of the *o* vowel mistakenly suppose it to be long, and consequently accent it.

But I was wrong. It turns out that our modern word comes from a medieval Latin *plēthōra*, from a Greek word πληθώρη (*plēthōrē*). The *o* in the penultimate syllable was definitely long. The OED reports that the 1731 edition of Nathan Bailey's Dictionary had 'the etymological pronunciation' *pleˈthōra*, but that the 1742 and 1755 editions of the same book have *ˈplethora*. And that's what most of us say today, despite the etymology.

1.8   diocese

The area that an Anglican or Roman Catholic bishop controls is a *diocese*. How do we pronounce this word? More trickily, what is its plural? In England there are a number of *dioceses*. How do we say that? And the derived adjective is *diocesan*, as in *Diocesan Board of Finance*. Where does the stress go?

If you had asked me that when I was aged nine or ten, I think I would have been able to reply confidently: ˈdaɪəsɪs, ˈdaɪəsiːz, daɪˈɒsɪzn. But that's because my father was a vicar, and these were everyday words in our house. As far as I know, those were also the pronunciations used by everyone else concerned with ecclesiastical administration, at least in our diocese (Liverpool). It means that *diocese* must have been attracted in its phonetics to the singular-plural alternation we see in such Greek-via-Latin-derived words as *crisis*, *thesis*, *basis*, *oasis*, *emphasis*, *neurosis*, *ellipsis*, *analysis* and *axis*. (Compare also *this* and *these*.)

	singular		plural
crisis	ˈkraɪsɪs	*crises*	ˈkraɪsiːz
thesis	ˈθiːsɪs	*theses*	ˈθiːsiːz
diocese	ˈdaɪəsɪs	*dioceses*	ˈdaɪəsiːz

However, this obviously produces a mismatch between sound and spelling. More to the point, most people are not from clergy families and may have no experience of ecclesiastical terminology. Not surprisingly, they tend to pronounce both *diocese* and *dioceses* the way they are spelt, with a regular sibilant-stem plural, making *diocese* perhaps ˈdaɪəsiːs or even ˈdaɪəsiːz and for *dioceses* appending the usual additional-syllable ending ɪz (or əz).

Jack Windsor Lewis points out that this word was spelt *diocess* from the sixteenth century to the end of the eighteenth; this was the only form recognized by Dr Johnson and the other eighteenth-century lexicographers, and was retained by some (notably by *The Times* newspaper) into the nineteenth century. During that century, however, *diocese* (as in French) became the established spelling.

The general issue I faced when compiling LPD was: do I prioritize the pronunciation used by those who use the word regularly, day in day out? Or do I heed those speakers for whom the word is a relatively unfamiliar written term? I chose the first, namely ˈdaɪəsɪs; other dictionaries, in this case at least, tend to choose the second, -siːs or -siːz.

There's a similar problem with *cervical*, where medical specialists generally use penultimate stress and a long *i* but the general public uses initial stress and a short *i*.

1.9   West Indian islands

Thoughts on returning from abroad: if you fly with Virgin Atlantic or British Airways from London to *Antigua* in the West Indies, you find everyone from passengers to check-in staff to the aircraft captain pronouncing it ænˈtiːgə, just as the locals do. But if you fly there from San Juan or New York on an American airline, as likely as not it will be referred to as ɑːnˈtiːgwə, with a Spanish pronunciation (sort of). Probably this is because Americans are much more likely than Brits to have learnt some Spanish at school, and of course the name does look Spanish and was originally Spanish, so that those unfamiliar with the name tend to assume it *is* Spanish, despite the island's three and a half centuries of speaking nothing but English. The Brits, on the other hand, mostly have French, rather than Spanish, as their main foreign language (if indeed they know a foreign language at all), and perhaps anyhow retain some ancestral memory of how to pronounce the names of former colonies.

Why, though, do we pronounce this Spanish-derived name without the **w** it has in Spanish? For the town of Antigua in Spanish-speaking Guatemala we indeed retain it. I don't know the answer. As a Spanish word *antigua* is anˈtiɣwa (it is the feminine form of the adjective *antiguo* anˈtiɣwo). We preserve this **w** when we anglicize the names *Paraguay*, *Uruguay* and *Guatemala*: so why do we treat *Antigua* differently? I don't know why, but we do.

Antigua's twin island is Barbuda, pronounced – by those who are familiar with it – as bɑːˈbjuːdə. It tends to crop up mainly in the official name of the country, *Antigua and Barbuda*. Non-locals therefore often need to pronounce this name, and they do tend to say it without its **j** as bɑːˈbuːdə, which is what it would be if it were Spanish-speaking and not just Spanish-derived.

You see something similar to *Antigua* with *jaguar*. In the UK we anglicize it very thoroughly as ˈdʒægjuə, while the Americans are more likely to go for a Spanish-style ˈdʒægwɑːr. In *Nicaragua*, however, do I detect a slight movement in Britain away from the anglicized ˌnɪkəˈræɡjuə in the direction of -ˈrɑːɡwə, as in AmE?

Another West Indian island with a tricky pronunciation is *Dominica*. Locally, and locals would insist correctly, it is stressed on the penultimate: ˌdɒmɪˈniːkə. Those not familiar with the island tend to assume that it has antepenultimate stress, dəˈmɪnɪkə. Fans of Chomsky and Halle's *Sound Pattern of English* (Harper & Row 1968) will see that the disagreement relates to differing views about the length of the penultimate vowel: if long, then stress-attracting, but if short – as in *Monica*, *Veronica*, *America*, *angelica* and many others – then stress-repelling. In the case of Dominica matters are made worse by the existence of a similarly named but quite distinct West Indian country, the Dominican Republic. Its name is normally pronounced with the expected antepenultimate stress. (Dominica, also known as the Commonwealth of Dominica, is the island located between Guadeloupe and Martinique in the eastern Caribbean. Its official language is English, the unofficial language French Creole. The Dominican Republic, aka Santo Domingo or Dominicana, occupies the eastern half of the island of Hispaniola, the western half being Haiti. Its language is Spanish.)

1.10   place names

Driving to Gatwick Airport a few days ago to meet an arriving passenger, I passed through the village of *Burgh Heath*. As on previous occasions when I have travelled that route, I wondered idly how it's pronounced. Is the first word bɜː or ˈbʌrə?

When I got back home I looked it up in the *BBC Pronouncing Dictionary of British Names* (Oxford University Press 1990, second edition), which says it can be either. Just not bɜːɡ.

I further learnt that Burgh in Norfolk is ˈbʌrə, but Burgh in adjoining Suffolk is bɜːɡ. Things are different in the north of England: Burgh-by-Sands in Cumbria is metathesized to brʌf, which must mean that for many locals it's more like [brʊf].

It's worse than *-ough*.

One day I wanted to go to a funeral on the outskirts of Birmingham. To reach my destination the map said I had to look for the road leading to *Alcester*. Er... what was that? I checked with my brother, who lives not too far away, and he said it was ˈɔːlstə. Then I looked in LPD and found that I agree.

And there's no call for Americans to feel superior to the wacky British. In the States you never know what will happen with Spanish names. I remember passing through *Salida*, Colorado. That's the Spanish for 'exit', and it was at the mouth of a canyon, so I thought that in English it would be səˈliːdə. But the local radio station announcers, who should know, pronounced it səˈlaɪdə.

Even English-derived names can be surprising. I remember driving through *Placerville*, California, and discovering to my surprise that it was not ˈpleɪsə-vɪl but ˈplæsə-vɪl.

My correspondent John Cowan points out that ˈplæsə is the standard AmE pronunciation of *placer*, a deposit of gravel which contains particles of gold or other precious minerals. *Placer mining* is the kind you do with a pan in which you wash the gravel, letting it flow over the lip of the pan along with most of the water, leaving the heavier gold behind. Despite appearances, the word is derived from Spanish *placer*, which may be of Portuguese or Catalan origin. Another correspondent, William Pitfield, adds that Burgh Heath gave its name to the local telephone exchange, covering a significantly larger area, including the place where he grew up. He doesn't recall any of the locals calling it anything other than ˈbʌrə *Heath*, at least among themselves. The exception was in the days before Subscriber Trunk Dialling, when it was wise to ask the operator for bɜː *Heath*, as otherwise they were liable to look for it under *Borough* and then assure you that the exchange didn't exist.

1.11   Madejski

Any visitor to Reading, on the way from London to Bristol, will be struck by the road signs everywhere pointing to the Madejski stadium. Why does the stadium have a Polish name? And how do people pronounce it?

Reading Football Club's stadium is named after John Madejski, one of the wealthiest people in the UK, the club's benefactor. He was born in Britain, with an English mother, but his father was Polish, an airman who was stationed here during the Second World War. As a Polish name, *Madejski* is pronounced exactly as spelt. The Polish diphthong written *ej* is similar to the English vowel in *face*, so the name would anglicize very easily as məˈdeɪski. However, English people do not know much about the pronunciation of foreign languages, except to some extent French. So they do not expect the letter *j* to stand for anything other than dʒ or (in foreign words) ʒ. And the resultant *məˈdeʒski would violate English phonotactics and thus be impossible. In fact, I am told that the usual pronunciation of the name in Reading is məˈdʒeski or məˈdʒedski, as if spelt *Madjeski* or *Majedski*. The metathesis makes it pronounceable.

1.12   Charon

A few years ago astronomers were discussing just what a planet is and exactly which heavenly bodies qualify as pukka planets. One of the candidates for planetary status is Charon, Pluto's moon. One TV news presenter called it ˈʃeərən. It is, however, traditionally pronounced in English with k, just as are other Greek words and names spelt *ch-*: *Charybdis*, *chemistry*, *chiropractic*, *chlamydia*, *Chloë*, *chlorine*, *chlorophyll*, *cholesterol*, *choreography*, *Christ*, *chromosome*, *chronograph* and also (usually) *chimera*, *chiropody*. Pronunciation dictionaries are unanimous for initial **k** in *Charon*: ˈkeərən, -ɒn.

Long before his name was given to the moon of Pluto, Charon was a figure in classical mythology: the grim ferryman who ferried dead souls across the river Acheron (or Styx) in Hades. I well remember Charon from Virgil's *Aeneid*, book six, line 299. As a teenager I was required to learn off by heart 20–30 lines of it:

> *portitor has horrendus aquas et flumina seruat*
> *terribili squalore Charon, cui plurima mento*
> *canities inculta iacet, stant lumina flamma,*
> *sordidus ex umeris nodo dependet amictus.*

> 'A frightful ferryman serves these waters and streams, in terrible filth, Charon. On his chin is an unkempt white beard, his eyes stand out with flame, a dirty tunic hangs knotted from his shoulders.'

Virgil's hexameters make it clear that the first vowel in *Charon* was actually short in Greek and Latin:

> terrībĭllī squāllōrĕ Chălrōn, cuī | plūrĭmă | mentō

The Greek form, Χάρων, makes it clear that his second vowel was long. So perhaps we ought to be saying ˈkærən (or even ˈkærəʊn) rather than ˈkeərən.

I found most of the Latin literature I studied at school and university pretty uninspiring. But the sixth book of the Aeneid was an exception. Virgil's lines about the lost souls yearning to be transported across the river really have that tingle factor:

> *huc omnis turba ad ripas effusa ruebat,*
> *matres atque uiri defunctaque corpora uita*
> *magnanimum heroum, pueri innuptaeque puellae,*
> *impositique rogis iuuenes ante ora parentum:*
> *quam multa in siluis autumni frigore primo*
> *lapsa cadunt folia, aut ad terram gurgite ab alto*
> *quam multae glomerantur aues, ubi frigidus annus*
> *trans pontum fugat et terris immittit apricis.*
> *stabant orantes primi transmittere cursum*
> *tendebantque manus ripae ulterioris amore.*

> 'To this place there rushed a whole crowd, pouring out onto the river bank: mothers and men and the lifeless bodies of great-hearted heroes, boys and unwed girls, young men placed on the funeral pyre before their parents: as many as the leaves that fall in the woods at the first frost of autumn, as many as the birds that flock together onshore, leaving the deep abyss, when the cold weather drives them across the sea to warmer lands. They were standing there, praying to be carried across first, and holding out their hands in yearning for the opposite bank.'

1.13   Judea

BBC TV showed a rather well done series on Roman history, *Ancient Rome: The Rise and Fall of an Empire*. One episode focused on the story of the Jewish Revolt, which swept through Judea in AD 66, and a disgraced general's attempt to put it down. I noticed that every single actor pronounced *Judea* as dʒuˈdeɪə. But when I was doing Ancient History at school it was most definitely dʒuˈdiːə (or rather the derived-by-smoothing dʒuˈdɪə). As far as I know, that's still what people say in church, too.

Judea or Judaea is the Latin name, via Greek Ἰουδαία, of the southern part of ancient Palestine. Two millennia ago, in those languages, it was pronounced something like juːˈdaia – but in both languages subsequently became juːˈdeːa. The regular development of this in English is dʒuˈdiːə or dʒuˈdɪə. Other names with a written *e* deriving from Latin *ae* and Greek αι include *Egypt* and *Ethiopia*. In English they still have iː. Other words with final stressed *-ea* include *idea*, *diarrh(o)ea*, *Thea* and *Korea*. I have not heard eɪə in any of them. For comparable cases, in which a traditional iː now faces competition from an upstart eɪ, we have to look to *nucleic* and the *-eity* words: *spontaneity, homogeneity, simultaneity* and, above all, *deity*. Indeed, for *deity* 80% of the BrE respondents in my 1988 pronunciation preference poll (reported in LPD) preferred the eɪ form. Merriam-Webster gives both possibilities, while prioritizing iː – as it also does for *Judea*, for which British dictionaries haven't yet caught up with the possibility of eɪ.

1.14   Chagos

The *Chagos* islanders were forced from their homes at gunpoint in the 1960s, as an entire British colony was handed to the US so that a monitoring station could be built in the Indian Ocean. The exiles now live in the slums of Mauritius where they belong neither socially nor economically. They're campaigning to return to the Chagos Islands.

On BBC Radio 4 I heard two contributors discussing the issue. One of them pronounced the name of the archipelago ˈʃɑːɡɒs, the other ˈʃæɡɒs. This suggests that neither of them had consulted the BBC Pronunciation Unit. Possibly, as experts on the subject, they felt they didn't need to. Because what it recommends is ˈtʃɑːɡəʊs.

In view of the fact that the islands were discovered by Vasco da Gama and presumably named in Portuguese, we should expect the spelling *ch* to correspond to ʃ rather than tʃ (which is what it would imply in Spanish). The adjacent islands, Mauritius and the Seychelles, are French-speaking, which would again favour *ch* = ʃ. Until 1965 the Chagos Islands were administered as part of Mauritius. I can quite see that Americans (who now run the islands and who usually know some Spanish) would in all likelihood pronounce the name ˈtʃɑːɡəʊs.

1.15   proceed and precede

Every now and again my students would reveal that they were confused about the words *precede* and *proceed*. Accounts of phonetic processes and allophonic rules often refer to a preceding consonant, or to something being preceded by a vowel, and so on. In the sequence ABC, B precedes C and is preceded by A.

But students sometimes write this as a 'proceeding' consonant, or being 'proceeded' by a vowel. Worse, since to proceed from can mean to follow, they sometimes interpret my spoken *precede*, which they imagine to be *proceed*, as meaning 'follow', so that they also have the meaning the wrong way round.

In theory, the distinction between the ɪ of *precede* and the ə (weakened from əʊ) of *proceed* ought to be robust. After all, in my own speech and in that of most of my students *valid* doesn't rhyme with *salad*, nor *rabbit* with *abbot*; the initial syllables of *finesse* and *phonetics* differ. But in practice, clearly the distinction may not be robust: weak *pre-* and *pro-* can get confused.

And I have just detected one of my favourite authors, Jared Diamond, committing the reverse mistake. In his marvellous book *Collapse* (Penguin 2006), on p. 501 of the UK paperback edition, we read that 'LA smog generally [gets] worse as one *precedes* inland'. Oh dear. What a precedent.

1.16   hypernymy and thrombolysis

One of our students chose *hypernymy* as a dissertation topic. How do we pronounce this word? Where does the stress go? I would say that following the pattern of *synonymy* sɪˈnɒnəmi it must clearly be haɪˈpɜːnəmi. But not everyone finds this obvious. Yet if you go along with Chomsky and Halle in *The Sound Pattern of English* (MIT Press 1968), native speakers of English have as part of their grammar (= their implicit knowledge of the language) a complex set of rules allowing them to produce the appropriate word stress and vowel qualities for English words, while the words themselves are specified in our mental lexicon without indication of stress placement and possible vowel reduction.

Chomsky and Halle were wrong, of course. The fact that anyone was uncertain about how to pronounce *hypernymy* bears this out. I have recently noticed another counter-example to the SPE principle. Every adult native speaker knows the words *paralysis* and *analysis*. Some also know one or more of *catalysis*, *dialysis*, *electrolysis* or some fifty other technical words with the same ending. All have antepenultimate stress: pəˈræləsɪs, əˈnæləsɪs, kəˈtæləsɪs, daɪˈæləsɪs, ˌelekˈtrɒləsɪs, etc.

Some years ago I was diagnosed with a heart condition and underwent an angioplasty procedure. Since then I have attended the cardiac support group run by my local hospital. One of the techniques for treating a heart attack or stroke is known as *thrombolysis*. But I have noticed that the cardiologists, cardiac surgeons, paramedics and nurses don't call this **θrɒmˈbɒləsɪs**, which is what you would predict on the basis of all the other *-lysis* words. They call it ˌ**θrɒmbəʊ ˈlaɪsɪs**. Ah well, language doesn't obey rules as much as some linguists would perhaps like.

In my lectures I sometimes talk about *allophony*. Guess how I pronounce it. Remember that everyone agrees that *telephony* is **təˈlefəni** and *cacophony* is **kəˈkɒfəni**, and that I am someone who knows the rules and plays by them. But millions of native speakers don't.

1.17   amiodarone

We learn something new every day. When my cardiologist started me on a drug called *amiodarone*, he pronounced it ˌ**æmiˈɒdərəʊn**, and that's what my GP said, too. But shortly afterwards I went for a blood test. The phlebotomist called it ˌ**æmiˈəʊdərəʊn**.

So should it be **ɒ** or **əʊ**? A short *o* or a long one? Who cares? The spelling's the same, which is what matters for the pharmacist who has to dispense it.

As with so many learned, scientific or technical words, the spelling is fixed while the pronunciation fluctuates. (Having boned up on heart disease, I am almost inclined to say it fibrillates.) That's because instead of hearing other speakers and imitating what they say, we often create a pronunciation for ourselves on the basis of the spelling, using the reading rules of English, which are notorious for their uncertainty.

1.18   French, German or Welsh?

An announcer on Classic FM radio referred to the painter *Gauguin* not as **ˈɡəʊɡæ̃**, which is the usual semi-anglicized pronunciation used by educated English people, but as **ɡaʊˈɡæ̃**. It was not so much the American-style end-stressing of the French name that caught my attention, as the interpretation of orthographic *au* as if it were German rather than French. (Think *Spandau* and *Strauss*.)

Mind you, the convention that maps French **o** (orthographically *au*, *eau*, *ô*, etc.) onto English **əʊ** (GOAT) is rather odd. It would be phonetically more accurate to equate it with English **ɔː** (THOUGHT). And in the cases spelt *au*, including *Gauguin*, this would also coincide with English orthographic habits. So **ˈɡɔːɡæ̃**, anyone?

Evidently, the foreign-language spelling *au* is something of a trap. I also heard another radio presenter, a BBC person this time, repeatedly pronounce the name of the Welsh parliamentary constituency *Blaenau Gwent* as **ˈblaɪnaʊ ˈɡwent**.

The Welsh plural ending -*au* (as in *blaenau* 'tops, heights', plural of *blaen*) has various pronunciations in the varying regional forms and stylistic levels of Welsh: in careful formal speech **aɪ**, or in the north **ai**, and in everyday speech more usually **e** or **a**, or in Anglo-Welsh even **ə**. But nowhere is it **au**.

The only people who might say 'blaɪnaʊ are those who do not know Welsh and who make a false inference on the basis of what they know about the relation between spelling and sound in German or some other irrelevant language.

Reading rules for *au* in non-English words:

- in French words **əʊ**, reflecting French **o** (*gauche*, *mauve*, *chauvinist*);
- in German, Spanish, etc. words **aʊ** (*Frau*, *Spandau*, *gaucho*);
- but in Welsh words **aɪ**. So it's *Blaen*[aɪ] or *Blaen*[ə] *Gwent*. The Welsh count 1, 2, 3 as *un*, *dau*, *tri*, which sounds like English *een*, *die*, *tree*.

1.19   Loony what?

In 2006 the *Guardian* carried the news that Prince Charles is buying a country estate in Wales. The name of the estate, *Llwynywormwood*, attracted my attention because it is a mixture of Welsh and English that doesn't really seem to be fully at home in either language. The Welsh part *Llwyn-y-* might be considered by the English to be unpronounceable, since in Welsh it is ɬʊɪn ə. Not only is there the difficulty of ɬ, but also the ʊɪ is a diphthong, making ɬʊɪn one syllable. The English part -*wormwood* won't do in Welsh, since its second syllable violates Welsh phonotactic rules, which do not allow **w** before **ʊ**.

In Welsh, *llwyn* means 'bush' or 'grove'. The linking *y* is the Welsh definite article, as in *Pen-y-bont* (head-the-bridge) 'Bridgend'. So the whole name might be anglicized as *Wormwood Grove*. Apparently its Welsh name is actually *Llwyny-wermwd*, with the proper Welsh equivalent of *wormwood* as the second element.

The Welsh spelling *ll* stands for a voiceless alveolar lateral fricative ɬ. It comes in many Welsh names (*Llanelli*, *Llangollen*, *Llandudno*, *Llywelyn*). Non-Welsh speakers in attempting this sound may well produce **xl**, **θl**, **kl** or, at best, **ɬl** instead. However, in Welsh consonants at the beginning of a word are subject to mutation in particular positions, which means that after most Welsh prepositions (among other things) any word with initial ɬ is said with plain **l** instead, e.g. *o Landudno* 'from Llandudno'. This provides a justification, if any were needed, for non-Welsh people to pronounce word-initial *Ll-* simply as **l**: which indeed we do in the name *Lloyd* (Welsh *llwyd* 'grey'). And I heard somewhere that the *Llwyni* ('Groves') Estate in one south Wales town is generally known as the *Loony* Estate.

For those who don't want to attempt the Welsh version ˌɬʊɪnə'wermud, I think – failing a recommendation from the BBC Pronunciation Unit – I would recommend the anglicization ˌluːɪnə'wɜːmwʊd, though this does make it sound unfortunately like a *loo* in some sort of forest.

Worse, the nearby village is *Myddfai*. That's Welsh ˈməðvai. What's the betting we hear ˈmɪdfeɪ?

1.20   Richter

Whenever there's an earthquake, the newsreaders make references to the *Richter* scale. They mostly pronounce it either ˈrɪxtə or ˈrɪçtə. But Charles Richter, the creator of the earthquake magnitude scale, was not from a German-speaking country, and the newsreaders' otherwise admirable familiarity with German pronunciation is here misapplied. He was an American, born in Ohio. Being American, he naturally pronounced his name ˈrɪktɚ, and we should do the same (or, in the case of us non-rhotic speakers, as ˈrɪktə).

This information is readily available from the BBC Pronunciation Unit and in the *Oxford BBC Guide to Pronunciation* (Oxford University Press 2006). It is explained in some detail in LPD. But newsreaders don't always heed offered advice.

1.21   Punjab and feng shui

The British seem to have a kind of unstated but deep feeling that foreign words shouldn't contain ʌ. I'm not sure whether Americans and speakers of other non-British accents share this feeling.

You can see the effect I am referring to in the name of the Indian province of *Punjab*. Older readers may remember Peter Sellers as an Indian doctor singing to the patient Sophia Loren:

> I remember how with one jab
> Of my needle in the Punjab
> I cured the beri-beri and the dreaded dysentery...

...correctly making the first syllable of *Punjab* rhyme with *one* wʌn (though not correctly rendering the length of the vowel in the second syllable).

But more often these days I hear people saying things like ˌpʊnˈdʒɑːb, pronouncing the first vowel not as ʌ but as ʊ.

Yet in Hindi, Urdu and Punjabi/Panjabi the name of this province is *Panjāb* (in Hindi, phonetically pə̃ndʒɑb). The Hindi/Urdu vowel transliterated as short *a* (i.e. the first vowel in *Panjāb*) is regularly mapped onto English ʌ. Compare the word *pandit*, pronounced in Hindi as pə̃ɳɖɪʈ and in English as ˈpʌndɪt (and usually spelt correspondingly as *pundit*). Hindi *pakkā* becomes BrE *pukka* ˈpʌkə. But *pundit* and *pukka* are so well integrated that people don't realize that they are of Hindi origin. Evidently we don't feel them to be foreign in the way that *Punjab* is perceived to be.

It's the same with the name of the Welsh nationalist party *Plaid Cymru*. The word for Wales is ˈkəmri in Welsh and ought to be ˈkʌmri in English. But English people persistently say ˈkʊmri.

And now from Chinese along comes *feng shui*, Mandarin ¹fʌŋ ³ʂuei. Aficionados know that the approved English pronunciation is not the *fen ʃuːi suggested by the Hanyu Pinyin spelling but rather fʌŋ ʃweɪ. Yet... foreign words don't have ʌ. So we get people saying fʊŋ ʃweɪ.

1.22   ylang-ylang

One word that I keep hearing (mis)pronounced on television is not a proper name, but a vocabulary word: *ylang-ylang*. One commercial current a few years back proclaimed that Air Wick could fill your house with the delightful fragrance of jə‿læŋ jəˈlæŋ.

Oh dear. Dictionaries tell us that *ylang-ylang*, also written *ilang-ilang*, is a Malaysian and Filipino tree, *Cananga odorata*, with fragrant yellow flowers from which a perfume of the same name is distilled. The word comes from Tagalog, where it takes the form *álang-ílang*. (Just how this got converted into its modern English form is not clear.) Reference books are unanimous that this is to be pronounced ˌiːlæŋ ˈiːlæŋ (or with final stress, and with the possibility of ɑ rather than æ in AmE).

I think this error may come from children's reading schemes in which the letter A is called æ, B is bə and so on, so that the letter Y is called jə. And the voice-over person can never have read Chaucer, where words such as *yclept* might have helped.

Those who follow the Olympics will have noticed that one of the classes of sailing boat competing there is an *yngling*. This was one of the words I added to LPD for its new (third) edition. You won't find it in many other dictionaries. The original Ynglings were the oldest known Scandinavian dynasty, part historical but part mythical. As a Norwegian word it would presumably be pronounced ˈʏŋlɪŋ, i.e. starting with a close front rounded vowel.

But now the name is applied to sailing boats. There is an International Yngling Association, which according to Wikipedia describes the boat as an 'agreeable cross between a planing dinghy and a keelboat'. Apparently the designer, Jan Herman Linge, wanted to build a keelboat for his young son, and named it Yngling, the Norwegian (and Swedish) word for 'youth, young man'; the name is unrelated to the dynasty, the House of Yngling. Etymologically, the word would correspond to English *young* plus the *-ling* of *weakling, duckling*.

And how do we pronounce it in English? In LPD I show it as ˈɪŋlɪŋ, and I believe this to be the usual pronunciation among those who sail that kind of boat.

But I heard an enthusiastic TV commentator call it a **ˈjɪŋlɪŋ**. You can see how this pronunciation might suggest itself to an English speaker unaccustomed to the idea that *y* at the beginning of a word could stand for a vowel.

This was no doubt the inspiration for the facetious *Guardian* letter-writer yesterday who said he was 'delighted to see that the ancient art of yngling has at last been recognised as an Olympic sport. I can't wait to see how we Brits fare in the tongling and tiddle I pogling events'.

That will make sense only to Brits of a certain age who remember the Goons and their Ying Tong song.

1.23   Mbabane

I'm sure we all know that *Mbabane* is the capital of Swaziland in southern Africa.

This name is extraordinarily difficult to anglicize. In the local language, siSwati, it is pronounced **mbaˈbaːne**. The initial nasal is non-syllabic, part of the prenasalized voiced bilabial plosive **mb**. You find this kind of thing in all the Nguni languages (the term Nguni covers Zulu and Xhosa and one or two others as well as siSwati, all more or less mutually intelligible).

We can't cope with this sound in English. Nor can we cope with an initial cluster **mb-**. So, as with *Mbeki, Ndola* and *Nguni*, we have to insert a schwa before the nasal to make it pronounceable in English. (An alternative tactic would be to insert the schwa after the nasal, thus **məbæˈbaːni**.)

Whereas the resulting **əmˈbeki, ənˈdəʊlə, əŋˈguːni** are fine for us, there is a further problem with a putative **əmbæˈbaːni** or **məbæˈbaːni** (and equally with possible variants having **ə** or **ɑː** in what is now the second syllable).

The same problem arises if we attempt an initial syllabic nasal, m̩bæ-. These are problematic because the phonetic structure of English words is subject to what is sometimes called the 'Teutonic Rule', namely that the first two syllables of a word cannot both be lexically unstressed. In words with the main stress on the third syllable or later, we need a secondary stress on the first or second syllable.

Attempting to put this secondary on the first syllable, unfortunately, would violate another rule of English phonetics, namely that schwa can never be lexically stressed.

Even putting it on the second syllable, thus əmˌbæˈbɑːni, or əmˌbɑːˈbɑːni, is still rather awkward. Perhaps we should go with AmE and make the first syllable ˌem-. This at last gives us a form that is truly pronounceable in English: ˌembəˈbɑːni. I wonder what non-Nguni-speaking native speakers of English who live there actually say.

By the way, I have discovered that in the 1880s one Michael Wells was one of the earliest entrepreneurs to set up an industry in Mbabane, namely a brewery. Since I know that my grandfather Edward Wells was a brewer in South Africa in the 1900s, I surmise that this was probably my great-grandfather.

1.24   brand names

Volkswagen, Weetabix, Whiskas… brand names are a familiar part of every native speaker's vocabulary, and often thoroughly global. Yet ordinary dictionaries mostly don't include them.

Whether we want to tell EFL students how we pronounce them, to reassure native speakers on what to say, or to document the current state of the language for the instruction and delectation of future generations, brand names (trade names, commercial names, trademarks) do in my view deserve a place in a pronunciation dictionary.

When Jones was editor, there were, I think, no brand names in his *English Pronouncing Dictionary* (EPD). So the likes of *Mazawattee, Dolly Blue* and *Craven A*, now only of historical interest, remained undocumented. Even *Coca-Cola* was not mentioned. The publishers of EPD's successor, the *Cambridge English Pronouncing Dictionary* (Cambridge University Press 2011), have now changed its policy about trademarks and include them.

Brand names are not without their problems. Many years ago I noticed that various pronunciations of *Hyundai* were in use in British television advertisements, though they now seem to have settled on ˈhaɪʌndaɪ – very different from the Korean source hjəːndɛ. The American version, ˈhʌndeɪ, is closer.

From the English pronunciation of *Kyocera*, ˌkaɪəˈsɪərə, you'd never guess that it is an abbreviation of *Kyoto Ceramic* (Kyōto Seramikku).

The modern lexicographer has resources unknown to earlier generations. If I want information on a trade mark, I can go on line and consult Wikipedia or Google. Sometimes the brand owner's website even carries an indication of how the name is to be pronounced.

Recently I was trying to discover how to pronounce *Freixenet*. On the company's British website I found clips of their television advertisements, in which the voice-over clearly says ˈfreʃənet. In the original Catalan, on the other hand, this word has final stress: frəʃəˈnɛt. The company's American website is useless in this respect, offering no video or sound clips, just the ambiguous specification 'pronounced fresh-eh-net'.

The German electrical brand *Braun* is usually brɔːn in English, even though this word, the German equivalent of *Brown*, happens to coincide with the English word in both sound and meaning. Spelling pronunciation rules.

For *Nestlé*, on the other hand, we have generally abandoned our earlier ˈnesl̩ in favour of ˈnesleɪ.

As for *Audi* – which in English, as in German, is ˈaʊdi – the slogan *Vorsprung durch Technik* does present problems to English speakers. In German it is ˈfoːɐʃpʀʊŋ dʊʀç ˈtɛçnɪk. But non-German speakers are not familiar with the idea that the letter *V* can stand for **f**, and they do not understand the German distribution of **ç** and **x**, both spelt *ch*. Anyhow, the cluster ʀç – a uvular fricative (or approximant) plus a palatal fricative – is tricky by any standards. (Actually, Germans often make it dʊʀç, so we could attempt at least dʊəx.) We usually say something along the lines of ˈvɔːsprʊŋ dɜːx ˈtexnɪk.

1.25   Sexwale

No, that isn't a misprint for something else. Tokyo *Sexwale* is a leading South African politician.

In the Bantu languages of South Africa, the letter *x* can stand for at least three sounds, depending on the language: a lateral click, a palatoalveolar fricative or (as in IPA) a velar fricative. Conveniently for the phonetically unsophisticated speaker of English, the first and last of these map onto English **k**. So it would probably be safe to pronounce his name seˈkwɑːleɪ (or perhaps sɪˈkwɑːli).

In the name of the language *Xhosa* the *X* stands for a voiceless alveolar lateral click, ‖ (or in old money ʖ). The following *h* shows that the accompanying velar component is aspirated, so in full we have ˈk͜‖ʰɔːsa. This spelling convention applies in Zulu, too.

In Tsonga, the letter *x* stands for ʃ. This is presumably due to Portuguese influence, since most speakers of Tsonga live in Mozambique. But in Venda (aka TshiVenda) the letter *x* stands for the voiceless velar fricative **x**.

Mr Sexwale's background is Venda, although he was born in Soweto. The name of the company he founded, Mvelaphanda, is certainly a Venda word.

The BBC Pronunciation Unit confirms that the orthographic *x* in this name is pronounced as a velar fricative.

So in English we should call him se'xwɑːleɪ or, failing that, se'kwɑːleɪ.

> 'When we were little,' the Mock Turtle went on at last, more calmly, though still sobbing a little now and then, 'we went to school in the sea. The master was an old Turtle—we used to call him Tortoise—'
>
> 'Why did you call him Tortoise, if he wasn't one?' Alice asked.
>
> 'We called him Tortoise because he taught us.'   From *Alice in Wonderland* by Lewis Carroll

The pun works perfectly in non-rhotic accents (= most English, Welsh and southern-hemisphere accents) providing you use the pronunciation of *tortoise* that I grew up with, namely 'tɔːtəs.

But every now and again I hear people say 'tɔːtɔɪs or 'tɔːtɔɪz. I think these must be fairly recent spelling pronunciations. In LPD I gave them a warning triangle.

The OED is not very clear about how the spelling came to be *-oise*, given an origin in the Latin *tortūca*, French *tortue*. The earliest (fifteenth-century) English spellings included *tortuce*, *tortuse*, *tortose*, as well as the French *tortue*. Nevertheless, the spelling *tortoise* is also quite early (mid-sixteenth century). There seems to be a possibility that the final sibilant may have arisen from, or been reinforced by, a genitive form as in *tortue's shell* (tortoiseshell).

The 1913 OED entry for this word also reported a pronunciation 'tɔːtɪs, which I have never heard.

We have a similar situation with *porpoise*, though here the etymology and history are rather different. The form *porpoys* goes back to Middle English, a borrowing from Norman French, based on some unattested Latin form of the type *porcus piscis* 'pig fish'.

As with *tortoise*, so with *porpoise*. The pronunciation I recommend in LPD is ˈpɔːpəs, with a warning triangle for ˈpɔːpɔɪs, ˈpɔːpɔɪz.

For both *tortoise* and *porpoise* Merriam-Webster reports only -əs.

I remember a misunderstanding when I was a boy. A dead porpoise had been washed up on the beach in Cumbria where we were on holiday. When we told the cleaning lady about it, she thought we were telling her about a dead cat – a poor puss.

1.27   continental and English values

On BBC World television news I was struck by how one of the weather forecasters pronounced the name of the capital of Nigeria, *Lagos*. Its usual pronunciation in BrE is unquestionably ˈleɪɡɒs, with the vowel of FACE. But what I heard was ˈlɑːɡɒs, with the vowel of START. I've also heard the occasional ˈlɑːɡoʊs from Americans.

This reflects a general difficulty we have in English when reading aloud proper names that look Spanish or Portuguese. What are the correct reading rules to use? Do we give stressed vowels in open syllables their 'continental' values or their 'English' values? In the first case we'll read the letter *a* aloud as ɑː, *e* as eɪ and *i* as iː. In the second, *a* will be eɪ, *e* iː and *i* aɪ. Our usual pronunciation of *Lagos* has the English values.

When we see the name *Toledo*, the continental values are appropriate for the place in Spain, but the English values for the place in Ohio. Another Spanish city is *Vigo*, which we nowadays pronounce in English with the vowel of *league* (= continental); but for *Vigo Street* in central London it was traditionally the vowel of *tiger* (= English). *Granada* in Spain has ɑː, but *Grenada* in the West Indies has eɪ.

The problem is particularly acute in the western USA, where there are large numbers of Spanish-derived place names. Does *Coronado* in California have ɑː or eɪ? Compare on the one hand *bravado* and *Colorado* (= continental, but locally æ) and on the other hand *tornado* and *Barbados* (= English).

As well as the Lagos in Nigeria, there's another Lagos in Portugal. Its local pronunciation is presumably ˈlaɡuʃ or ˈlaɣuʃ, so I suppose in English it'll be ˈlɑːɡuːʃ. And then there's yet another in France, laɡoːs.

1.28   my liege, we are besieged

Vassals (and wives) in Shakespeare often address their lord as *my liege*. The pronunciation given in dictionaries is liːdʒ. But I keep hearing Shakespearian actors (of both sexes) pronounce it as liːʒ.

The first dictionary to mention this variant seems to have been *Webster's Third International* (1961). You will still not find it in most dictionaries.

It's not only *liege*. I have heard the ʒ variant in *siege* and *besiege*, too. So what is it about dʒ after high front vowels? Is this some kind of contamination from *prestige* -iːʒ or *beige* beiʒ?

Then there is the corresponding position after other long vowels. Most English people, or at least those with any kind of familiarity with French, pronounce *rouge* and *luge* with ʒ, as in French. I have heard it in *deluge*, too. Water-colour artists know about *gamboge tint*, often pronounced with ʒ. And most English people seem to use ʒ rather than dʒ in *raj*, which is not French at all. (Nor, for that matter, is *Beijing*.)

So we seem to favour the fricative rather than the affricate after a long vowel. Is this an incipient sound change? Well, I've not heard anyone pronounce *huge* as hjuːʒ… yet.

1.29   Rothersthorpe

The service area that I know as Rothersthorpe Services on the M1 motorway in the English midlands has been renamed Northampton Services.

This got me idly thinking: how is it that we know immediately how to interpret these three *th* spellings? Obviously the pronunciations are ˈrɒðəzθɔːp and nɔːˈθæmptən (or minor variants thereof). So ð, θ, θ: but given that the spelling *th* is used indifferently for both θ and ð, how do we know which one to use where in an unfamiliar place name?

The spelling-to-sound rules can be summed up as saying that word-initial *th* spells θ except in function words such as articles and determiners. Word-medial *th* is ð in Germanic words but θ in Greek or Latin words. In the present discussion we can ignore word-final position.

At first it looks as if getting these names right is crucially dependent on recognizing morpheme boundaries. We have to be able to see that *Rothersthorpe* – an obviously Germanic name – consists of *Rothers* plus *thorpe*. The initial *th* in -*thorpe* therefore counts as being initial and hence voiceless. Compare *Scunthorpe* and indeed the surname *Thorpe*. The medial *th* in *Rothers*-follows the rule by being voiced. This is no doubt reinforced by the well-known place name *Rotherham*.

Northampton is slightly trickier. Although we say θ in *north*, we say ð in *northern*, *northerly* and place names such as *Northall*, *Northam*, *Northenden*, *Northiam*, i.e. when *th* is medial – yet θ in *Northumberland*. The distinguishing feature of *Northampton* and *Northumberland* seems to be that the vowel after the *th* is strong, thereby attracting the dental fricative into (syllable-) initial position and ensuring that it is voiceless. Perhaps that applies to *Rothersthorpe*, too, where the strong vowel attracts the second dental fricative into the last syllable. So it is not the morphology we depend on, but the syllabification.

Another place name with repeated *th* is *Rotherhithe* in London. Its polite pronunciation is ˈrɒðəhaɪð, but a correspondent wonders about ˈrɒðəraɪð, which he feels sounds 'more Sarf London'. Indeed, in non-rhotic accents such as received pronunciation (RP) and London **r** and **h** are mutually exclusive in names such as *Leatherhead* and *Wolverhampton*. The standard pronunciation retains the **h**, thus ˈrɒðəhaɪð, ˈleðəhed, ˌwʊləˈhæmptən. Local working-class accents tend to drop **h**, giving ˈrɒðəraɪð, ˈleðəred, ˌwʊlvərˈæmptən. Dropping the **h** in these names is comparable to dropping the **h** in phrases such as *over here, a bigger house*: if the **h** goes, linking **r** is automatically triggered. But dropping the **h** is clearly stigmatized and regarded as uneducated: it would indeed sound 'Sarf (= south) London'.

Rotherhithe also has a variant *Redriff*, which attests not only H dropping but also a centuries-old case of TH fronting. In 1665 Samuel Pepys wrote of walking to *Redriffe*. According to Ekwall, the name comes from Old English (OE) *hrȳther* + *hȳth* 'landing place for cattle'. But according to others, the first element is OE *redhra* 'sailor'.

The only times I have passed along Redriff Road, Rotherhithe, were while running the London Marathon. The marathon course takes the runners right around the Rotherhithe peninsula.

1.30   Campbell

Campbell is a pretty common surname throughout the English-speaking world.

The mismatch between its pronunciation and its spelling has always puzzled me. We pronounce it ˈkæmbl̩ yet the spelling has an irrelevant ('silent') *p* before the *b*. Why?

The origin of the name *Campbell* lies in a Scottish clan name. The Campbells occupied an extensive area of Kintyre and the western Highlands. According to the *Oxford Names Companion* (Oxford University Press 2002), which incorporates *A Dictionary of Surnames* (1988) by Patrick Hanks and Flavia Hodges, its likely etymology is Scottish Gaelic, in which *cam* means 'crooked' and *beul* 'mouth'. So *Cambeul* or *Caimbeul* was a nickname, 'wrymouth', apparently borne by the clan founder Gillespie Ó Duibhne, who lived at the beginning of the thirteenth century.

According to Wikipedia, there is a separate surname *Campbell*, of Irish origin, from the Irish *Mac Cathmhaoil* meaning 'son of the battle chieftain' (though personally I'd have thought that an Irish name of that spelling would yield the English form *McCall*).

But what about the spelling? As so often, it turns out that Norman scribes and/ or lawyers writing in Latin were to blame. They came up with an elegant Latin equivalent of the Gaelic name, turning it into *de Campo Bello* 'of the fair field'.

Just as the *b* in *debt* and *doubt* is down to Latin etymologizing, so is the *p* in *Campbell*.

1.31   malapropisms

When people speak of some man having an enlarged ˈprɒstreɪt or undergoing a ˈprɒstreɪt operation, is this just a non-standard pronunciation of ˈprɒsteɪt *prostate*?

Not really. Rather, it reflects a confusion between the words *prostate* and *prostrate*. People who pronounce the gland in question as the ˈprɒstreɪt will also want to spell it *prostrate*. For them, the gland and the word meaning 'lying flat, face down (in exhaustion or submission)' are perceived as homonyms.

Actually, since the latter is a relatively learned and unfamiliar word, they may know only the glandular meaning.

I wonder what they make of the words of the hymn.

> All hail the power of Jesu's name,
> Let angels prostrate fall;
> Bring forth the royal diadem
> And crown him Lord of all.

A similar case is the frequent confusion between *silicon* (chemical element, Si) and *silicone* (polymeric compound, used e.g. for breast implants). Referring in writing to a 'silicone chip' or in speech to a ˌsɪlɪkəʊn ˈtʃɪp is a solecism.

In a pronunciation dictionary, ought ˈprɒstreɪt to be included as a variant pronunciation of *prostate*, perhaps with a sign to show that it is not considered correct? My answer is no. We cannot cater for Mrs Malaprop. But it can be difficult to know where to draw the line.

1.32   ho, ho, ho

How do we pronounce the name of the letter *H*?

All dictionaries agree that it is eɪtʃ. Only LPD gives an alternative possibility, heɪtʃ, which it marks with the symbol § to show that it is not the RP form. I added a note, 'The form heɪtʃ is standard in Irish English, but not BrE or AmE'. This claim is possibly too sweeping, but on visits to Irish universities I had noticed Irish academics at all levels using this form. I was particularly struck by the expression piː heɪtʃ diː *PhD*.

At that time, twenty or thirty years ago, calling the letter heɪtʃ was perceived in England as simply wrong, a pronunciation likely to be used only by the illiterate and uneducated – the people who were prone to H dropping and to hypercorrect H insertion.

But things seem to have changed. Nowadays many younger Londoners, at any rate, call the letter *H* heɪtʃ. I have taught undergraduates who would defend this as the correct pronunciation, perhaps on the grounds that the name of a consonant letter should contain an instance of the corresponding consonant sound.

So I included the question of *aitch* or *haitch* in the online survey of pronunciation preferences that I conducted in 2007.

As reported in the third edition of LPD (2008), the overall voting figures were 84% for the traditional form, 16% for the newcomer. Comparing the preferences of different age groups shows that **heɪtʃ** is indeed an innovation that appears to be spreading rather fast. As many as 24% of those born since 1982 voted for it.

It's sometimes claimed that we divide on religious lines. I mentioned this point 25 years ago in my *Accents of English* (Cambridge University Press 1982, vol. 2, p. 432) in the chapter about Ireland.

> The letter *H* itself [. . .] is called **heːtʃ**, at least by Catholics. (This is in fact widely considered a sectarian shibboleth, with the Protestants calling it **eːtʃ**, cf. RP **eɪtʃ**.)

It's clear that in London, at least, this no longer applies: in no way is the **h-** pronunciation restricted to Roman Catholics or those taught at Catholic schools. Shortly after I wrote this I had a conversation with one of the youngest members of my partner's family, who was then aged five. 'He knows the names of the letters,' I reported, 'and one of them, he declares, is **heɪtʃ**. His family are Methodists, educated at state schools.'

1.33   d'oh, doh... duh

What does Homer Simpson say when he realizes that he has said or done something stupid?

You'll find the interjection spelt variously as *d'oh*, *doh* or *duh*. It's a kind of euphemism for *damn*.

Of course it's not really Homer who says it, but the actor Dan Castellaneta, who plays the part of Homer.

From analysis of TV clips of the cartoon I can report that it's pretty clear that he, at least, pronounces this interjection as **doʊ** (though in some cases it seems almost to approach **daʊ**). It is thus a homophone of *dough*, and is often pronounced with a special harsh or constricted voice quality. Like all exclamations, it is always said with a falling, or at least a non-rising, nuclear tone.

The interjection spelt *duh* is different. Whereas Homer says *d'oh*, and was perhaps the first to do so, *duh* was in use in AmE long before the Simpsons appeared on the scene, going back at least to Laurel and Hardy. It is pronounced **dʌ**, or like *duck* without the final **k**, and is thus not a homophone of *dough*. The meaning of *duh* is different, too: it is used to comment on someone else's stupidity, while *d'oh* is a comment on one's own stupidity.

1.34   ring in the old ear

Tinnitus is the perception of sound in the absence of corresponding external sound: an auditory disorder in which you hear a ringing in your ears.

How do we pronounce it? Is it tɪˈnaɪtəs, with stress on the penultimate, or ˈtɪnɪtəs, within initial stress? Dictionaries differ.

Here's what the American Tinnitus Association says:

> TINNITUS is pronounced either ti-NIGHT-us or TIN-i-tus. Both pronunciations are correct; the American Tinnitus Association uses ti-NIGHT-us.

I remember my colleague Michael Ashby telling me he thought that in LPD I ought to have prioritized ˈtɪnɪtəs, for BrE at least. On reflection I rather suspected he might be right. My problem is that, being a classicist by training, I am perhaps too strongly influenced by my awareness of the quantity of the second vowel in Latin, *tinnītus*, which implies penultimate stress and aɪ in English.

It was one of the items about which people voted in the BrE survey I carried out in 2007. The results were interesting. Overall, respondents preferred ˈtɪnɪtəs by a wide margin. However, the one age group for whom tɪˈnaɪtəs made a strong showing was those aged below twenty-six years. There is no sudden recent swing towards studying Latin in our schools, so I am at a loss to explain this.

1.35   /Who did you say were all liars?

I heard an ad on a commercial radio station enumerating some of the many attractive features of Greece, including ˈkriːʃn̩ olive groves.

I don't know if this is phonetics or more properly morphology, but surely the adjective from *Crete* is more usually *Cretan* ˈkriːtn̩.

At first I assumed that *Cretian* was simply a mistake. A check in the OED, though, shows that things are more complicated. Here's the OED's etymology for *Cretan*, a. and n:

> ad. L. *Crētānus*. The forms used in the various translations of the Bible are, in Acts ii. 11 *Cretes* (Middle English (a 1400, ed. A.C. Paues), Geneva and A.V.), in Titus i. 12 *Cretayns* (Tindale and Coverdale), *Cretyans* (Cranmer), *Cretians* (Geneva and A.V.); Reims and Douay have *Cretensians*, and R.V. *Cretans* in both places.

My *Cassell's Latin Dictionary* (1887, last revision 1928) confirms *Crētānus*, and adds a variety of other forms for a dweller in *Crēta*, *Crētē*, noun or adjective – among them *Crēs*, *Crēsius*, *Crēticus*, but no **Crētiānus*.

So it's really just the Geneva Bible and the Authorized Version (aka the King James version) that speak of *Cretians*. Here are the A.V. verses in question.

> Cretes and Arabians, we do hear them speak in our tongues the wonderful works of God. – Acts 2:11

> One of themselves, even a prophet of their own, said, the Cretians are alway liars, evil beasts, slow bellies. – Titus 1:12

There's also a metrical foot called a *cretic* (‾˘‾). Another fascinating fact: in Modern Greek the word for 'Cretan' (Κρητικός) and the word for 'critical' (κριτικός) are homophones.

Anyhow, I think an olive grove ought to be *Cretan*.

1.36   anglicized Welsh place names

In Gwent, southeast Wales, in areas where the English language displaced Welsh centuries ago, there are nevertheless plenty of small villages with names that are obviously Welsh, both in appearance (their spelling follows Welsh spelling conventions) and in meaning (in Welsh they mean something). I wonder how they are in practice pronounced by their monoglot English-speaking inhabitants.

Between Chepstow and Newport, for example, just across the border from England, we find villages called *Mynydd Bach*, *Gaerllwyd* and *Pen-y-cae-mawr* ('small mountain', 'grey castle', 'top of the big field'). In standard Welsh they would be ˈmənɪð ˈbaːx, ˈgəɪr ˈɬʊɪd, ˈpen ə kəɪ ˈmaʊr.

Many of these village names are listed in the recently published *Dictionary of the Place-names of Wales* by Hywel Wyn Owen and Richard Morgan (Gomer Press 2007), but without any systematic indication of pronunciation. None of them are mentioned in the *BBC Pronouncing Dictionary of British Names* (Oxford University Press 1990, second edition).

Let's consider the elements of the place names one by one. As an English name, though of Welsh origin, *mynydd* becomes *Mynd* **mɪnd** in the name of the Shropshire hill *The Long Mynd*. *Gaer* is the mutated form of *caer*, which gives us *Car* kə in *Carmarthen/Caerfyrddin* and *Carnarvon/Caernarfon*. Welsh *Llwyd* becomes English *Lloyd* lɔɪd. *Pen* anglicizes with no difficulty; the article *-y-* becomes English **i** in for example *Pontypool/Pont-y-pŵl*; and *-cae-* gets reduced to kə in *Gwaun-cae-Gurwen* ˈgwaɪn kəˈgɜːwən.

Of course what I ought to be doing, instead of speculating, is going out there and interviewing local people. I don't have anyone from east Gwent here in London that I can consult, but I do have someone from further west, a lady from near Neath. She says she speaks no Welsh, and indeed remembers from her schooldays that there was only one child in her class who spoke Welsh at home, which made him something of an outsider. (This was before the days of Welsh–English bilingual education.) When I asked her about the village of *Blaengwrach*, she had no hesitation in pronouncing it as **blaɪnˈgraːx**. Similarly, she confidently pronounces *Llanelli* as ɬəˈneɬi. So she clearly has the non-English consonants x and ɬ in her system. She has the usual anglicization of *Pontypool* with -**i**-, but pronounces *Pontypridd* as **pɒntəˈpriːð**, with Welsh-style -**ə**-.

I asked her about *Mynydd Bach*. Straight away: ˈmʌnɪð ˈbaːx. So members of the non-Welsh-speaking majority in Wales can often nevertheless pronounce Welsh names in a Welsh, as opposed to an anglicized, way.

(Jack Windsor Lewis points out that although this lady and other non-Welsh-speakers like her may 'have the item ɫ in her system', many actually pronounce not exactly ɫ but perhaps rather ɫɫ or, worse, xl or θl, none of which would pass muster in a phonetics exam.)

1.37   Jersey *h*

Jersey, in the Channel Islands, was in the news for a time because of a child abuse scandal. The former children's home then under investigation was called Haut de la Garenne, in the parish of St Martin.

It is striking that radio and television newsreaders pronounced this name with initial **h**, despite the fact that they must all be aware that in French the letter *h* at the beginning of a word is silent. Indeed, all British newsreaders must certainly know enough French to be aware that the French for 'high', *haut*, is pronounced **o**. (Let's not get involved in the question of so-called *h aspiré*.)

The BBC Pronunciation Unit tells me, 'Our newsreaders are following our advice by pronouncing the h-. This is the local pronunciation according to staff we consulted at BBC Radio Jersey. We tend to check Channel Island place names directly with people there because the level of anglicisation of French-looking names, though usually high, can be a bit unpredictable.'

Although the 1990 *BBC Pronouncing Dictionary of British Names* does not include any entry for *Haut de la Garenne*, its Channel Islands Appendix does list fourteen French-looking names spelt with *h-*. Thirteen of them are pronounced with **h**, including *Hacquoil*, *Hautes Capelles* and *Houiellebecq* **ˈhuːlbek**.

I don't know anything about Jèrriais (French *jersiais*), the Norman French dialect of Jersey, but presumably it has retained historical **h** despite the disappearance of **h** from standard French.

Or is it to be explained as spelling pronunciation, like the **h** in *Terre Haute*, Indiana?

1.38   Friern Barnet

In north London, in the London Borough of Barnet, is a place called *Friern Barnet*.

The earliest recorded form of this name is *Frerenbarnet* (1274). The first part of the name, *Freren*, is the Middle English (from French, from Latin) for 'of the brothers', and refers to its early possession by the Knights of St John of Jerusalem.

Not too far away there is another place, Monken Hadley. It is so called after the monks of the monastery which was once there.

As *Monken* is to *monk*, so *Friern* is to *friar*. In Friern Barnet there is a Friary Park.

Obviously, therefore, you would expect *Friern* to be pronounced ˈfraɪən, just like *friar*. And that is indeed how many people say it.

Others, though, call it frɪən. Presumably this variant arose as a spelling pronunciation, on the analogy of words like *pier* pɪə, *fierce* fɪəs and so on. (But compare *fiery* with aɪə.)

Both forms are given in Graham Pointon's *BBC Pronouncing Dictionary of British Names* (Oxford University Press 1990, second edition). Both are duly recorded in EPD and LPD. But the *Oxford Dictionary of Pronunciation for Current English* (Oxford University Press 2001) has only ˈfraɪən, which I think is OK prescriptively but not descriptively.

1.39   veterinary

My bedside radio comes on at 06:30. It is set to BBC Radio 4. So in the early morning every Saturday I get a dose of *Farming Today*.

One day there was a discussion about vets (i.e. animal doctors) and the problems that arise from the fact that working with companion animals (cats, dogs, rabbits) is nowadays much more lucrative than working with farm animals. This causes a shortage of vets prepared to work down on the farm.

Naturally, the word *veterinary* was used repeatedly. I was struck by the fact that the only pronunciation I heard, whether from farmers, from vets themselves or from their teachers at university, was ˈvetn̩ri or the phonologically equivalent ˈveʔn̩ri, ˈvetənri. Only three syllables, only one **r**.

Dictionaries tend to show only spelling-based forms such as ˈvetərɪnəri, with more consonants and more syllables.

In LPD I do give both types, though with priority to forms that have **r** near the beginning as well as near the end. You have to infer ˈvetn̩ri by unpacking the rather complex ˈvet ᵊn ər‿|i. (Perform this operation by ignoring the raised and italic letters and the cutback line, and compressing the last two syllables into one.)

Actual usage is clear – at least as exemplified in *Farming Today*. Three syllables only.

1.40   Marcel Berlins and Sarkozy

The columnist Marcel Berlins pronounces his name ˈbɜːlɪnz, and would like everyone else to do so too. In an article in the *Guardian* he complained about the BBC's 'widespread mangling of the [then] president of France's surname'. 'The three syllables *Sarkozy*', he continued, 'should be stressed pretty much equally'.

It is ridiculous to suggest that we should pronounce all three syllables of *Sarkozy* with equal stress: we're speaking English, a language in which no non-compound three-syllable word has three stresses. (In compounds, perhaps

OK: *deep-sea-blue*.) I assume Berlins is really calling for final stress, which is what with our English ears we tend to hear in French words: **saʁkɔˈzi**.

I expect American announcers pronounce it with final stress. But the BBC is not American.

The name is originally Hungarian, and Hungarian has initial stress. So that could be seen as justifying stress not on the last syllable but on the first. All the same, only an out-of-touch pedant would demand retention of the Hungarian stress.

In BrE we tend to give French words penultimate stress. That's how we mostly say *cliché*, *cachet*, *idée (fixe)*, *Calais*, *Orly* and many others. It's how many of us would stress *Chirac*, and I think it's fine to do it in *Sarkozy*.

Actually, in Hungarian the name is *Sárközy*, so that the middle vowel 'ought' to be ø, as if spelt *eu* in French. In English this Hungarian vowel would normally map onto ɜː (the NURSE vowel), not əʊ (the GOAT vowel). So should we be saying **sɑːˈkɜːzi**? I think not.

The Hungarian spelling also implies that the initial consonant should be not **s** but **ʃ**, which is something that, like the French, we can happily ignore.

1.41   repertory

In an interview that I found on the internet, my eminent colleague and old friend David Crystal is quoted as saying 'I've been in an amateur repartee company for many, many years...'

For someone so verbally dexterous and quick-witted, perhaps that explains a lot. *Repertory*, *repartee*.

Actually, *repertory* is phonetically quite an interesting word. It's OK for the Americans, since they maintain a strong ɔː vowel in the *-ory* ending. But we Brits weaken it to schwa, which leaves weak vowels in three successive syllables: **ˈrepətəri**. As usual, the penultimate schwa is subject to possible disappearance through compression, giving just **ˈrepətri**.

So perhaps it's not surprising that it sometimes gets misheard.

1.42   Penwortham

Penwortham is a village on the outskirts of Preston, Lancashire. Those who live there call it **ˈpenwə(r)ðəm**, with initial stress. (Preston is on the edge of the shrinking rhotic area of Lancashire, so there may still be a few people who pronounce it with -**r**-.)

Non-locals, particularly southerners, tend to assume that it's **penˈwɜːðəm** (or -ˈwɜːθəm), with penultimate stress; they're wrong.

(I don't know how the Australians pronounce the place with the same spelling in South Australia.)

This is one of several such place names in the north of England. In Lancashire just near where I lived as a boy is the mining village of Winstanley. We called it ˈwɪnstənli, but those unfamiliar with the place, and indeed bearers of the corresponding surname, almost all seem to say wɪnˈstænli. The *BBC Pronouncing Dictionary of British Names* gives both. Etymologically, the name derives from the OE proper name *Wynnstān*, modern Winston, plus *lēah* 'wood, clearing', which explains its initial stress.

Just over the summit of the Pennines as you go east into Yorkshire lies Todmorden. I've always known this place as ˈtɒdmədən, though according to the BBC PDBN it can also be ˈtɒdmɔːdən. But not tɒdˈmɔːdən, which is what parachuted-in TV reporters tend to go for.

Conversely, we all know about Newcastle (upon Tyne), which locals stress on the *-cas-* but most other people on the *New-* (a stressing 'firmly established in national usage', in the words of the BBC PDBN). But Newcastle(-under-Lyme) in Staffordshire has initial stress, and so do various other *Newcastles*.

Just to keep us on our toes, however, near Todmorden there is Mytholmroyd. That's actually ˌmaɪðəmˈrɔɪd, with final stress.

I console myself with the thought that all of this must be good for the sales of pronunciation dictionaries.

1.43   hello?

How do we spell and pronounce this greeting? You can find any of three spellings: *hello*, *hallo* and *hullo*. If I am not mistaken, Americans always spell it *hello*. (My Webster's Collegiate also gives *hollo*, but perhaps this is a different word.)

We can agree on its usual pronunciation: həˈləʊ. But instead of a schwa it can sometimes in BrE have a strong vowel in the first syllable; and this strong vowel may correspond to any of the spellings *hello*, *hallo*, *hullo*. In the first syllable, as well as ə I think I've heard e, æ, ʌ and I also suspect I've heard the stress on the first syllable, though maybe this was in stress-shift positions.

The way to determine whether or not there is a secondary stress on the first syllable is to see whether stress shift is possible. And here there is a bit of a problem.

As far as I can tell, stress shift happens only if *hello* (however spelt) is followed by the name of the person being greeted, i.e. a vocative. To trigger stress shift, this vocative has to be accented.

The difficulty is that final vocatives are normally not accented.

Furthermore, as far as I can see the intonation pattern under stress shift has to be fall plus rise.

\Hello, | /Mary.

I don't think you can say:

*\Hello, Mary.

though of course you can say the neutral

>Hel\lo, Mary.

(or the same thing with a rising or falling-rising nuclear tone).

This stress shift triggered by the anomalous accenting of a vocative is paralleled by the cry of despairing British tennis fans,

>\Come on | /Tim!

where logic would lead you to expect the unremarkable

>(')Come \on, Tim!

But in *Hello, Mary* the stress shift itself is anomalous, too, given that the usual first vowel in *hello* is ə. The only explanation seems to be that we're dealing with intonational idioms.

1.44   Lucida

How do you pronounce the font name Lucida?

Actually, Lucida is not the name of a single font but rather of a family of fonts: hence the names Lucida Sans Unicode, Lucida Grande, etc. They were designed by Charles ('Chuck') Bigelow and Kris Holmes in 1985.

The question is whether we should say ˈluːsɪdə (or with lj-), just like *lucid* plus a final schwa; or whether it should be luːˈsiːdə or even a great-vowel-shifted luːˈsaɪdə or an Italianate ˈluːtʃɪdə.

As an Italian word, meaning 'shining, lucid' (f.), *lucida* is indeed ˈlutʃida. Spanish has both *lúcida* and *lucida*, again feminine adjectives, with slightly different meanings. The first is ˈluθiða, ˈlusiða and the second luˈθiða, luˈsiða.

However, we are talking here about English, not Italian or Spanish. And in English we look to Latin.

English *lucid* is taken from the Latin adjective *lūcĭdŭs*. Since the penultimate *i* is short, the regular Latin stress rule means that stress goes on the antepenultimate, the *lū-*. Dropping the masculine ending *-ŭs*, as is usual, yields English ˈl(j)uːsɪd. The feminine form of the adjective is *lūcĭdă*, with the same stress. Keeping the feminine ending, we would get ˈl(j)uːsɪdə.

There are no other English words ending *-ida* that might provide an analogy, except perhaps in a learned singular of such zoological taxonomic terms as *Psittacidae, Vespidae, Ovidae*, all with antepenultimate stress.

The penultimate-stressed *armada* and *pagoda* do not provide models. The first comes via Spanish from the Latin feminine past participle *armāta*, with a long penultimate vowel and therefore penultimate stress. The second is from Portuguese, 'probably ultimately from Persian *butkada* idol temple' (*Concise Oxford Dictionary*) and so not Latin-derived.

Charles Bigelow tells me that he and Kris Holmes (the designers of the Lucida typeface) pronounce it ˈluːsɪdə, just like *lucid* plus a final schwa. 'Frankly, we don't object to any of the pronunciations. We're just glad to hear that people are using it.'

He adds, 'Because Lucida was designed to optimize legibility in early laser printing and computer screen display, we wanted to give it a name that could suggest it was made of light and was clear despite the low resolutions of screens and printers at that time, but we didn't want the name to be a mere description. "Lucidus" or "Lucido" might have been fine, but the success of Futura, Optima and Helvetica led us to consider a name ending in the Latin feminine singular. Maybe it was just superstition that a name could influence popularity.'

So it's ˈluːsɪdə.

1.45 phonetic numerals

Many people are familiar with the NATO/ICAO 'phonetic alphabet' (*alfa*, *bravo*, *charlie*, *delta*, *echo*, *foxtrot*...). In LPD I list these 'communications code names' under each alphabetic letter.

In the NATO/ICAO scheme it is not only the letters that are supposed to be pronounced in specified ways, but also the numbers. Their pronunciation is indicated by respellings, hopefully to avoid any confusion. The two best-known special pronunciations are *fife* for 'five' and *niner* for 'nine' – a sensible way to avoid confusion between the two over a crackly radio channel.

But one confusing respelling is *fower* for 'four'. In discussion of this recommended pronunciation people tend to assume that it's meant to rhyme with *flower* (perhaps because it's immediately preceded by *tree*). Probably, though, this respelling originated in an attempt to train people to say something like ˈfəʊə rather than the monosyllabic, non-rhotic fɔː. I very much doubt whether it was intended that radio operators should actually say ˈfaʊə.

The question, then, is whether *fower* is meant to rhyme with *flower*, *tower* or rather with *grower*, *mower*. *Fower* seems also to be the Scots dialect spelling for *four*.

An instructional CD-ROM I have (the excellent 'VFR RT Communications', produced by Oxford Aviation Training) pronounces the word ˈfaʊə when introducing the pronunciations in isolation – but then goes on to pronounce *four* in the usual way [i.e. fɔː] in examples of actual transmissions. Some speakers on the CD do make more of an effort to say ˈfəʊə during transmissions, it's true; but none goes so far as to say ˈfaʊə. All this confusion could have been avoided if only the NATO people had used IPA to describe what they meant! But then pilots aren't trained to read IPA...

Or they might even have asked a phonetician to advise on making respellings unambiguous.

1.46   Llantwit Major

A German teacher of EFL asked me, on behalf of one of his students, how to pronounce the name of Llantwit Major, a small town in the Vale of Glamorgan.

This is an English-speaking area, and *Llantwit Major* is actually its English name: in Welsh it is called something else. Nevertheless, the name looks Welsh, with the characteristic initial *Llan-*.

So I was interested recently to see on TV a feature about the place. It was striking that the locals all pronounced the name with an ordinary voiced approximant initial l. The visiting reporter, on the other hand, made a great effort to produce a Welsh *ll*, ɬ. He shouldn't have bothered. It's ˈlæntwɪt ˈmeɪdʒə, as confirmed by the *BBC Pronouncing Dictionary of British Names*.

The Welsh name is *Llanilltud Fawr* ɬaˈnɪɬtɪd ˈvawr. *Fawr*, the mutated form of *mawr*, just means 'great, big', and corresponds to the Latin *Major* of the English name. According to the *Dictionary of the Place-names of Wales*, both the English *Llantwit* and the Welsh *Llanilltud* have the same Welsh origin, *llan-* 'church' plus *Illtud*, the name of a monk who reputedly established a monastery there in the sixth century. English *-twit*, according to the authors, is traceable to an early variant *Illtwyd* from an Irish (!) genitive *Illtuaith*.

There's a BBC web page where you can hear audio files of the pronunciation of various Welsh place names. Trying it out, I was struck by the way the speaker pronounces the Welsh *ll* (e.g. in *Llandeilo, Llangwm, Llanddewi Brefi, Benllech*). Instead of the standard voiceless alveolar lateral fricative ɬ, he uses a voiceless palatal fricative ç.

I'm not sure whether this delateralization counts as a speech defect. I have come across it before, in the speech of a Welsh-speaking undergraduate we had at UCL a few years ago. But it is certainly not the mainstream pronunciation, and I do not think it ought to be given to the general public as a model.

1.47   apostasy

The egregious Archbishop Akinola of Nigeria was reported as wanting to save the Anglican Church from apostate leaders. I have not heard him personally say *apostate* aloud (and he now apparently denies that he said it), but when he was reported on BBC radio the reporter pronounced it as ˈæpəsteɪt.

However, the only stressing of *apostate* given in dictionaries is əˈpɒsteɪt, with penultimate stress.

Historians know the word as the appellation of Julian the Apostate, Roman Emperor 355–63 AD. In the modern world, 'apostate' is a favourite word not only of intolerant evangelical Christians but also of Islamic jihadist extremists denouncing their political opponents.

Why, though, is it standardly pronounced *a'postate*, with the stress on the penultimate? Why doesn't it follow the antepenultimate pattern of other trisyllables in *-ate* such as *'delegate*, *'vertebrate*, *'reprobate*? I am not sure what the historical answer is, but it must be something to do with the fact that unlike them *apostate* does not contain the Latin participial ending *-āt(us)*, in which the vowel is long. It comes from Greek, and consists of a prefix *apo-* and a stem *-stăt-* with a short vowel. Literally, it means one standing (*stat*) away (*apo*) from something. In classical Greek ἀποστάτης *apostatēs* meant a runaway slave or a deserter.

Presumably this Greek origin is also the explanation for the unexpected spelling of the corresponding abstract noun *apostasy* ə'**pɒstəsi** (Greek ἀποστᾰσία *apostasia*; compare *stasis*).

The same applies to *ecstasy*, *fantasy* and *idiosyncrasy*, which are also Greek-derived. Confusingly, it doesn't apply to Greek-derived *democracy*, *theocracy* and other *-cracy* words, which have -κρᾰτία *-kratia* in Greek and follow the familiar spelling pattern of Latin-derived *accuracy*, *celibacy*, *delicacy*, *candidacy*, *profligacy*, etc.

1.48   pwn

What is to *pwn*, and what is a pwn? According to Wikipedia, this is a leet slang term (see http://en.wikipedia.org/wiki/Leet), originating as a mistyping of *own* and meaning to own in the sense of being able to dominate or humiliate a rival. It is used in the internet gaming culture 'to taunt an opponent who has just been soundly defeated' (charming!).

Facebook users who have installed SuperPoke can give someone else a virtual pwn.

So how do you pronounce it? Wikipedia offers a range of possible pronunciations ranging from **poʊn** through **puːn** to more imaginative suggestions such as **pə'oʊn** and **pwəʔ'n̩**.

The past participle is apparently sometimes *pwn3d*.

My first feeling on encountering this word *pwn*, though, was that it should be pronounced **pʊn**, which is how it would be if it were Welsh. (Or if spelt *pŵn*, then **puːn**.) According to my Welsh dictionary there is indeed a Welsh word with this spelling and pronounced **pʊn**, though it means 'pack, burden'. For complicated but predictable reasons of Welsh phonology, its plural is *pynnau* '**pənai**.

I'll take that as a virtual pwn.

My friend Tim Owen tells me:

> I am a frequent user of message boards and forums. *Owned* and *pwned* (alternatively *ownt*) have been around fairly commonly since I first started surfing regularly in 2003. Every time I use it and have heard it (which runs into hundreds of times), it's consistently been pronounced as the word *own* prefixed with a **p**.

So for BrE that's **pəʊn**, then.

I see the word has now spawned a derivative *pwnage*.

1.49   Entwistle

I was struck by the fact that two presenters on BBC television pronounced the surname *Entwistle* as ˈenʔwɪsl̩. Others, like me, pronounce it ˈentwɪsl̩. Why the difference? Why my surprise? It's not because I wouldn't glottal a **t** between **n** and **w**: I am perfectly happy to say *slantwise* as ˈslɑːnʔwaɪz.

It's all to do with syllabification. The medial consonant sequence **ntw** is one of the few such sequences that allow two phonotactically well-formed possible places for the syllable boundary, **nt.w** or **n.tw**.

Like many English surnames, this one is derived from a place name. *Entwistle* is a village between Bolton and Blackburn in Lancashire. There's another place in Lancashire called *Oswaldtwistle*, and a Derbyshire village called *Tintwistle*. So it's natural for anyone who knows of these places to see *-twistle* as a separate morpheme.

According to my syllabification rules, dubious consonants go with the more strongly stressed of the flanking syllables, unless there is a major morpheme boundary blocking this. In the first case we would have ˈent.wɪs.l, where the **t** is in an environment that favours glottalling. In the second case we would have ˈen#twɪs.l, where **t** cannot be glottalled because it is syllable-initial.

The announcer's pronunciation of *Entwistle* is therefore what would be predicted in the absence of a morpheme boundary. Mine, on the other hand, is what is to be expected if there is a morpheme boundary between *En-* and *-twistle*.

I looked up the etymology of *Entwistle* in the *Oxford Names Companion*. Its origin is OE *henna*, 'water hen' (or perhaps *ened*, 'duck') plus OE *twisla* 'tongue of land in a river fork'. So the historical morpheme boundary corresponds to my contemporary perception. That explains my non-use of a glottal stop in this word (and also my non-use of pre-fortis clipping for the first vowel plus nasal). That's why it's ˈen.twɪs.l̩.

1.50   Chinese into English

A correspondent wrote to complain about the 'mangling' of Chinese names by English speakers, particularly that of the tennis player Zheng Jie.

'Why', he asked, do commentators 'insist on saying something like ʒʌŋ ʒiː when something like dʒəŋ dʒeə is quite close to the proper pronunciation and perfectly easy in English?'

In Chinese her name is written 郑洁, Pinyin *Zhèng Jié*, pronounced ⁴tʂəŋ ²tɕiɛ (or you may find it easier to think of the distinctively unaspirated obstruents as devoiced dz̥, dʑ̊). *Zheng* is the family name, *Jie* her personal name.

A reasonably thorough anglicization would be ˈdʒʌŋ ˈdʒɪə, or as a halfway house perhaps ˈdʒəŋ ˈdʒiːe. (Those who have a monophthongal SQUARE vowel could pronounce the personal name dʒeə, i.e. dʒɛː.) So why do commentators not say something like that?

I've commented from time to time on the problem of **dʒ** in foreign names. We are so brainwashed by the influence of French that we find it difficult to believe that any foreign language has an affricate **dʒ** rather than a fricative **ʒ**. Hence pronunciations such **tɑːʒ** in *Taj Mahal* instead of **tɑːdʒ**. Hence **ʒ** instead of **dʒ** in *Zheng*.

In the case of Chinese *zh-* this tendency is exacerbated by the prevalence of *zh* as a respelling for **ʒ** and as a romanization of Cyrillic ж (*Zhukov, Zhivago*).

And there's always *Beijing*, which ought to have **dʒ** rather than **ʒ** in the middle. How difficult is it to use a perfectly ordinary sequence of English phonemes **beɪdʒɪŋ** in saying a name? The BBC Pronunciation Unit gives very clear guidance on this. But it's one thing to tell announcers and commentators what they ought to do, another thing to get them to actually do it.

1.51   inter(n)ment

One of my social duties from time to time is to create service sheets for religious services, including in particular funerals. Many of the deceased are buried rather than cremated, and in a big city like London that means that after the funeral service is held in church the actual burial takes place in a cemetery located possibly several miles away. So the service sheet has to tell you where this will be.

Rather than 'burial', people tend to prefer to use the posh word 'interment'. The trouble is that many of them think it is spelt *internment* and pronounced correspondingly. In the service sheets I make myself I spell the word correctly, of course. But at several funerals I have attended the service sheet has been created by someone else, and they have got it wrong.

As we literate people know, *internment* **ɪnˈtɜːnmənt** is imprisonment without trial. You can see how readily it might be confused with *interment* **ɪnˈtɜːmənt**. Think of the common pronunciation of *government* with a single nasal, **ˈɡʌvəmənt**.

A further stage in the confusion is pronouncing this noun as **ˈɪntəmənt**. It does admittedly look confusingly like words with the prefix *inter-*. If *interval* is **ˈɪntəvl̩**, you might reasonably expect *interment* to be **ˈɪntəmənt**.

The verb *to inter*, stressed on the last syllable, has been in English since the fourteenth century, and its derivative noun *interment* likewise. Just think, instead, of

> The evil that men do lives after them;
> the good is oft interred with their bones.

Shakespeare might have written

> The evil that men do lives after them;
> the good is often buried with their bones.

But he didn't.

2   English phonetics: theory and practice

Including discussion of topics such as compression and weakening, not always well described in standard textbooks

2.1   assimilation

A Japanese correspondent asked about the pronunciation of the word *classroom*, having heard a visiting lecturer from the UK pronounce the word it with ʃ instead of s before the **r**. This pronunciation is not recorded in dictionaries. He asked whether it is a common pronunciation in RP in particular and in BrE in general.

I can't find any discussion of this possibility in the literature, although I think it is by no means unknown. I do mention the possibility in one of my lecture handouts, where I list various environments in which the assimilation of /s/ to [ʃ] may occur.

DEALVEOLAR FRICATIVE ASSIMILATION
/s, z/ → [ʃ, ʒ] before /ʃ, ʒ/, and perhaps before /j, r, tʃ, dʒ/ *this shop*, *this student*

You can get this wherever **s** and **r** abut: across word boundaries as in *this reason*, between the parts of a compound as in the *classroom* my correspondent heard, or indeed within a word as in the compressed version of *nursery* **ˈnɜːs(ə)ri**, **ˈnɜːʃri** or *grocery*.

There can be assimilation of **z** to ʒ in the same environments, e.g. *miserable* **ˈmɪʒrəbl̩**.

I have no statistics about how widespread this assimilation is. I don't do it myself, and it's not a mainstream pronunciation.

I suspect that the assimilation product may in some cases not be identical with an ordinary ʃ, ʒ, but rather a kind of retroflex ʂ, ʐ, anticipating the place of articulation of the **r**.

Rather more widespread, and on the increase, is **s** → ʃ before **tr**, as in *strong*. Many of my native-English students have this at least as an optional variant.

The **str** → **ʃtr** assimilation joins the **stj** → **stʃ** → **ʃtʃ** assimilation as phonostylistic phenomena we shall have to think of telling our EFL students about. I call them 's-affricate assimilation'.

2.2   internal intrusive r

At the cardiac support group organized by my local hospital I collected a new example of word-internal intrusive **r**: *meta-analysis*.

The speaker, a general practitioner, used this word several times, and each time pronounced it as ˌmetərəˈnæləsɪs.

A *meta-analysis*, in statistics, is a large study that combines the results of several smaller studies.

Actually, as the classicist in me protests, this word is not well-formed from the point of view of Greek. In classical Greek, prefixes ending in a vowel, such as *meta-* (but also *para-, cata-, ana-, epi-,* etc.), lose the vowel if the following stem has an initial vowel (or *h* plus a vowel). We see this in *metempsychosis, category* and *metonymy,* and also in *method* and *cathode.* So the word ought to be *metanalysis.*

Indeed, the second edition of the OED does not include *meta-analysis,* but only *metanalysis. Meta-analysis* was added in the third edition (2001), with the British pronunciation correctly shown as including an optional **r.** Interestingly, the third edition records that unhyphenated *metanalysis,* and with it the verb *to metanalyse,* belongs not to statistics but to linguistics. The first citation for the verb is from Randolph Quirk, in his 1962 book *The Use of English* (Longman), where he wrote that 'when the French word *crevice* ... was introduced into Middle English, its connexion with "sea food" caused people to metanalyse the final syllable as *-fish* ("crayfish")'. The first citation for *metanalysis* is from Jespersen in 1914.

Somehow it's not surprising that the linguists get the Greek right, while the statisticians, medical or otherwise, don't.

2.3   royal toil

Does *mile* rhyme perfectly with *trial*? Does *owl* rhyme with *vowel*? Does *oil* rhyme with *royal*? I suspect that for most English people the honest answer to all three questions is 'yes'. (I'm prepared to concede that it is not so for everybody, and in particular not for Geordies, as well as not for the Welsh and the Scottish.)

This is part of the more general collapse of the contrast between long vowel or diphthong plus **l** and long vowel or diphthong plus **əl.**

You'd never guess, though, from the entries in pronouncing dictionaries (let alone general dictionaries). Yet Gimson, when I was a student of his in the early 1960s, was already then pointing out that the historical distinction between the end of *mile* **maɪl** and the end of *trial* **traɪəl** was no longer made in practice. *Owl* and *vowel, oil* and *royal* are now usually pronounced so as to rhyme exactly.

In LPD I apply a complicated convention – perhaps too complicated – to try and allow for the rhymes to be identical, while not insisting that they must be. The raised schwa (denoting an optionally inserted sound) in the transcriptions of *mile* **maɪᵊl** and *oil* **ɔɪᵊl** allows for the 'breaking' that leads some speakers to insert a schwa glide between the vowel and the **l.** The slur mark (undertie) in the transcriptions of *trial* ˈtraɪ‿ᵊl and *royal* ˈrɔɪ‿ᵊl allows for possible 'compression', i.e. the squeezing of the two syllables into one. If *mile* gets a potential schwa and *trial* gets compressed, they end up rhyming perfectly. Similarly for *owl* and *vowel*.

LPD also allows for the possibility of 'smoothing', i.e. the loss of the ɪ element in *trial* and the ʊ element in *vowel*. That's how people like me can end up with *trial* and *vowel* as near-rhyming monosyllables **traːɫ, va̠ːɫ**.

2.4   wronger

I heard a TV presenter say 'You're placing undue reliance on a price of oil which is already wrong and which may well end up *wronger*.' He pronounced the last word **ˈrɒŋə**.

It is rare to catch sight of this comparative in the wild. *Wrong* is the only monosyllabic adjective ending in ŋ other than *long, strong, young*. The comparative and superlative forms of these latter three are irregular inasmuch as they are pronounced with -g-: **ˈlɒŋgə, ˈjʌŋgɪst**, etc. Is this because of some minor rule concerning the pronunciation of comparatives and superlatives of all adjectives ending in ŋ, or because *long, strong, young* are lexical exceptions? *Wrong* provides a possible test case to answer this question. If it too has -g-, then there seems to be some general rule in operation. But if it doesn't, the other three are exceptions.

The difficulty is that *wronger* is rarely encountered, because *wrong* is not a readily gradable adjective: things are either right or wrong, rather than having degrees of wrongness. But as the instance I heard shows, this is not always the case. The presenter's pronunciation of *wronger*, which is also my own, demonstrates that – for him and me at least – *wrong* follows the ordinary rule for comparatives, which means that *long, strong* and *young* must be exceptions.

2.5   compression

By the term 'compression' I refer to variability in the number of syllables in a word or phrase. A compressed version of a word or phrase has one syllable fewer than the uncompressed version. In LPD I show sites of possible compression by using the special mark [‿].

Many words have two pronunciations, differing only in a segment that in one version is syllabic, e.g. **i, u, n̩, l̩** and in the other non-syllabic, e.g. **j, w, n, l**. This variability is exploited by versifiers, who can require a particular sequence to be pronounced either uncompressed or compressed, to fit the metrical requirements of the poem, hymn or song in which it appears.

The crucial point of compression is that the number of syllables is reduced by one when a syllable beginning with a vowel follows. In English (treating potential syllabic consonants as phonetic variants of schwa plus the consonant):

> *cycle* **ˈsaɪkl̩** – *cyclist* **ˈsaɪklɪst**, usually not **ˈsaɪkl̩ɪst**;
> *sparkle* **ˈspɑːkl̩** – *sparkling* **ˈspɑːklɪŋ**, usually not **ˈspɑːkəlɪŋ**, **ˈspɑːkl̩ɪŋ**.

In English this process is usually blocked if the following vowel is strong. There is no possibility of compression in the following (though there **is** the possibility, indeed the likelihood, of a syllabic consonant):

> *cattle* ˈkætl̩ – *catalogue* ˈkætəlɒg or ˈkætl̩ɒg, but not ˈkætlɒg;
>
> *summer* ˈsʌmə – *summarize* ˈsʌməraɪz or ˈsʌm̩raɪz, but not ˈsʌmraɪz.

There are other cases, too, where it fails. *Vitally* ˈvaɪtəli or ˈvaɪtl̩i does not rhyme with *nightly* ˈnaɪtli.

Jack Windsor Lewis has commented on 'a fast increasing minority tendency for General British speakers to favour the use of schwa plus (unsyllabic) consonant where previously syllabic consonants were the norm, e.g. in *cotton*, *garden*, *bottle* and *struggle*, and even increasingly in such items as *assembly*, *doubly*, *gambling*, *cackling*, etc., for which it is doubtful that they ever previously contained a syllabic consonant'. Usually there has to be a related word with a syllabic consonant to trigger this, so that e.g. *duckling*, *madly*, *ugly*, for example, are not usually affected but words such as *buckler*, *burglar*, *butler*, *inkling*, *spindly*, *stickler*, etc. may well (he thinks) soon be increasingly heard with an anaptyctic schwa by some British speakers.

I think Jack's observations are correct. I do quite often hear three-syllable schwa-containing pronunciations of words such as *threatening*, *doubling*, *gathering* (though I don't think I'd ever use such a pronunciation myself), and even of *simpler*. I've never yet heard a trisyllabic version of *gently*, though it's not uncommon in *subtly*.

2.6 compression in hymnody

I've been musing about the phonetics of hymns. One thing I have noticed is the way hymnodists exploit compression.

Thus the word *victorious* is pronounced uncompressed, as four syllables, in the dactylic rhythm of the British national anthem, and *glorious* likewise as three syllables:

> Send her victorious (ˈ*tum-ti-ti* ˈ*tum-ti-ti*)
> Happy and glorious
> Long to reign over us
> God save the Queen!

But they are to be sung compressed in a well-known hymn by Charles Wesley:

> Ye servants of God, (*ti-*ˈ*tum-ti ti-*ˈ*tum*)
> Your master proclaim,
> And publish abroad
> His wonderful name;
> The name all-victorious (*ti-*ˈ*tum-ti ti-*ˈ*tum-ti*)
> Of Jesus extol

> His kingdom is glorious
> And rules over all.

Another hymn in which *glorious* is to be sung compressed (= as two syllables) is:

> Glorious things of thee are spoken, (*'tum-ti 'tum-ti...*)
> Zion, city of our God;
> He, whose word cannot be broken,
> Formed thee for his own abode...

Compression can also operate across a word boundary. The relevant vowels, weak **i** and **u**, arise from the weakening of function words such as *me, we, she, the* and *you, to*. Compression means that **i, u** lose syllabicity, becoming **j, w** (or if you prefer **i̯, u̯**).

Both within a word and across a word boundary, compression can operate only if the following vowel is weak – one of **i, u, ə, ɪ**. Thus, within a word we can have compression in *victorious* vɪkˈtɔːri‿əs → vɪkˈtɔːrjəs, where the following vowel is the weak schwa, but not for example in *Victoriana* vɪkˌtɔːriˈɑːnə, where it is the strong **ɑː**.

Eighteenth-century hymnodists follow this principle pretty faithfully. Look for example at the last verse of Charles Wesley's *And can it be*. The hymn is in 8.8.8.8.8.8 meter. Each line is an iambic tetrameter: it consists of four feet, the first syllable of each foot being unstressed and the second stressed (except that the first foot may be trochaic, stressed-unstressed, instead of iambic – producing an 'initial choriamb'):

> No condemnation now I dread
> Jesus, and all in him, is mine!
> Alive in him, my living head,
> And clothed in righteousness divine,
> Bold I approach the eternal throne,
> And claim the crown, through Christ, my own.

In the penultimate line the phrase *the eternal throne* is to be scanned as four syllables, ðjɪˈtɜːnəl ˈθrəʊn, as *the* undergoes compression before the weak initial vowel of *eternal*.

Elsewhere in Wesley's hymns we find *the incarnate deity* as scanned six syllables, with *the* undergoing compression before the weak initial vowel of *incarnate*. He also scans *Immanuel* as trisyllabic ɪˈmænjwəl, with the **u** compressed to **w** before the schwa (compare *genuine* optionally pronounced as two syllables, ˈdʒenjwɪn) and he can make *to appear* two syllables, with *to* (prevocalic weak form **tu**) undergoing compression to **tw** before the initial weak schwa of *appear*.

However, Wesley would never (for example) have scanned *the only* or *to answer* as disyllables. Compression is allowed only before an unstressed vowel. Normally, this vowel must also be weak, as set out above. Exceptionally, though, the hymnodists allow compression before an unstressed but strong vowel, as in the Christmas hymn *Hark! The herald angels sing,* where *With the angelic host proclaim* must be scanned as **ðjænˈdʒelɪk**. Or perhaps we are intended to sing this with elision of the vowel of the article, *th'angelic* **ðænˈdʒelɪk**. But if that were the case I think Wesley would have spelt it in that way.

2.7   GOAT compression

OK, this isn't about the maltreatment of smallholding livestock. No, it's about the possible weakening and subsequent compression of the vowel we use in the GOAT lexical set (see my *Accents of English*, pp. 146–7). In RP and similar accents this is the vowel whose strong version we transcribe əʊ. It used to have a weak version that Daniel Jones transcribed o in the first twelve editions of EPD, as in *November* noˈvembə. When Gimson took over the editorship, he replaced this (quite rightly) with plain schwa, thus nəˈvembə, and nowadays we reckon that in RP əʊ indeed normally weakens to ə: *micro̲cosm, bio̲sphere, pro̲ˈtest, Yello̲wstone*, possibly also *window̲-sill, tomorro̲w morning*.

But this doesn't apply prevocalically. How can we weaken the unstressed first vowel of, say, *o̲asis*? The answer is, we can't.

However, there are one or two words in which the GOAT vowel appears to weaken prevocalically to u. A good example is *tomorro̲w evening*. Weakening to u produces a candidate for compression, since this vowel can be compressed to w before a weak vowel, so losing its syllabicity. One word in which this can happen is *following*, where ˈfɒləʊɪŋ, ˈfɒluɪŋ can be compressed to ˈfɒlwɪŋ. This also applies in the archaic *(thou) followest* ˈfɒlwɪst, as proved by verse scansion. As usual, hymns show this well. *O Love that wilt not let me go* was written as late as 1882, and has the line *O light that followest all my way*, in which *followest* must, if it is to scan, be pronounced ˈfɒlwɪst.

2.8   analogical decompression

'Eng-ger-land! Eng-ger-land! Eng-ger-land!' chant the patriotic football crowds, cheering on the English team. But why do they feel the need to add an extra syllable? Why do they change change ˈɪŋ.glənd into ˈɪŋ.gə.lənd?

There's nothing phonotactically difficult for English speakers in syllable-initial gl. Why break up the cluster with an epenthetic schwa? Why the svarabhakti? (Some speakers don't have a g in *England*, but say simply ˈɪŋ.lənd. They have even less excuse.)

There's one other instance of this phenomenon in English that comes immediately to mind: the widespread pronunciation of *athlete, athletics* as ˈæθəliːt, ˌæθəˈletɪks instead of the standard ˈæθliːt, æθˈletɪks.

I have also heard *template* pronounced as ˈtempəleɪt instead of the usual ˈtempleɪt. (A hundred years ago it was a ˈtemplɪt. But nowadays the spelling pronunciation prevails.)

The explanation must be that the phonetic C+l sequences in these words could also arise from a process of compression (schwa deletion), as when *tingling* (from the verb to *tingle*) is compressed from ˈtɪŋgəlɪŋ to ˈtɪŋglɪŋ, ˈkæθərɪn *Catherine* to ˈkæθrɪn or ˈdʌbəlɪt *double it* to ˈdʌblɪt. (I ignore here the possibility of syllabic l̩ from əl, which is irrelevant to the argument.) Apply this process in reverse, and we get the svarabhakti forms. (But it doesn't explain why it applies only to a very few lexical items.)

This, together with morphological regularization, presumably explains the occasional ˈwɪntəri for *wintry* or riˈmembərəns for *remembrance*.

Eng-ger-land fans, don't let it spread any further. Please! Or as we say nowadays, *puh-leeze*!

2.9   compression anomalies

English seems to have a rule barring the compression of **i**, **u** to **j**, **w** when followed by a strong vowel, though it is fine before a weak vowel.

Hence we can compress *radiant* to two syllables, ˈreɪdiənt → ˈreɪdjənt but can't really do the same with *radiate* ˈreɪdieɪt. We can reduce *mutual* but not *bivouac*.

At least, that's the rule I've been teaching people for many years.

It also explains why *sierra*, *fiesta*, *Bianca*, *Kyoto*, which are all disyllables in the original language, get expanded to three syllables in English. Spanish ˈsjerra becomes English siˈerə, Japanese ˈkjooto becomes kiˈəʊtəʊ.

Given this, you would expect that French borrowings such as *moiré*, *joie (de vivre)* would be subject to the same pressure. But for some reason we're happy with ˈmwɑːreɪ and ʒwɑː. We don't feel any need to expand them to *muˈɑːreɪ and ʒuˈɑː – even though English has no native words with **mw**- or **ʒw**-. Funny.

2.10   oh, oh!

In the 'quantitative-qualitative' English transcription system introduced by Gimson in the sixties, which with minor adjustments remains our standard transcription today, there is just one change I sometimes wish Gim had not made. It concerns the symbol he introduced for the GOAT vowel, namely əʊ.

You can see why he wanted to change the symbol that had been standard until then, namely oʊ. In mainstream RP the vowel no longer had a back rounded starting point. Rather, the starting point had become central and unrounded. It was this change that he wanted to symbolize, but there are certain drawbacks to his choice of symbol.

- The letter ə had hitherto been used only for the weak vowel and the less prominent element of centring diphthongs. Using it for the more prominent part of a stressable diphthong confused matters, and still misleads beginners.
- People tend to mix up the symbols əʊ (GOAT) and aʊ (MOUTH), both in reading and in writing, because they look too similar to one another.

Both of these problems would have been avoided if he had chosen to write the GOAT vowel as ɜʊ. This would also have appropriately signalled that the first element in GOAT is more or less identical in quality with the vowel in NURSE.

Even better, arguably, would have been to stick with oʊ. This symbol would have required some flexibility in interpretation, since the quality of the starting point is indeed nowadays some way from o (cardinal 7). (But we go on writing the STRUT vowel as ʌ, even though its modern quality is some considerable way from cardinal 14 – see 2.25 below.)

If we had kept oʊ as the RP symbol, we would have been able to use the same GOAT symbol in both of the accents taught to EFL learners, RP and General American. As it is, the use of different symbols implies a greater difference between BrE and AmE than really exists.

In my own teaching and authorship I have loyally continued to use Gimson's system, including əʊ, because I appreciate the importance of having a standard system that all reference books agree in using. Except for works edited by Clive Upton, that's what we have, and I'm glad that we do. And even Upton uses the əʊ symbol.

2.11   stressing schwa

The discussion in 2.10 above raises the further question: can ə on its own (i.e. not as part of a diphthong) ever be stressed?

In a universal framework, yes of course it can. There are a fair number of languages around the world in which stressed schwa is attested, starting in Europe with Welsh, Romanian and Bulgarian. The Welsh for 'mountain' is *mynydd* ˈmənɪð; the Romanian for 'apple tree' is *măr* mər; the Bulgarian for 'I am' is съм səm. (No prizes for seeing the Indo-European connections here: Latin *mont-*, *mal-*, *sum*.)

But what about English? You do occasionally get a phonetically stressed schwa in English through the restressing of a weak form, e.g. *(be)cause* kəz, the adverb *just* dʒəst and *going to*, *gonna* gənə. But lexically there are no stressed schwas in English.

Unless... like some authors we use ə for the vowel in *luck*, *cup*, *done*, etc. (= my lexical set STRUT). Many American writers do this, notably Trager and

Smith and their disciples, who claim that the STRUT vowel and the commA vowel belong to the same phoneme, being the stressed and unstressed allophones respectively. If they are co-allophones of the same phoneme, they should be written with the same symbol.

But that is a different issue.

2.12   Latin stress in English

The stress rules of Latin still have a kind of ghostly presence in modern English, as Chomsky and Halle showed in their *Sound Pattern of English*. In Latin a noun or adjective, if it has three or more syllables, is stressed on the antepenultimate if the penultimate vowel is short and followed by at most one consonant (*ˈfacĭlĭs*); otherwise it is stressed on the penultimate (*impeˈrātor*, *treˈmendus*). We have taken this principle into English and not only apply it to words derived from Latin but extend it to words from Greek and sometimes other languages. So we have antepenultimate stress in *ˈdeficit*, *ˈmiracle*, *ˈstamina*, *ˈmemory*, *ˈJupiter* (Latin) and *aˈnemone*, *geˈography*, *aˈnatomy* (Greek). All of these meet the criterion of having a short penultimate vowel followed by a single consonant sound. But we get penultimate stress in *creˈator*, *Ocˈtober*, *bronˈchitis*, *aˈroma*, with their long penultimate vowels, and equally in *treˈmendous*, *Deˈcember*, *aˈorta*, with more than one (historical) consonant between the penultimate and final vowels.

That is the etymological reason that we stress *poˈlygamous* (Greek -γαμ- -*gam-*, with short *a*) differently from *Polyˈphemus* (-φημ- -*phēm-*, with long *e*) and *poly ˈmorphous* (-μορφ- -*morph-*, with two consonants after the vowel).

A nice pair is *Diˈogĕnes* vs. *Dioˈmēdes*.

Faced with an unfamiliar word ending -VCV(C), we crucially need to know whether the penultimate V is long or short. If it is long, it will be stressed; if it is short, it won't be, and indeed will undergo vowel reduction.

Nearly everybody pronounces *diploma* with penultimate stress, because the *o* is long, **dɪˈpləʊmə**. (It comes from Latin *diplōma*, Greek δίπλωμα.) But I knew one person (now deceased) who called it a ˈ**dɪpləmə**, perhaps under the influence of *diplomat* ˈ**dɪpləmæt** (which originated as a French back-formation from *diplomatique*, and does not follow the Latin stress rule).

There's a kind of dinosaur called a *diplodocus*. I've always called it a dɪˈplɒdəkəs, which may or may not reflect the fact that I know that its Greek etymon consists of διπλό- *dipló-* 'double' plus δοκός *dokós* (short o) 'beam'. I was initially taken aback to find that one of my colleagues called it a ˌdɪplə ˈdəʊkəs. But she's not the only one. Our ordinary spelling, of course, doesn't indicate vowel length in -VCV(C) words. It's one of the biggest shortcomings of our spelling system.

And then there is the word *diaspora*. It has an etymologically short penultimate *o* (Greek διασπορά *diasporá*, 'sowing around, scattering'), and a corresponding traditional English pronunciation daɪˈæspərə. But there are also people who stress it ˌdaɪəˈspɔːrə. The spelling doesn't tell you whether the *o* is long or short: and that's the factor that determines the stressing. Because of the Latin stress rule.

The news we heard recently about the human remains identified as those of Richard III meant that several newscasters and commentators made use of the word *skeletal*. Those I heard on BBC Radio 4 all pronounced it with penultimate stress, as skɪˈliːtḷ. There is, though, an alternative pronunciation, with initial stress, ˈskelɪtḷ.

So this is a word like *palatal*, in which uncertainty about the quantity of the penultimate vowel leads to rival pronunciations, one having the antepenultimate stressing and penultimate vowel reduction predicted if the penultimate is short (ˈpalətal, ˈskelɪtal), the other having the penultimate stressing to be expected if that vowel is long (paˈleɪtal, skeˈliːtal). In the case of *palatal*, phoneticians and linguists have settled for the first, although anatomists prefer the second.

Since *skeleton* is derived from the Greek σκελετόν, where the epsilon spelling of the penultimate vowel indicates a short vowel, the regular pronunciation according to the Latin stress rule is indeed the usual one, ˈskelɪtṇ.

Actually, the adjective-forming suffix *-al* is normally disregarded for purposes of the stress rule: we keep the stress on the adjective in the same place as it has for the naked stem, thus from ˈperson we form ˈpersonal (despite the long ō in Latin persōna). From ˈuniverse we have ˌuniˈversal, because the extra syllable in the adjective means that Chomsky and Halle's Alternating Stress Rule comes into play. So in *skeletal*, which does not involve an extra syllable compared with *skeleton*, it would be expected that the stress would be located on the same syllable as in *skeleton*.

And please don't ask about *adjectival*, because I don't understand why it's ˌædʒɪkˈtaɪvḷ, either.

2.13   gemination and degemination

Geminated (double) consonants are quite common in English. They are never found within a morpheme, but arise across (i) morpheme boundaries and (ii) across word boundaries, wherever one element ends in a given consonant and the following element begins with the same consonant:

(i)   *meanness* ˈmiːnnəs, *guileless* ˈgaɪlləs, *nighttime* ˈnaɪttaɪm, *midday* ˌmɪdˈdeɪ;

(ii)   *nice sort* naɪs sɔːt, *big girl* bɪg ɡɜːl, *bad dog* bæd dɒg.

Phonetically, geminated consonants are pronounced like ordinary ones but with extra duration. In the case of plosives, there is a single articulatory gesture but with a longer hold phase.

same man /seɪm mæn/ = [seɪmːæn], *rub both* /rʌb bəʊθ/ = [rʌbːəʊθ]

This much is covered by our textbooks. But what I don't remember seeing much discussion of is <u>de</u>gemination in English, the process whereby a geminate is simplified, i.e. two consonants are reduced to one.

Degemination is the norm in derivational (fossilized) morphology, but the exception in inflectional (productive) morphology. So inside the lexicon there are plenty of cases of degemination such as:

dis + sent = dissent dɪˈsent (cf. *consent*), *in + numerable = innumerable* ɪˈnjuːmərəbl̩; *abbreviate, addiction, aggregation, allocate, connotation, immigration, immature*

– though even here we sometimes override degemination to emphasize the meaning of a prefix, as in *dissuade* dɪ(s)ˈsweɪd (cf. *persuade*), *illegal* ɪ(l)ˈliːgl̩.

Germanic affixes are not subject to degemination. So alongside the Latinate *innumerable* we have *unnecessary* with geminated nn and cases like *meanness*, *guileless* in (i) above. *Entombment* is an interesting case: -*ment*, despite its Latin origin, 'came to be treated as an English formative' (OED), which means that *entombment* ɪnˈtuːmmənt has geminate mm.

What got me thinking about all this was hearing a Conservative MP on the radio pronouncing the phrase *a good deal better* with just a single, ungeminated d. This option is something I drew attention to in LPD, and something I sometimes do myself, though I admit it is a minority choice and probably becoming less frequent. It is also irregular, in the sense that we don't degeminate other dd sequences (*good dog, bad deal*).

Cannot is a special case. When *can* and *not* come together the result is not *can not* kæn nɒt but kænɒt (which in spoken styles is then usually further reduced to *can't*).

Jack Windsor Lewis has pointed out the 'commonplace' possible degemination in *some more* sə ˈmɔː, *good `deal*, *take `care* and *prime `minister*. Degemination in *prime minister* (as praɪˈmɪnɪstə) is certainly widespread: I am not so convinced about *take care*, which doesn't feel right to me with just one k.

The possible elision of t in *sit down, let go, whaddya want* is not degemination, though it is obviously similar, and similarly lexically restricted.

When the suffix -*ly* is attached to a stem ending in l, there are several possibilities, partly lexically determined. Recall that degemination is the loss of one of two identical consonants; compression is a reduction in the number of syllables.

A. stems ending in syllabic l (or əl)

1.   degemination with compression, so that the adverb has the same number of syllables as the adjective. Examples: *gentle* 'dʒentl̩ → *gently* 'dʒentli, *simple* → *simply*, *single* → *singly*, *noble* → *nobly*, *able* → *ably* (and similarly for the suffix *-able* or *-ible*: *possible* → *possibly*, *visible* → *visibly*, *reasonable* → *reasonably*, *understandable* → *understandably*, etc.).

2.   degemination with variable compression. Sometimes compressed, sometimes pronounced with -əli or -l̩i. Adjectives ending in *-ical*, thus *historic(al)* → *historically*, *surgical* → *surgically* usually -ɪkli. Adjectives ending in *-ful*, thus *peaceful* → *peacefully*, *beautiful* → *beautifully* -fli. Also *double* → *doubly*, *special* → *specially*.

3.   degemination without compression. Other adjectives ending in *-al*, thus *natural* → *naturally*, *vital* → *vitally* 'vaɪtəli or 'vaɪtl̩i, *racial* → *racially*.

B. stems ending in non-syllabic l

1.   degemination. Example: *full* → *fully* 'fʊli (perhaps the only categorical example).

2.   variable degemination. Examples: *whole* → *wholly*, *dull* → *dully* 'dʌli or 'dʌlli.

3.   no degemination. Examples: *pale* → *palely* 'peɪlli, *vile* → *vilely*, *cool* → *coolly*, *futile* → *futilely*.

2.14   reductions in casual speech

Someone asked me how a phonetician would transcribe *There you go!*, so I wrote down for him 'ðeə ju 'gəʊ. 'OK,' he said, 'but what if it was said like this?' – and he produced something like ej'gə. 'Has anyone attempted to produce systematic transcriptions of this type of speech?' he asked.

I referred him to various publications that attempt to do just that, or something like it – Linda Shockey's *Sound Patterns of Spoken English* (Blackwell 2002) and Gillian Brown's *Listening to Spoken English* (Longman 1990, second edition). I also mentioned Jack Windsor Lewis's EFL-oriented *People Speaking* (Oxford University Press 1977). (There is now also Richard Cauldwell's excellent and self-published *Phonology for Listening* of 2013, www.speechinaction. org/phonology-for-listening.)

I also suggested that such reduced versions could (in principle) always be derived by rule from careful versions. We may not be sure of all the rules, but in this particular case there appears to be no difficulty in deriving the reduced version by rules of quite general applicability:

input	ˈðeə ju ˈgəʊ
1. reduce *you* to its weakest form, **jə**	ˈðeə jə ˈgəʊ
2. drop the second element of diphthongs	ˈðe jə ˈgə
3. drop initial **ð**	ˈe jə ˈgə
4. drop all stresses except the nuclear accent	e jə ˈgə
5. drop phrase-internal schwa	e j ˈgə
= output	

QED, or, as young people say these days, ta-dah!

2.15   abject haplologies

We've all heard *library* pronounced as ˈ**laɪbri**, or *probably* as ˈ**prɒbli**. Some of us know that these are examples of haplology, defined as the omission of a repeated sound or syllable.

I remember at school, when I was in the classical sixth, the teacher wrote φιλόγος on the board instead of φιλόλογος. 'Please sir,' I said, 'you've committed a haplology.' (I was a real smart-arse as a teenager.) The teacher replied sarcastically, 'I have made a simple mistake'.

If I'd been even smarter, I'd have known that the term for a written as opposed to a spoken example is a *haplography*.

Anyhow, I heard a new phonetic haplology the other day. It was from a medical consultant giving a talk on blood pressure. She repeatedly referred to the instrument used to measure blood pressure, the *sphygmomanometer*, as a ˌ**sfɪgməˈnɒmɪtə**.

In the BBC Radio 4 panel game *Just a Minute* the panellists have to attempt to speak for sixty seconds on a given topic without hesitation, deviation or repetition. In one episode I listened to, one of the topics was what is usually written as *quantitative easing*. I would pronounce the first word here as ˈ**kwɒntɪtətɪv**. However, the chairman (Nicholas Parsons), and everyone else on the programme as far as I could tell, pronounced it ˈ**kwɒntətɪv**. Formally, I suppose this too is a haplology. A repeated consonant gets deleted along with its support vowel.

The OED has a separate entry for *quantitive*, which it regards as 'irregularly' formed. It adduces citations from 1626 onwards. In *Just a Minute*, given that the chairman specified the topic as ˈ**kwɒntətɪv** easing, I wonder whether panellists would have been penalized for deviation if they had referred to ˈ**kwɒntɪtətɪv** easing. You're allowed to repeat the words on the card (but no others) without penalty. So perhaps repeated ˈ**kwɒntətɪv** ought to have been allowed, but not *quantitative* ˈkwɒntɪtətɪv, since that was not exactly the word the chairman had specified as part of the topic. Are the 'words on the card' those that the chairman utters, or those that are written?

Americans and some others prefer ˈkwɒntəteɪtɪv, a variant which I imagine would be resistant to haplology.

2.16   the happY vowel

I still receive a number of queries from students puzzled by 'the happY vowel' (shown in many dictionaries and textbooks as i, as opposed to iː or ɪ).

The point is that the last vowel in *happy* and all other similar words can sound like the iː of *fleece* or like the ɪ of *kit* or something intermediate between them. The distinction between iː and ɪ is 'neutralized' in certain phonetic environments. There are many thousands of other examples besides *happy – very, coffee, valley, spaghetti, sanity, suddenly*; also the second vowel in *various, radiation*.

Current pronunciation dictionaries and other works use the notation i to show these cases in which the distinction between FLEECE (iː) and KIT (ɪ) does not apply. Where it does apply, they write iː (as in *green, bead, feet, reach, seating*) or ɪ (as in *grin, bid, fit, rich, sitting*), as appropriate.

There is a corresponding neutralized back vowel u, as in *thank you, incongruous, situation*.

More technically, it seems to be right to recognize two distinct vowel systems in English. The strong system (in RP) covers ɪ e æ ɒ ʌ ʊ iː eɪ aɪ ɔɪ uː əʊ aʊ ɪə eə ɑː ɔː ʊə ɜː, while the weak system covers not only i u ə but also ɪ ʊ, as in *finishes, executive*. Weak vowels occur only in unstressed syllables, although strong vowels may be either stressed or unstressed.

The vowels ɪ ʊ therefore belong to both systems. As a weak vowel, however, ʊ is increasingly replaced by ə. Various other accents, e.g. Australian, lack the distinction between weak ɪ and ə, or at least give it a very low functional load. Thus English seems to be moving towards a weak system of three vowels only: i u ə.

Vowel weakening involves a switching between the strong system and the weak system. We see this:

- in words with strong and weak forms, e.g. *can* kæn – kən;
- and in alternations such as *preside – president, variety – vary, anatomy – anatomical*.

One of the reasons our spelling system is less than transparent is that it generally writes the strong and weak alternants identically.

The happY vowel is good news for speakers of languages such as Spanish, for whom the distinction between iː and ɪ is difficult. Where we write i, they needn't bother to make that distinction.

2.17 crazes and crazies

The *Guardian* newspaper carried the following correction:

> A mishearing led us to quote the psychoanalyst Adam Phillips as saying that 'anybody who's been in the therapy profession for any length of time will know that there have always been crazies'. In fact, he was referring to crazes.

I am one of those who pronounce *crazies* and *crazes* identically, as ˈkreɪzɪz. They are absolute homophones for me, so I can sympathize with anyone who 'mishears' one for the other.

Nevertheless many other native speakers of English – the majority, I should think – make a distinction between the two. Either their happY vowel (the final vowel in *crazy*) is tenser, [i], or they use a schwa in the plural ending after a sibilant (*crazes*), or both.

That is why modern pronunciation dictionaries, including LPD, use the special symbol **i** for the weak happY vowel. It covers both an **iː**-like quality, for those who use it, and an **ɪ**-like quality, for those like me who use that. So we write *crazies* as ˈkreɪziz, and *crazes* as ˈkreɪzɪz (or ˈkreɪzəz).

Other potential homophones to test include: *bandied – banded, studied – studded, taxis – taxes, Rosie's – roses*.

You find the happY vowel both at the end of words like *happy* and also within a word before a vowel, in words such as *glorious*. Behind this use lie two main considerations. One is saving space when specifying pronunciation in a dictionary or vocabulary list. If I pronounce ˈhæpɪ but the majority of English speakers say ˈhæpiː – i.e. if like Jones and Gimson I identify the final vowel with that of *kit*, while they identify it with that of *fleece* – then we save space by using a special symbol, **i**, distinct from both, rather than by transcribing each such word twice (and there are a very large number of them).

But the other reason is a more sophisticated one. English arguably distinguishes two vowel systems, strong and weak. Weakening means switching from the strong system to the weak, making a strong vowel weak. Thus ə is the weak counterpart of strong æ, ɒ, ʌ (and various other vowels), as we see in the strong and weak forms of *at, of, us*. In exactly the same way, **i** and **u** may be seen as the weak counterpart of strong iː, uː, as seen in *me* and prevocalic *you, to*. Because the weak-vowel system is much smaller than the strong-vowel system, in these positions we have a neutralization (or, in Trubetzkoy's terminology, an *Aufhebung*, 'annulment') of some of the phonemic oppositions present in the strong-vowel system.

These are not the only neutralizations we find in English. The opposition between **t** and **d**, exemplified in *tamp* vs. *damp*, is neutralized after tautosyllabic **s**, as in *stamp*. So logically we might introduce a new symbol, say **T**, to show it, and instead of **stæmp** write **sTæmp**. What applies to the alveolar plosives also applies to the labials, as in *pin – bin – spin*, and to the velars, as in *core – gore – score*.

As a further example, within the strong-vowel system, there is the neutralization of iː (*bee*) vs. ɪə (*beer*) in the environment _rV, as in the first syllable of *serious*.

But the practical needs of EFL learners inhibit us from going any further down this path. Even the happY vowel is puzzling enough for many of them.

2.18   banded or bandied?

A journalist in the *Financial Times* spoke of a derogatory term being 'banded about' by hip-hop artists. What he meant, of course, was *bandied about*, from the verb *bandy about* 'to mention an idea, name, remark, etc. several times, especially in order to seem impressive'. There is no verb *band about*.

Bandy is one of the words that ends with the happY vowel, which we nowadays write **i**, representing the neutralization (non-distinction) of iː and ɪ in weak final position, and ranging phonetically between tense [i] and lax [ɪ].

The conditions for *bandied* and *banded* to be homophonous, as they presumably are for the journalist in question, are twofold. First, the happY vowel must be realized with a quality and quantity identical to those of /ɪ/, and secondly the past tense/past participle suffix -*ed* must be pronounced as ɪd, not as əd.

Since my own pronunciation satisfies these two criteria, the words are homophonous for me, ˈbændɪd. I therefore have to be careful to spell each one appropriately. But Tony Blair, for instance, with his pervasive use of ə in weak syllables, would presumably make a difference between them. So would anyone who has an [i]-like quality for the presuffixal happY vowel of *bandied*. Some speakers have both these characteristics. The trend is towards distinguishing the two words as [ˈbændid] *bandied* vs. [ˈbændəd] *banded*.

Other relevant pairs are *candied – candid, taxis – taxes, studied – studded* and even *Billy's – Bill is*. In the first of these it is a matter not of an inflectional ending, but of the adjectival suffix -*id*. But this usually seems to agree with -*ed*.

2.19   the status of schwa

Ought schwa to be included in the phonemic inventory of English? After all, it only occurs in the weak-vowel system, and all other vowels in that system are already members of the strong-vowel system. So isn't schwa equivalent to the **T** in s**T**æmp we discussed above (2.17), and wouldn't it make sense to write *panda* as either ˈpændæ, ˈpændɒ or ˈpændʌ rather than ˈpændə?

This is essentially what the first edition of the OED did, using notations such as ă. It was abandoned in later editions.

In some words (not *panda*) this kind of analysis is supported by the use of strong vowels in singing. Transcribing *angel* as ˈeɪndʒĕl (where ĕ = weakenable

e) could be justified on these grounds, even though in all kinds of speech other than singing we say ˈeɪndʒəl.

But it is precisely cases such as the second syllable of *panda* that present an interesting case. There is no style of speech in which we use anything other than ə for the vowel in this word, and no grounds other than orthographic for choosing one of the alternatives shown rather than another. As long as it remains a weak vowel, the final vowel of *panda* contrasts only with what I write i and u, i.e. the vowels of *happy* and *thank you*. Compare *panda* and *handy*. As long as we know we are in the weak vowel system, schwa does indeed represent a neutralization of e, æ, ɒ, eə, ɑː, ɔː, ɜː, as we see in the strong/weak alternation of the function words *them, at, of, there, are, for* and *sir*.

Actually, there's a problem with e, in the endings *-ed, -es, -est*, which for most speakers of RP and similar accents weakens not to ə but to ɪ. (In closed syllables there is a slightly larger weak-vowel system, which includes ɪ.) Such speakers formerly also weakened it to ɪ in *-less* and *-ness*, but now mostly weaken it to ə. So we have the awkward anomaly that e can have two different neutralization forms, even for the same speaker.

However, the main argument against this line of thought is rather different. It is that we never know from the general structure of a word whether a given unstressed syllable will select its vowel from the strong system or from the weak system. Alongside words like *gymnast* (with -æst, strong system) we have words like *modest* (with -ɪst, weak system). Think about the unstressed final syllables of *phoneme, Kellogg, cuckoo, syntax, torment* (n.) – all strong. No neutralization there! Chomsky and Halle have some pointers to what's going on, but in many cases it remains arbitrary whether or not vowel weakening occurs.

In this respect English differs strikingly from, say, Russian, where weakening is highly predictable once you know where the word stress is located.

2.20   charted and chartered

Every day the *Guardian* newspaper publishes 'Corrections and clarifications'. One day in 2006 the paper included an apology for writing 'unchartered territory' (they meant 'uncharted'), and another for saying that a minister had 'tended his resignation' (they meant 'tendered'). The next day they apologized for allowing the writer of a letter to the editor to say '... eating initiatives are having an affect on our school children', with the undesirable effect of suggesting that he did not know the difference between 'affect' and 'effect'.

I am showing my age when I reveal that for me not only does *chartered* ˈtʃɑːtəd sound different from *charted* ˈtʃɑːtɪd and *tendered* ˈtendəd from *tended* ˈtendɪd but also that for me *affect* (verb) əˈfekt is not a homophone of *effect* ɪˈfekt.

All my twenty-year-old native-English students seem to have *affect* and *effect* as homophones, both with ə-. An awful lot of them pronounce *-ered* and *-ed* as homophones too, both with -əd. Evidently the *Guardian* reporters who misheard or misspelt *tend(er)ed* and *chart(er)ed* do the same.

In England it seems to be along the east coast that the drift from weak ɪ to ə is at its most general: in Norfolk, for instance, or in Geordieland. Elsewhere, it is a well-known characteristic of southern-hemisphere English, as well as of most rhotic accents. Among public figures, Tony Blair is one who uses a striking number of schwas where traditional RP would have ɪ.

Although in EFL we traditionally teach that the verb ending *-ed* is pronounced -ɪd after alveolar plosives (as in *waited, faded, painted, landed*), at least one recent EFL textbook prescribes -əd.

2.21   singing strongly

Being the son of an Anglican clergyman, I have been accustomed from my earliest years to singing hymns, both at school and in church. The pronunciation used in hymn-singing is subtly different from ordinary conversational pronunciation. It is 'over-articulated': in particular, there is less vowel reduction. The ending *-ed* after alveolar plosives is usually **ed** rather than ɪd or əd. The ending *-(e)s* after sibilants is usually **ez** rather than ɪz or əz. The endings *-less* and *-ness* are unreduced **les, nes**. Not all vowels are strong, however. The preconsonantal indefinite and definite articles retain schwa: ə, ðə.

So when we sing we pronounce *praises* as ˈpreɪzez and *kindness* as ˈkaɪndnes, as well as singing *to* invariably as tuː. In *the morning* and *the sky*, however, *the* is ðə. When singing, we all make these modifications without conscious thought.

2.22   happY prefixes

In the 2008 revision of LPD I changed the entries for words with the unstressed prefixes *be-, de-, pre-, re-*. Instead of entries like these:

becalm **bɪ** ˈkɑːm bə-, §biː-
predict **prɪ** ˈdɪkt prə-, §priː-

– I put:

becalm **bi** ˈkɑːm bə-
predict **pri** ˈdɪkt prə-

The LPD symbol § denotes 'BrE non-RP'. For the last twenty years or so phoneticians have been using the symbol i for the weak close front vowel used at the end of words such as *happy, coffee, donkey* ('the happY vowel').

In conservative Daniel Jones-style RP this vowel is phonetically identical with the ɪ of KIT. But for many other speakers it is more like (or indeed identical with) the **iː** of FLEECE.

The environments in which I use **i** in the first and second editions of LPD are:

- word-finally: *happy, coffee, valley*;
- before a strong vowel: *variation, ratio*;
- and before a weak vowel: *glorious, convenient*.

I also use it:

- at the end of a combining form: *multilateral, polytechnic*;
- and in inflected forms in which **d** or **z** is added to a stem ending in **i**: *carried, carries*.

So it was a very natural extension to use it for the prefixes *be-, de-, pre-, re-*. It saves a little space, too.

Just as *studied* was a homophone of *studded* for Daniel Jones (and is for me), or *bandied* and *banded*, so now *descent* was/is a homophone of *dissent*. But there are other speakers who make a difference in such pairs.

2.23   happY endings

In the discussion of *bandied* and *banded* (2.18 above) I failed to mention a complicating factor: that there are people who have tense [i] for the word-final happY vowel, but change it to [ɪ] before inflectional **d** or **z**. Such speakers therefore have [i] in *bandy, taxi, study, coffee* but [ɪ] in *bandied, taxis, studied, coffees*. It follows that for them *bandied* can still be homophonous with *banded*, and *taxis* (cabs) with *taxes*, despite the [i] in the uninflected form. Other speakers, though, do not do this, but keep [i] even before an inflectional suffix. I have never come across anyone who distinguished the plural from the possessive. Probably *cities* and *city's* are homophonous for everyone.

You can get the same change of [i] to [ɪ] before *-ful* and *-ment*, giving [i] in *beauty, accompany* but [ɪ] (or even [ə]) in *beautiful, accompaniment*.

An even more interesting case is suffixes beginning with **l**: *-ly* and *-less*. I have [ɪ] in *happy, angry*, but often change it to [ə] in *happily* and virtually always in *angrily*. (As editor of LPD, Gimson gave priority to -rəl- in this word as long ago as 1977.) A more conservative pronunciation keeps ɪ in this position, a more progressive one ə.

For those who go all the way (like me) there is a further interesting consequence. The derived schwa can then trigger syllabic consonant formation, producing a syllabic **l̩** in *readily* ˈredl̩ɪ, with a laterally released **d**. *Mightily* then rhymes with *vitally*. Similarly, I think many, perhaps most, people say *funnily* and *penniless* with -nl̩-.

I wouldn't do that in *guiltily* or *unwieldily*, though.

2.24   some

A correspondent asked about the pronunciation of the word *some*. From the point of view of EFL there are three issues here:

- does this word have distinct strong and weak forms?
- if so, what is their distribution?
- if the distribution depends partly on whether this word is accented, when is it accented?

Let's take them in order.

In RP *some* has the strong form sʌm and the weak form səm. The weak form is susceptible to possible syllabic consonant formation, making it sm̩. I'll ignore this possibility in the remainder of the discussion. Despite ending in a labial rather than in an alveolar, this word is for many speakers also susceptible to assimilation of place of articulation, e.g. ˈsʌŋ kaɪnd əv... *some kind of...* I'll ignore this possibility, too.

As far as other accents are concerned, it depends on whether or not there is a robust contrast between ʌ and ə (as in RP) or not (as in many other accents). If there's no reliable contrast between the vowels, it makes little sense to distinguish strong and weak forms.

The distribution of strong and weak forms in RP is subject to the usual rules. The word is pronounced strong if stranded or accented, weak otherwise.

'Stranded' means followed by a syntactic gap. In the case of *some*, this would be because the noun that would otherwise follow has been deleted (ellipted). In (1) *some* has its usual following noun, so is weak. In (2) it is stranded, therefore strong, even though unaccented.

(1)   Would you like some coffee?
(2)   A: More coffee? Let me pour you some.
         B: No, thanks. I've still got some left.

The *some* in (2) stands for *some coffee*. But the word *coffee* has been ellipted ('is understood'). That leaves *some* stranded.

In *some more*, *some* is not stranded, so has its weak form.

Let me get you some more.

Some is unaccented when it is merely a quantifier (used like *a/an*, but before a non-count noun or a plural: *some salt, some books*). If the noun is present it must have its weak form, səm.

There's some milk in the fridge.
Go and get some potatoes.

Here are some more examples of stranded *some*, with the strong form.

(You're eating ice cream.) ˈI want some, | ˈtoo!
(Look, apples!) Why don't you ˈtake some?!

You could say that all 'pronominal' uses of *some* – all cases where *some* is not followed by its noun or noun phrase – represent stranding. That would cover cases like the following, where *some* is however likely to be accented.

(Milk?) There's 'some in the <u>fridge</u>.
(Potatoes?) There are 'some in the '<u>shed</u>.

When *some* has a more specific meaning, it is usually accented and always has its strong form **sʌm**.

(i)   as opposed to *others* or to *all*
         'Some 'insects are '<u>good</u> for the garden,
         | 'some are '<u>bad</u>, | and 'others are '<u>neutral</u>.
         A: All Cretans are liars.
         B: That's not true, | although 'some are.
         'Some cheese | is made from '<u>goat's</u> milk.
         It's 'all right for V<u>some</u>!
         (= unlike the rest of us, you [or they] have all the luck)
(ii)   meaning 'a considerable quantity of'
         It was 'some '<u>years</u> | be'fore she '<u>saw</u> him again
         It's been 'some '<u>time</u> | 'since we last '<u>saw</u> one another.
(iii)   as a determiner, 'some ... or other'
         'Some '<u>idiot's</u> | 'left the '<u>light</u> on.
         'Some day | I'll 'win the '<u>lottery</u>.
         'Some people | are 'just '<u>useless</u>.
         For 'some reason | she 'wasn't in'<u>vited</u>.
(iv)   exclamatory, 'very remarkable'
         That was '<u>some</u> | '<u>party</u>!
         They were '<u>some</u> | '<u>students</u>!

Compare

(i)   He put **səm** '<u>fruit</u> on the pizza.
         (as well as cheese, ham, etc.)
(ii)   He put '**sʌm** '<u>fruit</u> on the pizza.
         (I can't identify what fruit.) or (it was a remarkable fruit.)

See Churchill's defiant words to the Canadian parliament in 1941:

> When I warned [the French] that Britain would fight on alone, whatever they did, their Generals told their Prime Minister and his divided cabinet: 'In three weeks, England will have her neck wrung like a chicken.' 'Some '<u>chicken</u>; | 'some '<u>neck</u>!

– with the strong form, of course.

2.25   the symbol for STRUT

A student has taken me to task for using what he sees as inaccurate phonemic symbols for English.

> My /ʌ/ [he claims, very reasonably] seems to be far closer to [ɐ] than to (cardinal) [ʌ]; my /æ/ I believe to be far more like (cardinal) [a] than [æ]; my /u/ seems to be a kind of central/lax front vowel of the order of [ʉ], quite far from (cardinal) [u], my aɪ is far more like ɑɪ or ʌɪ, and my e is far more like ɛ than (cardinal) e. Now, I understand that phonemic symbols are merely conveniences, and aren't necessarily meant to convey any underlying phonetic reality. I also understand that, historically, it was also more difficult to type, for instance, the IPA symbol for a close central rounded vowel, ʉ, than u.

But he's still very unhappy about it.
   I replied along the following lines:

> When I first started phonetics myself, half a century ago, I had the same thought as you about ʌ: that it would be better written ɐ. I made a point of transcribing it like that in the transcription assignments I was set by my phonetics teacher.

> But when I came to be a phonetics teacher myself, and to publish books, it seemed better to stick with the same transcription that other people use. There are millions of people around the world who know that ʌ means the STRUT vowel of English; there are a few thousand, at most, who know or care anything about the cardinal vowel system.

> The same, mutatis mutandis, applies to /æ/ (better written /a/?) and to /uː/ (better /ʉː/?).

> Furthermore, if we want the same transcription system to apply to a wide range of different varieties of English, there are strong arguments in favour of sticking with æ and uː.

> It is possible that in another fifty years the discrepancies will have become too great: the tectonic plates will shift, and some new influential phonetician will establish a different notation. But not me.

2.26   the Teutonic Rule

The 'Teutonic Rule' of English says that the first two syllables of a word cannot both be lexically unstressed. In words with the main stress on the third syllable or later, we need a secondary stress on the first or second syllable.
   So what do I mean by 'lexically stressed'?
   In running speech, as we know, stress (in the sense of a rhythmic beat on a syllable) is very variable. Depending on intonation, speech rate and other factors,

we readily suppress the stress on some of the syllables which could have been stressed. This is 'utterance stress'.

'Lexical stress', on the other hand, is a fixed property of each word in the speaker's mental lexicon. Whatever happens in running speech, the second syllable in each of *regret, consider, decisively* remains lexically stressed, as we show by their dictionary transcriptions **rɪˈɡret, kənˈsɪdə, dɪˈsaɪsɪvli**.

These are all single-stressed words. What is the justification for considering some English words to be lexically double-stressed? i.e. to have two (or more) lexically stressed syllables?

The crucial point with multiple-stressed words is their susceptibility to 'stress shift'. Although in isolation we say the words *photographic, catastrophic* with the main stress on the penultimate syllable, and *afternoon, fifteen* with the main stress on the final syllable, in connected speech – as is well known – the first syllable of each of these words may have not just a rhythmic beat but also intonational prominence (= an accent), while the other stress may be suppressed.

photoˈgraphic	aˈphotographic ˈrecord
cataˈstrophic	a ˈcatastrophic ˈfailure
afterˈnoon	ˈafternoon ˈtea
fifˈteen	ˈfifteen ˈpeople

So far, so good: students of English phonetics know about this (I hope).

And this is where the Teutonic Rule comes in. Without a lexical stress ('secondary stress', 'pretonic stress') before the main stress, and consequent susceptibility to stress shift, words such as *photographic, catastrophic, afternoon* would not be phonologically well-formed.

Other pretonic stresses, though, are not dependent on the Teutonic Rule. The word *fifteen* has only two syllables, so it would conform to the Teutonic Rule even without a pretonic stress on the first syllable. How, then, can we determine its presence or absence? The only way is to examine its behaviour under stress-shift conditions.

Consider, as a test case, the word *bamboo*. In its dictionary entry, should the pronunciation read **bæmˈbuː** or ˌ**bæmˈbuː**?

First let it bear the intonational nucleus, and then put it in a sentence in which it is followed by a word bearing the nucleus, and see what happens.

1. It's ˈmade of bamˈboo
2. × a bamˈboo ˈtable
3. a ˈbamboo ˈtable

We say (1) and (3), but not (2). So *bamboo* must be lexically double-stressed, ˌ**bæmˈbuː**.

If we test *cosmetic*, we get:

1. It's ˈmerely cosˈmetic
2. a cosˈmetic ˈsurgeon
3. × a ˈcosmetic ˈsurgeon

We say (2), not (3). At least, that's what I do. So *cosmetic* is single-stressed, kɒzˈmetɪk.

Sometimes usage is divided.

1.   ˈbuying anˈtiques
2.   ? an anˈtique ˈchair
3.   ? an ˈantique ˈchair

Some speakers go for (2), some go for (3). For those who say (2) this word is lexically single-stressed; for those who say (3) it is lexically double-stressed. In LPD I want to cater for both. That's why I use the rather ungainly notation (ˌ)ænˈtiːk.

2.27   problems with lexical stress

It is sometimes difficult to decide how to mark word stress in a dictionary. A dictionary should ideally show lexical stress, i.e. the stress pattern that the word has when spoken in isolation with no special pragmatic factors in play (no special contrastive stress, for example). You can usually check this by making the word a one-word utterance, as an answer to a question such as *What's that? What's it like? What did he do? How did he do it?*

There's a particular difficulty with compound adjectives such as *God-given*, *hard-drinking*, *long-term*, *sabre-toothed*. Lexically it is probably correct to show them all with double stress (end-stress), so ˌGod-ˈgiven, ˌhard-ˈdrinking, ˌlong-ˈterm, ˌsabre-ˈtoothed.

The trouble is that all double-stressed words are candidates for stress shift. And adjectives like these are usually attributive: they precede a noun, itself likely to be stressed, so that in practice they undergo stress shift much more often than not.

our ˈGod-given ˈrights
a ˈhard-drinking ˈsailor
ˈlong-term ˈplans
a ˈsabre-toothed ˈtiger

It may feel slightly awkward to force them into predicative position:

What sort of rights are these? – God-given.
What kind of sailor was he? – Oh, hard-drinking.
What plans did you make? – Long-term ones.
What kind of tiger was it? – Sabre-toothed.

If we do this, however, I think it becomes clear that they are indeed double-stressed.

What sort of rights are these? – ˈGod-ˈgiven.
What kind of sailor was he? – ˈHard-ˈdrinking.

What plans did you make? – 'Long-'term ones.
What kind of tiger was it? – 'Sabre-'toothed.

If we answered the last question by saying

–'Sabre-toothed

then we would implicitly be contrasting *sabre-* with some other kind of tooth-edness. But sometimes this kind of contrastiveness becomes fossilized, as in *pear-shaped*, so that initial stress is the only possibility.

It's 'all gone 'pear-shaped.

There is also a problem in deciding whether to show words such as *one-size-fits-all* or *MRSA* with four stresses or (as they are usually pronounced) just with two; and likewise whether to show three or two lexical stresses in words such as *non-denominational*.

2.28   twenty-twenny

Americans, as we all know, tend to pronounce *twenty* as '**tweni** rather than '**twenti**. That's because they have an **nt** reduction rule that allows the deletion of **t** between **n** and a weak vowel, as in *winter*, *painting*, *center*, *counter*, *gentle*, *in front of* and all other cases satisfying this structural description.

Londoners, too, often say *twenty* in this way. But they don't lose the **t** in *winter*, *painting*, etc. (though they might make it a glottal stop). Londoners don't say 'wɪnə rather than 'wɪntə. In fact the only other cases for Londoners seem to be *plenty*, *wanted*, *went (away)*, *want to*, '**pleni**, '**wɒnɪd**, '**wen** (ə'weɪ), '**wɒnə**. (More generally, they can lose the **t** from *want* and *went* whenever they are followed by a vowel sound. There are also **t**-less reductions of *trying to* and *going to*.)

So we can say that for Londoners this is not a general phonological rule but a lexically specific one applying to just a few special cases.

And what about RP? In LPD I do mention the '**tweni** form as a BrE possibility, but with a warning triangle against it. Yet I am aware that some people who qualify generally as RP speakers do use it, as well as (some of) the other London reductions mentioned. Ought I to remove the warning triangle?

You may be surprised that I include *gentle* as one of the examples in the first paragraph above. Does it have **t** followed by a weak vowel, as required by the structural description of the rule? Well, yes, it does. I regard syllabic [l̩] as a realization of the underlying string /əl/. If this is right, then the **nt** reduction rule holds as long as it applies before the syllabic consonant formation rule is applied.

underlying form	/'dʒentəl/
nt reduction	['dʒenəl]
syllabic cons. formation	['dʒenl̩]
= surface form	

But this is not without its problems. Before another syllabic consonant, namely
[n̩], Americans don't reduce **nt** in this way. In words such as *Clinton*, *accountant*
they tend instead to use a glottal stop: ˈklɪnʔn̩. (American /t/ tends to be glottal
before a consonant in the next syllable.)

So the AmE **nt** reduction rule is a bit messy, because we have to allow it to
operate before syllabic ḷ (and syllabic r̩, as in *winter*), but not before syllabic n̩.
But those are the facts.

The word *continental* /ˌkɑntəˈnentəl/ is a nice example. In the first /nt/ the /t/
becomes glottal, while in the second it disappears. So we get [ˌkɑnʔn̩ˈenḷ].

Here's one way of doing the phonology, with some awkward rule ordering.

underlying form	/ˌkɑntəˈnentəl/
syllabic **n** formation	[ˌkɑntn̩ˈentəl]
T glottalling	[ˌkɑnʔn̩ˈentəl]
nt reduction	[ˌkɑnʔn̩ˈenəl]
syllabic **l** formation	[ˌkɑnʔn̩ˈenḷ]
= surface form	

2.29   phantom r

As we all know, the rulers of Burma would prefer that we call their
country *Myanmar*.

In Burmese, this name is essentially just a variant of the name *Burma*. It is
transliterated as *Myan-ma* or *Mran-ma*, and in the local language pronounced
something like **ma(n)ma**, as against **bama** for the traditional name.

Within the Burmese language, *Myan-ma* is the written, literary name of the
country, while *Bama* (from which English *Burma* derives) is the oral, colloquial
name. In spoken Burmese, the distinction is less clear than the English transliteration suggests.

So the situation is comparable to the former right-wing rulers of Greece, the
colonels who insisted on literary (katharevusa) *Ellas* rather than popular (dhi-
motiki) *Elladha*. Right-wing politics becomes associated with the more literary
form, left-wing with the more popular.

What interests me now, however, is the question of how Americans and other
rhotic speakers are supposed to pronounce this name. In both *Myanmar* and
Burma the English spellings assume a non-rhotic variety of English, in which the
letter *r* before a consonant or finally serves merely to indicate a long vowel:
ˈmjænmɑː, ˈbɜːmə.

So anyone who says the last syllable of *Myanmar* as **mɑːr** or pronounces
Burma as **bɜːmə** is using a spelling pronunciation based on British, non-rhotic,
spelling conventions.

In compiling LPD I faced a somewhat similar problem with the words *scarper* ˈskɑːpə 'vamoose, take off' and *sarnie* ˈsɑːni 'sandwich'. Americans don't generally know or use these words, but how would they pronounce them if they did? The first is believed to be derived from Italian *scappa!* or by rhyming slang from *Scapa (Flow)* (= go); the second obviously comes from *sandwich*. In neither case is there an **r** in the source; yet rhotic speakers in Britain and Ireland pronounce both with **r**.

Another example is the breed of dog called *shar pei*. This name is Chinese, 沙 皮 *shā pí* (or the Cantonese equivalent *sā pèih*): again, no etymological **r**.

People in the rhotic west of England tend to pronounce **r** in words such as *khaki*, even though there is no *r* in the spelling. The equivalence 'non-rhotic ɑː = rhotic ɑːr' is a deeply buried part of their phonological knowledge.

Under *marm*, the OED (2000, third edition) comments:

> Variant of MA'AM n.[1] In U.S. usage, it is not always clear whether the spelling with -*r*- is merely a graphic device to indicate lengthening of the vowel (especially in representations of the non-rhotic dialects of New England), or else represents a genuine intrusive /r/: rhotic /mɑrm/ can easily develop from /mɑːm/ by analogy with e.g. rhotic /hɑrm/ harm n. corresponding to non-rhotic /hɑːm/.

It asks us to compare the spellings *mars* and *marse* for *Mas'*, i.e. 'master'.

Think of the inner-city buses called *Hoppa*. Some British trade names of this sort, transparent to us non-rhotic speakers (= 'hopper' – geddit?), must be either baffling or irritating to rhotic speakers, not to mention non-anglophones). Eric Armstrong, writing from Canada, tells me he was baffled by the product names *Whiskas* (catfood) and *Polyfilla*.

> As a child, I had no idea that these were derived from words with -*er* endings. Their advertising makes the words sound just like we Canadians would read them. It wasn't until I went to the UK for a year in my early 20's that I began to 'hear' the **r** in those words.

He adds:

> As a voice trainer, I have to do mental gymnastics every time I use a book for actors written by a British (non-rhotic) trainer, such as Cecily Berry, who writes the ɑ vowel as *ar* and the ɔ vowel as *ore*, etc. North Americans and other rhotic speakers are just stopped dead in their tracks trying to figure these out. (Why can't they abandon these spelling conventions and use the IPA?)

As we say (or rather write) in England, you've got to larf.

2.30   Nadsat is non-rhotic!

You may have read the novel *A Clockwork Orange* by Anthony Burgess (first published 1962) or seen the 1971 Stanley Kubrick film based on it. It is set in an imagined England of the future, an England under Soviet domination. If so, you will either have recognized the Russian origin of various words in the slang put in the mouths of some of the characters, or alternatively have been thoroughly puzzled by them. For example, the protagonist Alex refers to the fellow members of his teenage gang as his *droogs*. This word is based on the Russian друг *drug*, 'friend'. Similarly, *klootch* means 'key', from Russian ключ *kl'uch*.

A correspondent from France tells me of his gratification the day he suddenly realized that:

- Burgess's British-inspired spelling *gulliver* actually meant голова *golova* (head)
- with *goober* he referred to губа *guba* (lip)
- with *morder* he referred to морда *morda* (muzzle, or a human's beastly face)
- with *rooker* he referred to рука *ruka* (hand).

Speakers of rhotic English, or non-natives, do indeed face this additional hurdle when deciphering Burgess's invented slang.

My own favourite Nadsat word is *horrorshow*, meaning 'good', which is cleverly antonymous. It comes from the Russian хорошо, transliterated *khorosho* and in Russian pronounced xərʌˈʃo.

2.31   non-rhotic loanwords

In Japanese there are plenty of examples of borrowings from English which rhotic speakers might find difficult to interpret. (To be honest, even we non-rhotic speakers do not always easily connect such borrowings to the English origin, either.)

Japanese has an **r**, but it is used only before a following vowel, i.e. in just the same positions where non-rhotic English allows it. So English *door* becomes Japanese *doa*.

An interesting example is the word *elevator*. When written in Japanese katakana it reads, in transliteration, *erebeetaa*, and is correspondingly pronounced.

Yet this word must have been borrowed from AmE, not from BrE, since we Brits call the apparatus in question a *lift*. Nevertheless, the American voiced tap t̬ of American *elevator* ˈeləveɪt̬ɚ is mapped onto Japanese voiceless **t** rather than onto voiced **d** or **r** (= tapped **r** in Japanese), while the American final r-coloured schwa ɚ is mapped onto a Japanese double **aa**.

It is regular for English **v** to be mapped onto Japanese **b**, and for **l** to be mapped onto **r**, i.e. [ɾ]. But that is not relevant to the current issue.

It also seems to be typical for loanwords to be taken from AmE but then pronounced as RP-style BrE interpreted in Japanese phonetics.

Take another example: *hamburger* becomes Japanese non-rhotic *hambaagaa* (though the place name *Hamburg* is Japanized as *hanburuku*).

Actually, there are two possible ways of making a non-prevocalic **r** fit in with Japanese phonotactics. One is to ignore it, as in the final syllable of *erebeetaa*. The other is to treat it like other non-prevocalic consonants, which for Japanese means adding an epenthetic **u** or **o**, as when *McDonald's* becomes *makudonarudo*.

The examples *door*, Japanese **doa**, and *beer*, Japanese **biiru**, illustrate these two possibilities. Apparently Japanese preserves the American **r** in *beer* because the word was originally borrowed from Dutch rather from English. Compare the loanwords *bia hooru* (beer-hall) and *bia gaaden* (beer garden), which show the expected treatment of English final **r**.

There are two interesting Japanese loanwords from German in which preconsonantal **r** is preserved in Japanese: *arubaito*, meaning a job on the side (German *Arbeit*), and the name of the composer *Moots(u)aruto* (Mozart).

2.32   Gordon Brown

In his regular parliamentary sketch in the *Guardian*, the late Simon Hoggart several times commented on the former UK prime minister Gordon Brown's 'peculiar ways of pronouncing certain words', among them *Bournemouth* and *reconciliation*. Most of us use -**məθ** in *Bournemouth*, and we start *reconciliation* with ˌ**rek-**. So Gordon Brown's -**maʊθ** and ˌ**riːk-** do sound bizarre to many people.

Hoggart comments that these pronunciations suggest a surprising lack of social awareness on Brown's part, since instead of following other people he seems to have been led to invent his own spelling-based pronunciations.

EFL learners, take note: using wrong pronunciations may convey a hidden unfavourable message about you as a speaker.

Another unusual pronunciation of Brown's commented on by Hoggart is that of pronouncing the word *iron* as spelt, **ˈaɪrən**. So for him it rhymes with *Byron* and involves the same sequence as *tyrant*. But I think that this is the usual Scottish form, and that Brown is merely doing what other Scottish people do. The usual English pronunciation of *iron*, on the other hand, namely **ˈaɪə(r)n**, must result from a historical metathesis by which -**rən** became -**ərn**. The **r** then as usual coalesces in rhotic accents with the preceding schwa in rhotic accents to yield **ɚ**, **ˈaɪɚn**, while in non-rhotic accents, being preconsonantal, it undergoes deletion, giving **ˈaɪən**.

The Scottish pronunciation of this word does have the advantage of making it clearly distinct from *ion*, wheras for non-rhotic speakers like me *iron* and *ion* are homophones.

2.33   an albatross on the balcony

The phonetician David Deterding tells me that for him all words with the spelling *alC*, where *C* is any other consonant, have the STRUT vowel ʌ – *albatross, altruism, algorithm, alcohol, balcony, calculate*... He points out that this does not happen before a clear l, since for him *allergy, Sally, callous, fallacy* and so on all have the usual front æ (TRAP) vowel. He says he doesn't know whether this is a widespread pronunciation tendency, or whether it is a personal idiosyncrasy of his own.

I have never come across it before. For most of us *balcony* and *albatross* have æ. So my reaction was that it may well be David's idiolectal idiosyncrasy. Allophonic lowering of short front vowels before l is widespread, but speakers do not usually perceive this as a change of phoneme.

I am aware that a similar treatment of e has been reported for New Zealand English, where words such as *shell* and *shelf* are perceived as having æ rather than e. But David says he doesn't do this. For *shelf*, he says, there is the usual allophonic lowering before dark l, but otherwise no difference from the vowel in *shed*.

I wonder if anyone else pronounces these words like David.

2.34   changes in English vowels

Here is a formant plot showing changes in certain vowels of 'Standard Southern British English', comparing the speech of elderly people, born 1928–1936, with that of twenty-somethings born in the 1980s. I have taken it from an article by Gea de Jong, Kirsty McDougall, Toby Hudson and Francis Nolan entitled 'The speaker discriminating power of sounds undergoing historical change: a formant-based study', which appeared in the *Proceedings of ICPhS Saarbrücken* (2007).

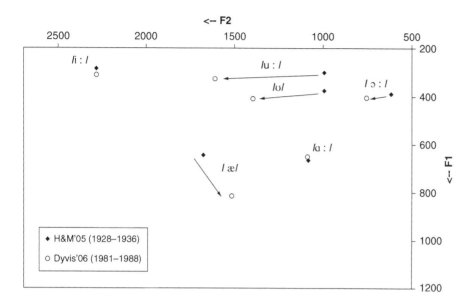

You will see it confirms the vowel changes that people have been commenting on for some time:

- the opening/backing of æ (TRAP)
- the fronting of **u:** (GOOSE) and **ʊ** (FOOT)
- – and also to some slight extent a fronting of ɔ: (THOUGHT).

What a lot can happen in fifty years!

The vowels **i:** (FLEECE) and **ɑ:** (START), on the other hand, have remained static.

2.35   Christmas puzzles

How do we account for the fact that 'Christmas *tree* and 'Christmas *cake* are single-stressed, while 'Christmas 'Day, 'Christmas 'Eve and 'Christmas 'shopping are double-stressed?

We do our 'Christmas 'shopping in order to get our 'Christmas cards and buy some 'Christmas presents, which we give on 'Christmas 'Day before our 'Christmas 'dinner, which includes some 'Christmas 'pudding. We might watch or listen to the Queen's 'Christmas 'speech or sing some 'Christmas 'carols round the 'Christmas tree. Later we eat 'Christmas cake or might pull 'Christmas 'crackers.

My colleague Petr Rösel writes to add 'Christmas 'stockings, 'Christmas 'holidays, 'Christmas 'Eve and the now almost forgotten 'Christmas box. For many families, he says, 'Christmas time means a lot of stress...

Compounds with the second element *Day* are just as arbitrarily stressed as those with the first element *Christmas*. We have single-stressed (early-stressed) *Boxing Day*, *St David's Day*, *May Day*, *Labo(u)r Day*, *Derby Day*, *Independence Day* and *Ascension Day*, but double-stressed (late-stressed) *Christmas Day*, *Easter Day* and *Michaelmas Day*.

These patterns, like all lexical patterns, can of course be overridden for contrast: *not Boxing Day but* 'Christmas Day.

As far as I can see, these lexical stress patterns are ultimately just arbitrary. There is no logic to them.

2.36   data processing under stress

How do you stress the compound *data processing*?

When asked, I said I thought that the usual stress pattern for this compound was double stress: ‚data 'processing. I could be wrong; like many recently coined compounds, it has perhaps not yet really settled down lexically. Meanwhile we give it a pragmatic stressing.

> ?(i) We're going to do some processing. | Today it'll be 'data processing.
> (ii) We've got some data. | Now we must move on to data 'processing.

Clearly, (ii) is the more usual implicit situation.

So this pragmatic effect seems to override the usual early-stress rule for compound nouns. But as the compound becomes more established it would be expected to fall into line and move towards 'data processing (and no doubt already has done for some speakers).

With *word processing*, on the other hand, we would never think:

> *(ii') We've got some words. | Now we must move on to word 'processing.

So it is always 'word processing, in accordance with the compound rule.

Compare also the American hesitation over the stressing of *Thanksgiving*, or the cases of other compounds where we don't all agree: *ice cream*, *armchair*.

This explanation may be a bit ad hoc. But it's the best I can manage.

2.37   a cab, innit?

A girl hurriedly dialled directory enquiries to book a taxi from her home in London to Bristol airport, using the cockney rhyming slang *Joe Baxi*.

But the operator told her they were unable to find anyone by that name. Seething, the youngster snapped back: 'It ain't a person, it's a cab, innit.'

The operator duly gave her what she asked for and put her through to the nearest supplier of cabinets.

The cabinet saleswoman seemed equally confused.

'Look love, how hard is it?' the caller fumed. 'All I want is your cheapest cab, innit. I need it for 10am. How much is it?' The sales adviser told her £180. The tantrum-throwing teenager left her address details and rang off.

The next morning, rather than being picked up by a cab, the young woman had the cabinet dropped off.

Allegedly.

The segments would have been the same in each case: **kæbɪnɪʔ**. Theoretically the two possibilities ought to have been disambiguated by prosody.

(1)   It's a \cab, | \innit?
(2)   It's a \cabinet.

(1) would be expected to have a longer æ than (2), and to have a second accent on the ɪn of *innit* (= isn't it). The æ in (2) would be expected to have shorter duration because it is subject to rhythmic clipping, aka foot-level shortening, due to the following unstressed syllables.

As we know, you can't always rely on prosody.

2.38   instances and incidences

It is sometimes very difficult indeed to hear the difference between *instances* and *incidences*. That is why some people confuse the two words. Here are a few cases thrown up by Google. You can easily find others.

> New incidences of human rights abuses in run-up to the Beijing Olympics revealed

> What incidences of racism have you ever had to personally deal with?

> Could you please supply me with any information/documents concerning how many incidences of assault between prison inmates ... have occurred.

In each case the writer must surely have meant *instances*. (Alternatively, in the last case they may have meant *incidents*, which for many people is a homophone of *incidence*.)

The confusion arises because *instance* and *incidence* may be pronounced identically in rapid speech. This is because of the possible disappearance of the vowel of the middle syllable of *incidence*. We can, and often do, go straight from the **s** to the **d**, omitting the weak vowel (ə, or a conservative ɪ) that would otherwise stand between them. Since under these circumstances the **d**, now abutting on a voiceless consonant, gets devoiced, the result is that the -sd̥- of *incidence* ends up very similar to the -st- of *instance*.

In moderately paced speech the deleted vowel seems to leave some compensatory lengthening of the preceding consonant: ˈɪn(t)sːd̥ən(t)s. In rapid speech, however, I think this subtlety of timing can be lost, making *incidence* as good as homophonous with *instance*.

This phenomenon has been termed 'pseudo-elision', as opposed to true elision where the deleted segment supposedly leaves no trace at all.

We find the same thing in words such as *trinity, comedy, Cassidy, quality, university* (can it rhyme with *thirsty*?). In *trinity* the tongue tip may remain in place on the alveolar ridge as we pass from the (lengthened?) **n** to the **t**, with no intervening vowel.

2.39   settee

A correspondent asked why **e** (the DRESS vowel) is found at the end of the first syllable in the word *settee*, given that this vowel is never found in final open syllables.

This word, seˈtiː, is one of a small number of words that have a short strong vowel in this position: another is *tattoo* tæˈtuː. Why? That's how it is. English is irregular.

Not surprisingly, some people (including me) usually pronounce it with a schwa, səˈtiː. Others, though, say it with **se-**, and that, I think, is the usual pronunciation.

When I was a boy our family had a piece of furniture we called a settee, so it is a familiar word for me. Nowadays, though, most people have a *sofa*.

My correspondent followed this up by asking about the word *divorce*, which is shown in LPD with ɪ at the end of the first syllable. Should that not, she asked, be i (happY) instead?

Yes, in LPD I transcribe *divorce* as **dɪ ˈvɔːs, də-**. Why do I not write the main pronunciation as **di ˈvɔːs**? After all, I now transcribe words such as *depend* as **di ˈpend, də-**, replacing the **dɪ ˈpend, də-, §diː-** of earlier editions.

In the third edition of LPD I decided to simplify the treatment of words with the weak prefixes *be-, de-, pre-, re-*. I exploit the existing notation **i**, which covers a range of possibilities from **iː** to **ɪ**, extending its use from words such as *happy, glorious, radiation* to these prefixes (see 2.22 above).

However, words spelt *di-* are different. In the first and second editions I did not give them a variant with **diː-**, because as far as I know such a pronunciation is not found. Their prefix vowel can only be ɪ or ə.

A nice potential minimal pair is *dissent* vs. *descent*. Probably most of us they are homophones; but not for everyone. I transcribe them **dɪ ˈsent** and **di ˈsent** respectively.

Yes, this does mean that ɪ is thereby left at the end of an open syllable. But in any case we need to recognize ɪ as one of the weak vowels, sometimes distinct from **i**, because of its appearance in words such as *finishing*. And as schwa shows (*banana* **bə-**, *commercial* **kə-**), there is no difficulty about syllable-final weak vowels.

Going back to the word *settee*, my correspondent asks whether it would be possible to divide it **set.iː**, rather than my **se.ˈtiː**. Although putting the t in the first syllable might seem to improve the phonotactics, I think it is wrong. Why? Because the **t** is strongly aspirated, which it would not be if it were syllable-final. (The main function of syllabification as I present it in LPD is to predict the correct allophones in those phonemes that are sensitive to syllable boundaries.) Conversely, lack of aspiration is what leads me to syllabify *nostalgic* as **nɒ.ˈstældʒ.ɪk**, leaving a syllable-final short strong vowel as awkward as the one in *settee*. Sometimes language is not neat and tidy.

The word *mistake* brings these various points together. We do not say it as **mɪs.ˈteɪk**, i.e. with an aspirated **t**. Despite its etymology, it must be **mɪ.ˈsteɪk**, since the t is unaspirated, just as in *stake*; because in English t is unaspirated after s in the same syllable. Furthermore, we are left with a first syllable ending in **ɪ**.

This analysis goes back to A.C. Gimson, who as editor of the fourteenth edition of EPD corrected the syllabification of *mistake* (as shown by the location of the stress mark) given in earlier editions. As evidence he took the study by Niels Davidsen-Nielsen, 'Syllabification in English words with medial *sp, st, sk*', published in the *Journal of Phonetics* 1974, 2: 15–45.

2.40   imma

I was struck by *imma* in a cartoon caption, presumably American, 'Imma get myself a snack'. It evidently means 'I'm going to', and I think is pronounced **aɪmmə**.

No doubt the initial diphthong can be reduced, too, to some kind of **a**.

One of my little campaigns over the years has been to try to persuade learners of EFL that there is a respectable weak form of *going to* that people ought to teach and learn, namely **gənə** (or before a vowel **gənu**). We Brits tend to fight shy of the spelling *gonna*, thinking of it as too American. Yet it is clear that we too can and do contract the words *going to* (but only when they are modal – so not in sentences like *I'm going to Brighton tomorrow*).

One stage further is the fusion of *I'm* with *gonna*. In my own speech this can produce **aɪŋ(ə)nə**. The nasality of the **m** of *I'm* coalesces with the velarity of the **g** of *gonna* to yield a velar nasal **ŋ**, in a kind of two-way assimilation. The following schwa can disappear.

But for *imma* the output is not a velar but a bilabial nasal that spreads over the following underlyingly velar and alveolar consonants. This assimilation is purely progressive, like **ˈrɪbm̩** for *ribbon* (2.49 below).

I have no idea what proportion of speakers, American or even British, go for **aɪmənə** or **aɪmmə** rather than the **aɪŋənə** or **aɪŋnə** that I would use.

Lynne Murphy, an American living in Britain and author of a blog on BrE–AmE differences, tells me she thinks that this is from AmE dialectal (and often humorously applied in other dialects) pseudo-aspectual *a*-prefixing. *I'm a-going to* → *I'm a-gonna* → *I'm-a*.

Phil Thompson reports from California that **aɪŋənə** has a variant **aämŋənə**. He thinks that the form implied by *imma* seems to indicate a southern or African-American Vernacular English (AAVE) speaker and hears it in his mind's ear as **amə** or **aːmə** or **āmə**. I was probably wrong in my speculation about possible double **mm** or syllabic **m̩**.

John Cowan writes:

> The form **ɑmə** began as AAVE basilect and has gone upmarket in the last several decades, like a lot of AAVE basilect (it's discussed in Dillard's *Black English*). It's an open question whether this is nasal assimilation as you explain, or derived from a Plantation Creole future/volitional particle *a* ('*I'm a-quit*'), or a mixture of both.

He says he has **aɪmənə** (not **aɪŋənə**) most of the time, and **aɪmə** occasionally. He claims that **aɪmənə** is now a standard pronunciation, while **aɪmgənə** strikes him as only suitable for formal or emphatic contexts.

With that, I'm'a declare this discussion closed.

2.41   terraced attacks

My summer course colleague Jack Windsor Lewis, listening to the radio news, reports hearing a disturbing account of police discrimination against less well-to-do homes. Apparently, a house in Forest Gate was raided by anti-ˈterəst forces. The many British people who live in terraced houses (for Americans, that's row houses) rather than in semis or detached houses might rightly feel aggrieved. (In case you haven't caught up, this was meant to be *anti-terrorist*.)

For some reason it reminded me of the Scotsman who took a week off work because he had a wee cough. (If you're teaching students about pre-fortis clipping, this minimal pair makes a change from *plump eye – plum pie* and *might I – my tie*.)

With aircraft cabin announcements, I often do a double-take when I hear about 'our co-chair partners' (actually, code-share partners). Because the **d** in *code-share* gets devoiced, the distinction between *co-chair* and *code-share* depends on nothing more than (i) fortis versus lenis and (ii) syllabification, both of which are pretty inaudible in this context: ˈkəʊ.tʃeə, ˈkəʊd.ʃeə. Oh, and perhaps the difference between an affricate on the one hand and a plosive plus a fricative on the other. Pre-fortis clipping is blocked by the morpheme boundary.

2.42   synthetic homographs

I've been doing a consultancy job for a publisher, listening to synthesized speech automatically generated for a handheld computerized dictionary currently under development – not isolated headwords, but phrases and sentences. Speech synthesis is much better these days than it used to be, but it still has some way to go, particularly in the matter of working out a plausible intonation pattern.

I've listened to a thousand randomly selected samples. So I can tell you both what the commonest type of error was, and what the worst type was. (How would the software have coped with the sentence I've just written? It ought to have been able to recognize the need for contrastive tonicity: *both what the commonest type of error was, | and what the worst type was.* Would it have succeeded? No.)

OK, then: the worst type of error was the wrong choice between homographs. English has a number of words where the same spelling is used for two words of different sound and different meaning. Thus *wind* (air movement) is **wɪnd**, but *wind* (turn, twist) is **waɪnd**; *entrance* (way in) is **ˈentrəns** but *entrance* (bewitch) is **ɪnˈtrɑːns**; *present* (noun or adj.) is **ˈprezənt**, *present* (verb) is **prɪˈzent**. In the thousand samples I listened to there were five errors of this kind. Obviously, choice of the wrong pronunciation would be seriously misleading for the dictionary user. (See further 2.48 below.)

However, the most frequent error was failure on the part of the speech synthesis software to recognize compound nouns and therefore to apply compound stress. In the great majority of cases of noun + noun in English it is appropriate to put the primary stress on the first element, as for example *adˈventure story*, *appliˈcation form*, *ˈmurder charge*. (Of course, you need to be aware of the occasional exceptions, such as ˌstrawberry ˈjam, ˌgang ˈwarfare.) The software got this wrong in 65 cases, constituting just over a quarter of all errors identified.

You could see this, alternatively, as a demonstration of a fault in English spelling conventions. In the other Germanic languages, compound nouns are written solid, with no space (thus German *Abenteuergeschichte*, *Anmeldeformular*, *Mordanklage*). So you can recognize them as such. English sometimes does this (*wintertime*, *railway*) but very often doesn't. If we wrote *adventurestory*, *applicationform*, *murdercharge* and so on, then the software (and millions of EFL students) might get the stress right.

2.43   mine and my

We all know the opening lines of *The Battle Hymn of the Republic*:

Mine eyes have seen the glory of the coming of the Lord; He is trampling out the vintage where the grapes of wrath are stored...

Given that these words were written in 1861, we may well ask why it begins *Mine eyes* rather than *My eyes*, which is what everyone writes and says today, and indeed wrote and said in the Victorian era.

From the thirteenth to the eighteenth centuries, *my* maɪ and *mine* maɪn were in complementary distribution as possessive adjectives before a noun. People said and wrote *mine* if the following word began with a vowel and *my* otherwise. (Before **h**, though, usage was divided.) This is the usage to be found throughout Shakespeare (1564–1616), the Authorized Version of the Bible (1611), and the Book of Common Prayer (1662).

Nowadays, as the OED puts it, *mine* qualifying a following noun is 'only arch. or poet. before a vowel or h; otherwise superseded by *my*'.

So Julia Howe, the writer of this hymn, was indulging in arch[aic] or poet[ic] language, which I suppose is fair enough. No doubt she was also echoing the words of Psalm 121 in the Prayer Book, *I will lift up mine eyes unto the hills.* Other hymn writers of this period, though, didn't hesitate to write *my anchor* and *my heart.*

The OED adduces a quotation from Swift's *Gulliver's Travels*, dated 1726:

> Till I had gotten a little below the level of mine eyes.

But that's their latest citation for *mine* before a noun. Anything more recent is indeed consciously archaic – either poetic (up to about a hundred years ago) or religious, or else jocular, as when you call an innkeeper *mine host.*

Martin Barry of the University of Manchester, who besides being a phonetician is also a cathedral choirmaster, reminds me of the fifteenth-century carol with the refrain *Lullay, mine liking, my dear son . . . mine own dear darling.* Why do we get *mine* before **l** and *my* before **d**?

2.44   um... er...

In a conference presentation I attended, Richard Cauldwell discussed the factors making for fluency in the language of trainee air traffic controllers.

His aim was to isolate the factors that led candidates to be judged as relatively fluent or non-fluent in their use of English. He found that to progress from level 3 (non-passing, 'pre-operational') to level 4 (passing, 'operational') you would need to:

- increase the average speed of your speech by 30% (from 100 to 130 wpm);
- make your speech units longer (words and syllables);
- increase the percentages of medium and fast speech units by 20%;
- reduce silent pauses to 15% of duration;
- use fillers to fill pauses.

Your fillers should not be distracting. (The term 'fillers' here is applied not so much to expressions such as *you know* or *sort of* as rather to hesitation noises.)

To progress to level 5 ('extended') or 6 ('expert') his data suggests that you would need to further reduce silent pauses (to 10%), and to eliminate or nearly eliminate ums and uhs.

Phonetically, *um* is most often **əm**. (To what extent do people say **ʌm** as use rather than mention?) The variant that Cauldwell spells *uh* is more usually written *er* in BrE, since it is phonetically like a long schwa, **ɜː**. To my way of thinking, the spelling *uh* is appropriate only for American **ʌ**.

In BrE we also have *erm* **ɜːm**. Other languages have other habits. In Japanese it's *anoo*, in German *äm* or *hm*. We do say *hm* in English, too, (or *hmm*), but it is not exactly a hesitation noise. As a longish **m̥mm**, a voiceless then voiced bilabial nasal with a falling tone, it shows doubt or disagreement, meaning something like 'I understand what you say, but I don't think I agree with it'. As **m̥m**, with shorter duration and an abrupt fall, it shows mild surprise and means much the same as 'Oh!' or 'Well, well!'

Unfortunately there are many academics (and others) whose fillers are definitely distracting and indeed annoying. I think public speakers, including lecturers and conference presenters, ought to train themselves not to um and er.

2.45   thou hast, he hath

I was brought up as an Anglican and have therefore been familiar since childhood with the Book of Common Prayer and the Authorized Version of the Bible. A consequence of this is that the old present tense second and third person singular verb forms (*thou givest*, *he giveth*) are part of my linguistic competence – not something learned by study, but part of my everyday knowledge of English. (They are, though, restricted to the liturgical, biblical and archaic-literary registers of the language.)

I have come to realize that for many other native speakers of English this is not the case. To begin with I was amazed to hear people stumbling over these forms and coming up with nonsense such as *thou giveth* or *I comest*.

OK, if you're not sure, the rule is:

- *-est* only in the second person singular (*thou*), present tense;
- *-eth* only in the third person singular (*he*, *she*, *it* or a singular noun), present tense.

Here, from the *New York Times Digest*, 7 January 2008, is a comment by Paul Krugman:

> You see, for 30 years American politics has been dominated by a political movement practicing Robin-Hood-in-reverse, giving unto *those that hath* while taking from those who don't.

No, it's *he/him that hath* and *those that have*. Look.

> For he that hath, to him shall be given: and he that hath not, from him shall
> be taken even that which he hath. – Mark 4:25

> Gather my saints together unto me; those that have made a covenant with me
> by sacrifice. – Ps. 50:5

One consequence of having these forms as a core part of my knowledge of English is that I also know that some of them have strong and weak forms in pronunciation. For example, *hath* has the strong form **hæθ** and the weak form **(h)əθ**. Similarly, *hast* has the strong form **hæst** and the weak form **(h)əst**. I find that I use these as naturally as I do the strong and weak forms of *has* or *have*.

I know that *(thou) sayest* is **ˈseɪ ɪst** but *(he) saith* is **seθ**.

I know a further interesting fact: that for *do* there are doublets *doest – dost* and *doeth – doth*. In each pair the first (**ˈduːɪst, ˈduːɪθ**) is used as a main verb, the second (strong forms **dʌst, dʌθ**, weak forms **dəst, dəθ**) as an auxiliary.

This makes me realize (*si parva licet componere magnis*) what it must feel like to be one of the last speakers of an endangered language.

2.46   rhotic

My own personal contribution to the English language is the word *rhotic*. In 1968, inspired by reading Labov's account of his fieldwork in NYC, I carried out an afternoon's fieldwork in Southampton asking random passers-by on the street about possible ice cream flavours, thereby inducing them to pronounce the words *vanilla* and *ginger* and recording the presence or absence of final r-colouring in their pronunciation of each. It was in reporting my findings that I classified the respondents as 'non-rhotic' (having no non-prevocalic r-colouring) or 'rhotic' (having r-colouring in *ginger* even when not followed by a vowel sound). The existing American term, *r-ful*, obviously sounded rather awful if pronounced in an accent like mine.

In due course the word was taken up by other phoneticians and sociolinguists.

But now people are using my word as a noun, in a different sense, which the 2010 edition of the OED has not altogether caught up with. This new sense is 'a non-lateral liquid consonant' (informally, then, an r-sound). Ladefoged and Maddieson's 1996 book *The Sounds of the World's Languages* (Blackwell) has a chapter entitled 'Rhotics'. Back in his 1984 book, *Patterns of Sounds* (Cambridge University Press), Ian Maddieson was still calling them r-sounds.

The earliest use of *rhotic* in this new sense that I can find is in R.M.W. Dixon, *The Grammar of Yidiɲ* (Cambridge University Press 1977). He reports the consonants of Yidiny as including:

- a trilled apical rhotic – *r*;
- and an apical-postalveolar (retroflex) rhotic continuant – *ɽ* [sic].

The term subsequently became established in descriptions of other Australian languages (which typically have two rhotics), and from there was taken up more generally. Bob Dixon was my colleague at UCL in the 1960s, and no doubt picked up the word from me there, although he then proceeded to use it in a different sense.

There is uncertainty in some quarters as to how to pronounce the word. I pronounce it with the GOAT vowel, though some use the vowel of LOT.

You can see their reasoning. After all, *-otic* has the LOT vowel in *antibiotic*, *asymptotic*, *demotic*, *erotic*, *exotic*, *hypnotic*, *narcotic*, *necrotic*, *neurotic*, *osmotic*, *patriotic*, *quixotic*, *sclerotic* and *semiotic*.

Note, however, that (with the exception of the maverick Cervantes-hero-derived *quixotic*) these words all involve the ending *-(o)tic* attached to what etymologically was a separate morpheme. Thus *demotic* includes the same Greek stem as *democracy* and *demagogue*, *neurotic* the same as *neuralgia*.

But *rhotic* is not derived from a stem **rh-* plus *-otic*. Rather, it is related to *rhō*, stem *rhōt-*, the name of the Greek letter P, ρ (= r). The name of this letter also lies behind *rhotacism* and *rhotacize*, which certainly have the GOAT vowel.

Hence my pronunciation ˈrəʊtɪk. For what it's worth, all the pronunciation dictionaries agree with me, as does the Concise Oxford.

Plus... it avoids the awkward potential homophonic clash with *erotic*.

2.47   progressive assimilation

An enthusiastic but non-native-speaking teacher of English phonetics offered the following phonetic version of *if you can understand what's written here*:

ɪf jə kŋ ʌndəˈstæm wɒts ˈrɪtn hɪə

What's wrong with this?

Personally, I normally keep *you* (weak form) as **ju**, rather than reducing it to **jə**. But that's not the point. There are plenty of speakers who would reduce *you* in that way.

There is a fairly drastic reduction of *understand*: elision of one stress and one consonant, assimilation of the newly final consonant. But that's OK.

No, it's the word *can*. Although we can say **kŋ** in contexts such as *you can go*, *they can be*, *we can do*, we absolutely cannot do so in *you can ask*, *they can always*, *we can only*.

So why not? What's the difference?

It's the phonetic context. This kind of assimilation can take place only phrase-finally or before a consonant (*go*, *be*, *do*), never before a vowel (*ask*, *always*, *only*).

Progressive assimilation (aka perseverative assimilation or lagging assimilation) is mentioned in most books about English phonetics, with such examples as *ribbon* ˈrɪbən → ˈrɪbm, *bacon* ˈbeɪkən → ˈbeɪkŋ. It is distinguished from ordinary regressive (anticipatory, leading) dealveolar assimilation of the familiar **tem bɔɪz, teŋ gɜːlz** type.

There is a constraint that the assimilation does not happen before a vowel. As far as I can recall, no one else has ever discussed this constraint. But it's real enough: you can say 'əʊpm before a pause, or before a consonant as in *opened*, *open them* – but not before a vowel as in *opening* or *open it*. The constraint holds even if you change the **p** to **ʔ**, as we often do.

Syllabic consonant formation, which changes schwa plus a nasal or liquid into the corresponding syllabic nasal or liquid, is an absolute precondition to this type of assimilation. The only possible input to the progressive assimilation rule is a syllabic **n̩**. The point is that if a syllabic nasal immediately follows a plosive, then there may be assimilation of place to that of the plosive.

n̩ → m / {p, b} _
n̩ → ŋ / {k, g} _

Thus from 'əʊpən *open*, syllabic consonant formation gives us 'əʊpn̩. Then by progressive assimilation we derive 'əʊpm̩. Similarly, for *ribbon* we have 'rɪbən → 'rɪbn̩ → 'rɪbm̩, for *bacon* we have 'beɪkən → 'beɪkn̩ → 'beɪkŋ̩, while for *organ* we have 'ɔːgən → 'ɔːgn̩ → 'ɔːgŋ̩.

Naturally, if the schwa remained it would prevent the nasal from directly abutting the plosive, so no assimilation could occur.

Secondly, if the nasal is also followed by a consonant then it will be a candidate for regressive assimilation as well. Sometimes these two assimilatory pressures reinforce one another, as when *steak and kidney* becomes 'steɪkŋ 'kɪdni, *organ grinder* becomes 'ɔːgŋgraɪndə, or *carbon paper* becomes 'kɑːbmpeɪpə. But sometimes they pull in different directions. In *steak and mushroom (pie)* the **k** of *steak* tries to make the **n̩** (= *and*) velar, while the initial **m** of *mushroom* tries to make it bilabial. I think it was Francis Nolan who showed that often in such cases both things happen simultaneously, so that we end up with a velar-bilabial, or indeed velar-alveolar-bilabial, nasal.

Thirdly, in AmE people do not make these assimilations nearly as readily as we Brits do, or perhaps at all. Nor do they assimilate to **m** before **w** (*ten ways* **tem weɪz**) as Brits do.

Fourthly, the corresponding assimilation clearly happens in German. For *haben Sie?* you will often hear Germans saying 'haːbmzi (or indeed 'haːmmzi, with additional regressive assimilation of nasality). But in German the English constraint of not-before-a-vowel doesn't apply. Thus *wir haben auch...* can be vɪɐ'haːbm 'ʔaʊx. It may be that the glottal hard attack of word-initial vowels is what makes this possible (though not all kinds of German apply this automatic glottal stop).

2.48   homographs

We have a number of cases in English of homographs: pairs of words spelt identically but pronounced differently. Looked at from the point of view of text-to-speech rules (which is the way non-phoneticians almost always do look at them) they must seem very puzzling, since by definition you cannot predict the pronunciation from the spelling.

So, as we all know, *wind* is **wɪnd** if it is moving air, but **waɪnd** if it is to turn or twist. *Entrance* (way in) is ˈ**entrəns** but *entrance* (bewitch) is ɪnˈ**trɑːns** (or ɪnˈ**træns**, depending on accent). *Present* (noun or adj.) is ˈ**prezənt**, *present* (verb) is priˈ**zent**. (See also 2.42 above.) *Tear* (eye water) is **tɪə**, but *tear* (rip) is **teə**; *sow* (female pig) is **saʊ**, but *sow* (seeds) is **səʊ**. And so on. Text-to-speech algorithms may need quite sophisticated ploys to achieve the right result in such cases.

Very awkwardly for text-to-speech and also for the EFL learner, the words *use*, *excuse*, *close* and several others have **s** or **z** in accordance with rules that are not always easy to formulate.

I have noticed people doing odd things with the endings *-ate* and *-ment*. The normal rule is for these endings to have a strong vowel in the verb, but a weak vowel in the related noun or adjective. So we have *separ[**eɪ**]ted* but *separ[ə]tely*, *complim[**e**]nted* but *my complim[ə]nts*. Every now and again, though, I hear native speakers, including radio and TV announcers, getting these wrong or at least violating the usual rule. I suppose that in a literate society such as our own it is difficult to maintain lexicophonetic distinctions that are not supported by the spelling. But I find it rather disturbing when someone says they want to *advoc[ə]te* or *implem[ə]nt* this or that policy.

3 Teaching and examining

Teaching and examining phonetics, including general phonetics and EFL

3.1 deceptive strings

In some phonetics oral exams we test the candidates on reading aloud short strings of phonetic symbols. Some of these are real English words – **dɪˈnaɪ**, **ˈpɜːpəs** and the like. Others look like English but are not, since they are not spellings but phonetic symbols, e.g. **ˈreply**, in which the last vowel is to be interpreted IPA-style as a close front rounded vowel; or **thumb**, where we need [**t**] followed by [**h**], a close back vowel, [**m**] and a final [**b**]. Candidates find these sequences remarkably difficult to perform correctly.

3.2 practical tests

The practical test we used to give our MA Phonetics students at UCL covered transcription, dictation and the oral component (performance and recognition).

The transcription passage was a colloquial dialogue to be phonetically transcribed and marked up for intonation. Here is a sample passage.

> A *Oh, hi there! I was wondering if I could have a word with you.*
> B *Yes, of course. What is it?*
> A *It's about that Birmingham job I mentioned. I've finally decided to go ahead and apply for it.*
> B *Well, good luck then. But what d'you want me to do about it?*
> A *I was hoping you might give me a reference, or at least put in a good word for me.*
> B *OK. You'll have to tell me what you want me to say, though. I'm not very well informed about your career to date, you know.*
> A *Oh, I'll cover all that in my c.v. What I need from you is more a character reference, saying that I'm trustworthy and honest and so on.*
> B *All right, then. Give my name to the recruitment agency and get them to write to me. I hope you get the job, though of course I'll be sad to see you go.*

Most of our non-native-speaking students did pretty well on this exercise the year it was set. Nevertheless, it is instructive to analyse the most frequent errors they made.

Words frequently transcribed wrongly included *then* as **ðən** instead of **ðen** (this word has no weak form) and *trustworthy* with **θ** instead of **ð**. We wouldn't penalize *Birmingham* with **-ŋg-**, given that that is how the locals pronounce it. We also allowed *of course* with **ɔf** instead of **əv**, although the latter is surely the usual form, voicing assimilation across a word boundary being unusual.

In the intonation markup, the most frequent errors were a failure to identify compound stress in *'Birmingham job*, *'character reference*, *re'cruitment agency*; failure to accent *ahead*; failure to deaccent *I mentioned* and *you know*. Only three of the eight candidates managed to locate the nucleus correctly in *what is it*; only two got the most plausible nucleus placement in *what d'you want me to do about it*.

3.3   faulty abbreviations

'Final alveolar consonants, i.e. /n/, are often subject to assimilation', writes an undergraduate in an examination answer.

But she doesn't mean *i.e.*, she means *e.g.* The first stands for 'that is', the second stands for 'for example'. 'The consonant /n/' is not the same as '(all) alveolar consonants'; it is an instance of an alveolar consonant.

Younger native speakers often confuse *i.e.* and *e.g.* Both these abbreviations stand for Latin phrases, *id est* and *exempli gratia* respectively. You could blame their confusion on the decline of classical learning: not many people learn Latin these days. On the other hand there are millions of people who don't know Latin but who manage to use these abbreviations correctly.

You might also think that we ought to have English abbreviations for English phrases. Foreign learners, in fact, sometimes suppose that to be the case. I have several times come across 'f.e.' or 'f.ex.' in English essays written by Germans. After all, the German equivalent of *for example* is *zum Beispiel*, abbreviated as *z.B.* I have to explain that 'e.g.' is the only way of abbreviating this expression in English.

Another English abbreviation I have seen invented by Germans is 'a.s.o.' What does it stand for? Obviously, 'and so on' (German *und so weiter*, *u.s.w.*). But the English for that is *etc.* It's Latin again: *et cetera*.

A popular (mis)pronunciation of this latter phrase is **ɪkˈsetrə**, as if it began *ex-*.

3.4   exotic sounds

Courses in phonetics often include a practical examination that requires the candidates to be familiar with 'all the sounds represented on the IPA chart' (or words to that effect). They are expected to be able to recognize these sound-types in nonsense words or substitutions and to perform them in isolation or in simple sequences.

However, in practice certain sound-types tend to be excluded, whether explicitly or implicitly. For example, with speech therapy students we usually require only a subset of the cardinal vowels: all the primaries **i e ɛ a ɑ ɔ o u**, yes, but among the secondaries only **y ø œ ɯ**. We don't bother with **œ**, with cardinal **ɒ ʌ** or with **ɤ**. On the other hand the MA Phonetics students, and candidates for the IPA exam, do have to cover these sounds.

The same applies to some of the consonants in the chart. Whereas everyone has to be familiar with those such as **ɸ ʂ ɣ q**, only advanced students would be expected to cope with the pharyngeals **ħ ʕ**. As for the epiglottals **ʜ ʢ ʡ**, I don't think we require anyone to master them for examination purposes.

I remember being surprised, many years ago, to find that students at another university with a well-regarded phonetics course were not taught the alveolopalatals **ɕ ʑ tɕ dʑ**. We certainly cover them in London, not least because of having to deal with Polish and Mandarin Chinese, in both of which languages alveolopalatals contrast with (somewhat retroflex) **ʃ ʒ tʃ dʒ**.

3.5   the Swedish sj-sound

A correspondent expressed dismay at the 'defeatist attitude' he found in an elementary textbook of Swedish when it came to the distinctive Swedish consonant **ɧ** (the '*sj-lud*'). It merely described it as 'similar to *sh* in *she* ... [but] difficult for foreigners to produce'.

In its section on Swedish, the *IPA Handbook* (Cambridge University Press 1999, p. 140) calls **ɧ** a 'voiceless dorso-palatal/velar fricative'. In the list of symbols (p. 167), it gives the phonetic value of 'hooktop heng' slightly differently, as 'simultaneous voiceless postalveolar and velar fricative'.

To this I would add that in my experience this articulation is often accompanied by lip protrusion. The overall effect is of a voiceless fricative with no very determinate place of articulation but rather a long channel constriction.

My advice to non-Swedes would be to start with a velar fricative **x**, add a simultaneous darkish **ʃ**, and protrude and round the lips.

First listen to a recording of *sju*, which means 'seven', and then practise saying it.

There is an entire book (in Swedish) devoted to this consonant (Lindblad, P. 1980. *Svenskans sje- och tje-ljud i ett allmänfonetiskt perspektiv*). The author describes two different variants of the sound. And that's not counting the retroflex **ʂ** that a few speakers use instead (and which of course most speakers use in words spelt *rs*).

Olle Kjellin, author of several books on teaching Swedish pronunciation to foreigners, sent a helpful comment.

> As for the kind of lip rounding, it has the same lip shape as the long 'o' sound (**uː**). I tell my learners to strongly whisper a long 'o', as if in a big theatre with a thousand spectators.
>
> A peculiar but important characteristic of the *sj* sound is that it does not get coarticulated with the vowel that follows, but should keep its *o*-like lip shape

at all times, even before front unrounded vowels. I have noticed the same thing about the English *sh* sound, as in *she*, although your twitch of the Orbicularis oris muscle is much slighter than ours.

I choose practice words with *o* following, e.g., *skjorta* 'shirt', *journalist*, *lektion* **lekˈʃuːn** and all those *-tion/-sion* words. Only after extensive practice do we turn to *skina* 'shine', *giraff*, *själv* 'self', etc.: **ˈʃiːna, ʃiˈrafː, ʃɛlːv**. Then finally we attempt the irritating word *sju* **ʃu** 'seven', which involves moving the tongue from back to front (**i**-like) position but without changing the lip shape even the slightest. That's the most difficult word, in my opinion and experience.

This lip shape, for me, is almost the same as for whistling. So, if I whistle the **uː** and **ʃ** sound, it will be the lowest bass whistle I can manage to whistle at all. Whereas the *hus* **uː** whistle will be about 800 Hz. Or preferably 1600 Hz, which is closer to its F2 frequency. The lower octave generally seems to be sufficient. It's quite fun and illustrative to perform this whistling glissando to demonstrate the 'true' pronunciation of *sju*.

Whistling the lowest note one can is also a good way of achieving cardinal 8 **u**.

3.6   pausing a problem

It is natural that EFL learners who have no such distinction in their native language can find it tricky to hear the difference between the GOAT vowel **əʊ** and the THOUGHT vowel **ɔː**.

What surprises me, though, is that even advanced learners may sometimes be unaware of the relationship between spelling and sound. This became clear as I was doing a guest ear-training session for the UCL summer course.

My phonetic dictation included the word *pose*. One of the class members wrote it as **pɔːz**. She had, however, correctly identified the word and its meaning, and so knew that it was spelt *pose*. When I pointed out that a word with the spelling *-oCe* (where *C* is any consonant letter) would surely not be pronounced with **ɔː**, she reacted in surprise. No one had ever told her that.

Yet this is a very simple rule: *nose, wrote, hope, alone, code, spoke* and many many others all have **əʊ**. (Words spelt *-ore* are of course an exception: *more, store, core*. But they are the only cases where *oCe* corresponds to **ɔː**.)

Other than to *or(e)*, the vowel **ɔː** typically corresponds to the spellings *au, aw*: *author, caught, law, drawn*. The spellings corresponding to **pɔːz** are *pause, paws* (and in accents like RP *pours, pores*). No one had ever told her that, either.

There are several very common words in which the spelling *oCe* corresponds to some vowel other than **əʊ**, as for example *come, love, some, gone, move*. This is one of the particularly poor design features of our traditional orthography. Nevertheless, poorly designed though it is, English spelling does offer some pretty reliable reading rules. Learners ought to be aware of them.

3.7   volcano

Parts of Montserrat, the island in the Caribbean, are threatened by an active volcano. (Contrary to what some people would have you believe, life still goes on in the 'safe zone' in the north of the island, where some five thousand people continue to live happily and safely.)

The Montserrat Volcano Observatory staff make regular reports on the current volcanic situation, both written and spoken, the latter on the local radio station ZJB. Not all the volcanologists and other experts are native speakers of English.

One specialist whom I heard giving a spoken radio report recently is a Dr D., whose first language is Italian. Listening to him, I was struck by the fact that each time he used the word *volcano* – a frequent and crucial word in his report, as you might imagine – he pronounced it *volc*[æ]*no*.

You would think that as a volcanologist working in an English-speakng environment he would have noticed by now that all his English-speaking colleagues, not to mention all the other half-billion or whatever native-English speakers in the world, pronounce it *volc*[eɪ]*no*. He must have made a wrong inference many years ago about the pronunciation of this word, on the basis of the spelling, and somehow become deaf to all the spoken evidence around him showing that he was wrong. (The error must be spelling-based, attributable to the uncertainty over whether the letter *a* represents eɪ or æ. It is not a matter of negative transfer from his native Italian, which would give what we would hear as *volc*[ɑː]*no*.)

Does this sort of thing matter? Well, yes, it does. The effect of his mispronunciation, on me at any rate, was to make me discount the value of what he had to say. If he doesn't register the abundant evidence about the pronunciation of this everyday word, why should we suppose that he pays proper attention to the evidence on which he bases his scientific findings?

'To seek to change someone's pronunciation – whether of the L1 or of an L2 – is to tamper with their self-image, and is thus unethical – morally wrong' (D. Porter and S. Garvin, 'Attitudes to pronunciation in EFL', *Speak Out!* 1989, 5:8–15). What rubbish! If some kind person were to teach Dr D. the correct pronunciation of *volcano*, they would be doing him a positive and useful service that would enhance his scientific credibility and thus his professional standing.

3.8   suddenly in Sydney

As part of a phonetic workshop I conducted at the University of Kōchi there was a question-and-answer session. There were seventy or eighty people in the audience, a mixture of students and schoolteachers, with a sprinkling of academics, and we asked them to submit their questions in writing, giving plenty of advance warning. The result was a surprisingly large number of questions, which ranged from the narrowly phonetic ('What is the difference between ˈsʌdn̩li and ˈsʌdənli?') to the general and personal ('Do you speak Japanese?', 'How many people do you have in your family?').

The question about the transcription of *suddenly* gave me an opportunity to talk briefly about nasal release and also about the abbreviatory convention I use in the LPD, where the word is transcribed ˈsʌd ᵊn li.

Japanese learners of English find nasal release very difficult. (They find lateral release even more difficult, for obvious reasons.) The Japanese version of *Sydney* is シドニー (*shidonii*); for them to pronounce it as two syllables, ˈsɪdni, with nothing between the **d** and the **n**, as native speakers of English do, presents a real problem.

Although I know a few words and phrases, and have plenty of theoretical and practical knowledge about Japanese pronunciation, the answer to whether I speak Japanese is a regretful 'No'.

3.9   perceptions of /æ/

Some weeks ago a German colleague, an excellent linguist but not a specialist phonetician, was telling me that he and his wife had taken a short holiday-cum-English language course in the Republic of Ireland. They were delighted with the holiday aspect, but he was worried about whether Irish English was a suitable model for learners such as himself to be exposed to. In particular, he complained, the Irish EFL teachers mispronounced – as he saw it – the English **æ** vowel of *that bad man*, making it [**a**] instead of the [ɛ] he was expecting.

I had to tell him that (i) on balance I think it is a good thing, rather than a bad thing, for EFL learners to be exposed to more than one variety of English; and

(ii) if he is concerned about deviation from the RP standard, the things that might well worry him about Irish English could include their use of plosives for θ, ð and of a fricative for intervocalic coda t, but not the quality of their æ, which is well within the range of variability to be found within England, let alone the remainder of the British Isles.

I think the problem is really the institutionalized perception in central and eastern Europe that English /æ/ (the TRAP vowel) is to be mapped onto a variety of the local short /e/ (phonetically [ɛ]) and not onto the local short /a/. In German, the English-derived loanword *Flashback* is pronounced ˈflɛʃbɛk. Polish has borrowed *flash* as *flesz*, Russian as флеш, Serbian as *fleš*. All too often, this leads to a failure by Germans and east Europeans to make any distinction in English between the vowels of *pan* and *pen*, *bat* and *bet*, or indeed *flash* and *flesh*. (Speakers of Spanish and Japanese, on the other hand, map English /æ/ onto their own /a/, and may therefore fail to distinguish *pan* and *pun*, *bat* and *butt*, *flash* and *flush*.)

The east European treatment of /æ/ rather shocks us native speakers of English – British ones, at any rate. We think of our TRAP vowel not as a kind of [e], but as a kind of [a]. After all, we call *Málaga* ˈmæləgə, *Hamburg* ˈhæmbɜːg, *Poznań* ˈpɒznæn and *Novi Sad* ˌnɒvi ˈsæd. We expect the equivalence to work the other way round, too.

3.10   misled by spelling

A correspondent tells me of an Italian lady of a certain age who is educated, cultured, intelligent, quite refined, self-aware and quite ready to criticize other people's mistakes. But when she speaks English – although her syntax is flawless – she has ɒ (the LOT vowel) in *London* and *money*. These are words she must have heard pronounced correctly with the STRUT vowel a million times! How can it be that she makes this mistake?

How indeed? I blame our crazy English spelling.

3.11   unaspirated /p t k/

Every now and again I get emails from Chinese correspondents worried about the statement found in textbooks to the effect that English voiceless plosives, usually aspirated, are nevertheless unaspirated after s, as in *spin*, *steam*, *skin*.

The statement is correct. There is an audible difference between the bilabial plosive in *pin* and that in *spin*. In the first it is aspirated, in the second it is unaspirated. This means that in the first there is a delay after the release of the bilabial closure before the onset of voicing for the vowel (the duration of this delay being known as 'voice onset time'): [pʰɪn]. In the second there is no such delay: [sp⁼m]. (The basic IPA offers no diacritic to mean 'unaspirated'; I show it by using a raised equals sign, part of the extension ExtIPA.)

It is difficult to hear the difference between unaspirated [**p⁼ t⁼ k⁼**] and devoiced [**ḅ ḍ g̊**]. Theoretically it depends on the difference between fortis articulation, for [**p⁼ t⁼ k⁼**], and lenis articulation, for [**ḅ ḍ g̊**]. But fortis-lenis is much easier to hear in fricatives and affricates, where it affects the volume of air flow and therefore the intensity of the turbulence, than it is in plosives.

Whereas we like to think of the English plosives as being basically voiceless vs. voiced (despite positional devoicing), it is clear that the Chinese ones are aspirated vs. unaspirated. Their representation in Hanyu Pinyin may be *p, t, k* vs. *b, d, g*, but their phonetic representation is usually reckoned to be /pʰ tʰ kʰ/ vs. /p t k/. Mapping these onto English /p t k/ vs. /b d g/ respectively works well, except after **s**. In that position Chinese EFL learners should be encouraged to use the sound that they usually map onto the English voiced plosive.

It may be interesting to note that when English words are borrowed into Welsh (which, like Chinese, has basically aspirated vs. unaspirated plosives), *spite* becomes *sbeit*, *spell* becomes *sbel*, *(di)scourse* becomes *sgwrs*, and *screw* becomes *sgriw*. But Welsh is inconsistent: for some reason, *studio* is *stiwdio*, not **sdiwdio*, and *station* is *stesion*, not **sdesion*.

3.12   Yokohama and the like

Languages differ in the syllable structures that they allow. We can distinguish (i) languages such as English or French, that allow both (a) consonant clusters and (b) one or more final consonants (a coda) in a syllable; and (ii) languages such as Hawai'ian, that do not allow them.

Speakers of type (ii) languages, with syllable structure [CV], may have difficulty producing the consonant clusters ([CCV]) and final consonants ([CVC]) they need when learning type (i) languages. When I discuss this topic in lectures, with reference to the learning of English pronunciation, I usually choose Japanese as my example of a type (ii) language, taking the place name *Yokohama* to illustrate the canonical syllable structure [CV]. *Yo-ko-ha-ma* = [CV CV CV CV].

A few days ago one of the audience, who had heard me lecture on this before, complained that I always use this same word as an example. Why not use some other examples for a change? OK, then, sticking with Japanese proper names: *Nakamura, Watanabe, Taniguchi, Toyota, Nagasaki, Hakodate, Nagano, Shikoku, Haneda, Narita*. And of course there are hundreds more.

More exactly, the canonical syllable structure is [(C)V]: the consonant at the beginning may be absent, leaving just [V]. That's what we have in the first syllable of *Okinawa, Ikebukuro, Akasaka* and in the first two syllables of *Ueno*. Furthermore, the vowel may be double rather than single, yielding a long vowel or a diphthong.

In Hawai'ian, all syllables comply with this [(C)V] structure: *Honolulu, Waikiki, Kamehameha, Oahu, Kahului*. The same applies to other (all other?) Polynesian languages: *Samoa, Papeete, Rotorua, Fiji, Tonga* **to.ŋa**.

Japanese, on the other hand, is not such a strict type (ii) language. Not all Japanese syllables have the structure [(C)V]. Some have a slightly more complicated structure. First, the consonant can have an associated palatal glide, as in *Kyoto, Ryuku*, giving a very limited possibility of [CCV]. Secondly, the vowel may be followed within the syllable by [N], a 'moraic' nasal, or by [Q], an obstruent agreeing in identity with the initial C of the following syllable. Since both [N] and [Q] are consonants, we do have some possible [CVC] syllable structures, though again highly restricted.

We can see these slightly more elaborate syllable structures in cases such as *Sendai, Namba* and *Hokkaido, Sapporo, Beppu*.

So the structural formula for a Japanese syllable is [C(j)VX], where X = [N] or [Q]. (The Japanese affricates romanized as *ch, j* and *ts* count as single consonants.) It's true, too, that Japanese **i** and **u** are devoiced or deleted in certain phonetic contexts, thus giving rise to phonetic (but not phonological) consonant clusters and coda consonants. So *sukiyaki* sounds as if it begins **ski-**, *ohayō gozaimasu* 'good morning!' seems to end -**mas** and *hajimemash(i)te* 'how do you do?' to have a cluster **ʃt**. But these are superficial details of allophonic realization.

Anyhow, that's why in Japanese *milk* gets transformed into **mi.ru.ku** and *McDonalds* into **ma.ku.do.na.ru.do**. And why Japanese EFL learners tend to want to do something similar in their English pronunciation.

Although I started this by talking about syllable structure, speakers of Japanese do not usually think in terms of the syllable: they think in terms of the 'mora'. A mora corresponds either to the [(C(j))V] part of a syllable, or to one of the elements [N], [Q] or [ː] (the second part of a long vowel). The elements [N], [Q] and [ː] cannot co-occur in the same syllable. It follows, then, that a syllable can comprise either one mora or two, but not more than two.

The Japanese word for 'bread', *pan* **pa-N**, has two moras, though we interpret that as one syllable. The proper name *Honshū* **ho-N-ɕu-ː** has four. *Hokkaidō* **ho-Q-ka-i-do-ː** has six. The English disyllabic word *corner* is borrowed into Japanese as the four-mora *kōnā* **ko-ː-na-ː**.

The mora is claimed to be the basic unit of timing in Japanese, in the same way that the syllable is claimed to be in syllable-timed languages and the stress-group (foot) in stress-timed languages. Awareness of the mora is also doubtless reinforced for literate speakers by the kana writing systems used for Japanese, in which there is one symbol per mora.

The devoicing or elision of certain high vowels does not affect the mora count. So *hajimemash(i)te* still comprises six moras despite the disappearance of the **i**.

A Japanese word or morpheme cannot begin with any of the elements [N], [Q] or [ː]. They are found only within a word, following a [(C(j))V] element and making a syllable with it. That is why we still need to talk about syllables in Japanese. Moras alone are not enough.

3.13   struggling to teach phonetics

I hesitated for some time before finally writing this piece (in December 2007).

A young man wrote to me recently. He is a student at a university which had better remain nameless. He is enthusiastic about phonetics, and has taught himself a good deal about the subject. He had already sent me a number of well-informed comments on various matters.

But he had never studied phonetics formally – till now.

> One of the modules in my third level course [he said] is linguistics. Today we began with phonetics. [...] I was eagerly anticipating my first official lecture on the topic, when I could experience the know-how of an 'expert'.

> I was shocked and dismayed at the misinformation propagated by my lecturer. I was spoilt for choice, but here are a few examples:

> - in the list [**p**, **b**, **t**, **d**, **m**, **n**], she said that only [**t**] was voiceless;
> - after introducing English **r** under the heading 'place of articulation', she said that the English phonetic realization of /**r**/ was one of the ways that the language was determined to be Germanic rather than Indo-European;
> - she described forwards slashes // as those used for phonetic (rather than phonological) transcriptions;
> - she said that the Spanish phoneme /**j**/ was glottal (she meant orthographic *j*, which would be correctly transcribed /**x**/) [in fact of course in standard Castilian it is velar, or at most uvular];
> - she said that the difference between English accents is absolutely never in consonants, always in vowels;
> - she said the difference between Australian and New Zealand English is slight (true), and that the differences concern *a* and *e* (I've no idea what that means, TRAP and DRESS, or FACE and FLEECE? Anyway it doesn't matter, because needless to say the main difference is in the KIT vowel);
> - she transcribed *tree* as /**tRi**/, dubbing it 'phonetic'.

> You might wonder why I go to the trouble of listing these, but when one feels passionately for a subject, one wants to see justice done to it. I just cannot understand how somebody with such a poor understanding of a subject could be allowed to teach it.

What can one say? I did a little web research. The university in question states, in the prospectus for the BA in question, that the programme 'provides a foundation in [...] Linguistics'. The teacher in question had recently completed a PhD in a branch of linguistics. Presumably, as a junior post-doc, she was told by the head of department that she must teach an introductory linguistics course covering phonetics. No doubt she has been struggling to do her best.

My correspondent says he is dismayed 'that anyone can get a PhD in any branch of linguistics without knowing about basic linguistic concepts such as competence/performance and grammaticality, and without knowing even elementary phonetics'.

All I could hope was that in due course the external examiner would realize what was going on, and flag it up. Or even the Head of Department.

But possibly the Head of Department did not know much phonetics and linguistics either.

3.14   accents and actors

Long ago, when I was young and unknown, I spent a lot of time looking into material I might draw on for the work that eventually became *Accents of English* (Cambridge University Press 1982). As well as pursuing all the written stuff I could lay my hands on, I enrolled in an evening class in Accents and Dialects, taught by a drama teacher whose name I have forgotten.

Each of the weekly three-hour sessions began with extensive warming-up exercises (going **bɑː bɑː bɑː, biː biː biː, buː buː buː** and the like). We then had a little bit of theory, and a coffee break. The second half was taken up by play-reading to practise what we had learnt (or what the teacher could demonstrate, or what we could do anyhow).

The 'theory' consisted mainly in learning the IPA symbols for RP.

People in the class obviously enjoyed it, and had an opportunity to imitate the speech varieties demonstrated to them. But for my own purposes I concluded that on this evidence the speech and drama people couldn't offer me anything of serious phonetic interest.

A recent article in the *Guardian* described a new CD set about English accents, the work of a former tutor of speech and drama at RADA and a well-known actress. Reading it, I saw that the speech and drama world is still a land of fantasy, not facts. The author's 'environmental theory of accent formation' attributes 'the directness of Geordie' to the way that 'in the north-east, the wind whips off the North Sea and smacks you in the face', while she tells an actor struggling with RP to 'imagine walking across a manicured lawn in England'; and for south Wales, she imagines the intonation 'rising to the tops of mountains and then descending to the bottoms of valleys'. Her advice to someone trying to sound Welsh is 'When in doubt, sing,' while remembering that for some vowels, e.g. in the word *here*, 'the tongue forms a curled, daffodil shape'. As for AmE, its 'colourful r sound' calls for 'speedy contraction in the tongue'; the actor should 'imagine riding a horse at full gallop and pulling back hard and short on the reins'. The letters **p** and **b**, she suggests, 'are softened by tapping the tongue lightly on the bottom teeth'.

I wish someone could persuade the drama schools of the value of real phonetic knowledge. Can't they see what nonsense it is to talk of tapping the tongue on the bottom teeth in order to make an American p-sound (or rather, letter)? Or curling the tongue into a daffodil shape?

We lucky people who know phonetics can simply say that in parts of south Wales *here* is pronounced **jœ:**. End of story.

Eric Armstrong, a voice, speech and dialect coach now working in Canada as Associate Professor of Voice at York University, supplied a thoughtful and valuable reaction to my rant.

> I was pleased to see your post on Actors and Accents. I'm not in the least surprised by your point of view. Far too many of my colleagues haven't enough knowledge to teach basic phonetics effectively, and essentially pass on what they were taught, continuing a tradition of ignorance that is decades if not centuries old.
>
> 'The speech and drama world is still a land of fantasy, not facts.'
>
> This is true, and perhaps to be expected. Actors are creative artists, not scientists. Most voice and speech trainers come to their work from the world of the theatre, not from the world of science, and their clients are uneasy with the world of science. In fact, many actors have made it clear that the reason they were drawn to their art was because of their disdain for science and math. To them, phonetics seems an odd combination of science and math-like symbols, things that they have failed at in the past, and notions that make them uneasy, fearful and angry.
>
> As I'm sure you're well aware, there are many types of learners in the world. We aren't all blessed with 'good ears' – so few seem to be auditory learners. I find that many actors are kinesthetic learners more than auditory ones, but there are also visual learners. The world of actor training is immersed in metaphor and imagery, as is the world of the professional actor. This is the language of art, not science, and it is used in an uninhibited manner – splashing around in the pool of metaphor – in order to reach a goal that may be beyond a performer who has a resistance to more linear thinking, rational explanation and concrete examples. Many high level actors work in an almost child-like sense of wonder, playing their way into new roles, with new physicalities and vocalizations. Short attention spans are, unfortunately, the norm. There are some who clearly have great ears, brilliant minds, agile tongues, and open hearts. As a colleague of mine once retorted, 'We used to call that "talent"'.
>
> Part of the problem the established voice and speech community faces in trying to embrace greater phonetic detail and more accurate usage of the tools available to us from the worlds of linguistics arises, I believe, from deeply held beliefs about the systems and methodologies in which people have been trained. When new data is presented to these trainers revealing

that their teaching methods are ineffective, cognitive dissonance, uncomfortable feelings arising from having two conflicting ideas or beliefs, forces them to justify what they have been doing in the past, and to devalue the new information. Often the systems and methods learned by trainers are the life work of their mentors, and so rejecting the concepts they learned means rejecting what is, in many ways, a beloved parent figure for them.

I think there is hope for the future of the speech and drama world. Teachers like Dudley Knight and Phil Thompson have found ways to bring greater phonetic detail into the conversation while keeping an actorly playfulness in their teaching. Their greatest innovation is in guiding the people they work with to explore the world of sounds available. One small example: making noises through gibberish play called 'omnish', an imaginary language of all the world's sounds. Actors love the kind of exploration where they do an oration in Omnish, and another actor provides simultaneous translation. Yes, to a scientist, it must sound silly. But silliness has great value to an actor! It frees her up, lets her connect to those new sounds in a joyous, unfettered manner, stripping away all those value judgments of sounds (and ultimately symbols) as being 'mere math'. And once she can hear those sounds in her own mouth, to feel the physical action required, then visualize the action of her articulators, she is ready to begin to learn how to write them down systematically with IPA.

There is no defense of inaccurate metaphor, I think. But actors need metaphor, and a trainer of actors is sorely lacking if they don't have it in their arsenal.

3.15   minimal pairs in action

We were having dinner on a cruise ship. For dessert one of our party had ordered cherry tart (the elegant Frenchified menu called it a clafoutis). But the waiter, who was Thai, brought us what looked like Black Forest gateau instead. We protested, and he took it away and brought us the correct order.

He explained that it wasn't his fault. He had asked the kitchen for *tart* **tɑːt**. But they had given him *torte* **tɔːt**.

Very few of the catering staff on the ship were native speakers of English. This was English as a lingua franca in action. It failed.

(At least, I suppose we have to say it's English. The words in question are loanwords.)

Distinguishing between minimal pairs, in perception and in production, is not just a classroom exercise. And don't say that bothering about that sort of thing is not important, and that the only thing that matters is communication, that the context will sort things out. Sometimes communication breaks down precisely because the context does not sort things out. Getting it wrong has a practical consequence.

In this case, the result was inconvenienced customers and an indignant waiter convinced it was not his fault.

3.16   a French user of English

I attended a university public lecture on cognition. The speaker's native language was French, but he spoke English fluently and fully intelligibly.

He had a number of typical French (mis)pronunciations: uvular **r**, no contrast between ɔː and əʊ (*law – low*), occasional spelling-based oddities such as 'ɒðə *other*, *infɔːmation*, *ˈripresent*, together with word stress errors such as *chaˈracterize*, *satisˈfy*. But most word stresses were OK, and he had a good robust contrast in iː–ɪ with its high functional load.

This was a good demonstration of the point that in EFL you can get away with quite a few pronunciation 'errors' as long as your speech overall is fluent, with good rhythm and acceptable intonation.

3.17   Taiwan English

Many thanks to Karen Chung for allowing me to reproduce this transcription of 'Taiwan English' – English as it might typically be pronounced by someone from Taiwan. Bear in mind that schools in Taiwan are all supposed to teach AmE, not BrE.

However, I think most of this would apply to English in much of mainland China, too, where BrE is the norm.

The instruction Karen gives her students is 'First, read the text out loud to decipher it, then write it out in regular English orthography.' Readers might like to try their hand.

ɛs ˈkjuz mi iz ˈðis ˈsɪt ˈtæk ən

ˈnɔ is ˈnɑt ˈsæŋ kju naʃ ˈwe ðɚ ˈizən ɪt

ˈjɛs is ˈnɑs æ̃ ˈwɔm ɪs biŋ ˈkoʊ fɔ sɔ ˈmɛni deɪs lɪs ɪz ma ˈfʌst ˈtãĩ tu ˈdʒɔk lɪs ˈmaŋθ du ˈdʒu laɪ ˈʒɔk iŋ

ˈwɛl ˈnɑ ˈɹɪ li ˈju ʃu ˈtɹaɪ ˈɪt ˈdʒɔk iŋ is maɪ ˈlaɪ ˈluk æ maɪ ˈdʒɔg iŋ ˈʃus ˈleɪ ɑ ˈmæt ĩ ˈiŋ gə lən æŋ aɪ ˈboʊ ˈlɛm iŋ ˈhɔŋ ˈkon ˈleɪ ɑˈɹɪ li gɔt

ɪf ˈju waŋt tu ˈlʌŋ ˈxaʊ tu ˈðʒɔk ju ˈnɪt ə ˈgu ˈpɛɹ aʃ ˈsus laɪ mãĩ

ˈwɛl aɪ ˈluk æ ˈlos mɛn ˈleɪ ɑ ˈɹɪ li ʂˈloʊ ˈleɪ ɑ ˈwok iŋ ˈnɔt ˈdʒɔk iŋ

ˈxu ɑ ˈju ˈtok iŋ əˈbaʊ də mæ̃ wɪf lɔŋ ˈxɛɹ hiz ˈxæt luks ˈfa ni
o læs ˈmaɪ ˈbɹɑ ðɚ o am ˈso ɹi aɪ ˈmin ðə ˈpʌ sən ˈnæs tu ˈxim lə ˈwã ĩ lə ˈstju pɪ ˈgɹiŋ ˈswe tɚ æn bəˈlæk ˈpæs ˈwɛl lə ˈmæ̃ ˈju ɑ ˈtok iŋ əˈbaʊ is ɑˈpi ˈʔi ˈtɪ tʃɚ æ̃ ˈbaɪ lə ˈweɪ hiz ˈo soʊ ˈmaɪ ˈxɑs bɛnd

Notice how:

• final consonants tend to be lost, particularly if the next word begins with a consonant; if present, they may be wrongly voiceless;

- consonant clusters tend to be simplified or broken up with an intrusive vowel;
- the voiceless dental fricative θ tends to be replaced by **s** or **f**, and the voiced ð by **l** or **d**;
- final nasals often have the wrong place of articulation, or nasalize the preceding vowel and are then lost;
- the vowels FLEECE-KIT, DRESS-TRAP-FACE and STRUT-START are often confused;

and so on.

You would think the loss of final consonants would be particularly devastating for intelligibility. However, this seems to be characteristic of some African-American English, too, and the results are apparently not too catastrophic.

3.18   the IPA Certificate

The year 2008 marked the centenary of the setting up of the International Phonetic Association's Certificate of Proficiency in Phonetics.

Here is the exact text of the IPA Council's decision establishing it (**m.f.** 23:5–6, 1908, p. 67). It is in phonetically transcribed French.

> **egzamẽ d fɔnetik**. a l ynanimite, lə kɔ̃ːsɛːj s ɛ prɔnɔ̃ːse ã favœːr d œ̃ sɛrtifika d etyd fɔnetik, a delivre ɔfisjɛlmã o nɔ̃ d l **af** par dez egzaminatœːr dymã kalifje. kɔm prəmjez egzaminatœːr (a defo də Sweet ki avɛ rfyːze) ɔ̃t ete nɔme :
>
> pur l almã, W. Viëtor;
> pur l ã̃ːglɛ, E. Edwards;
> pur lə frã̃ːsɛ, P. Passy.
>
> nu dɔnɔ̃ si-aprɛ lə mɔdɛl adɔpte.

So there were three Certificates: one for German, one for English and one for French. On the following page the **m.f.** shows a model of the French certificate. The various topics were:

Dictée phonétique française
Dictée en langue inconnue
Transcription
Lecture d'un texte phonétique
Lecture d'un texte orthographique
Questions théoriques
Prononciation en parlant.

Most of these topics remain in the examination to this day, though in recent years only the certificate in English has been examined. We still have dictation of English and of nonsense words (words in an unknown language), transcription, reading from a phonetic text and questions on theory. Only reading from an orthographic text and 'spoken pronunciation' have been dropped (since many candidates are now native speakers of English). The standard required has always been uncompromisingly high.

(The 1908 examiner for English, Ernest Edwards, was appointed to teach phonetics at UCL in 1903. It was he who recommended Daniel Jones as his successor at UCL to carry on his work.)

The IPA examination was particularly important at a time when few universities held examinations in the phonetics of foreign languages or indeed of oral proficiency in general. As this changed, the number of candidates fell. Latterly, though, it has been given an entire new lease of life by the IPA Certificate strand of the UCL Summer Course in English Phonetics, which culminates with sitting the examination.

You can read about it and download sample questions at www.phon.ucl.ac.uk/courses/ipaexam/ipa-exam.htm.

3.19   dead letters

From the IPA exam regulations:

> In the dictation of nonsense words or an unknown language, candidates should be prepared to recognise any sounds occurring in the IPA chart.

Let's leave aside the interesting question of whether any *sounds* truly *occur* in the chart, which on the face of it seems to betray a naïve confusion of speech (sounds) and writing (symbols).

Instead, here is something candidates sitting this and other examinations in practical phonetics might like to know.

There are a few symbols in the chart that you can ignore. You will not be tested on them. They stand for sounds that you will not actually be expected to recognize or reproduce.

Take, for example, the vowel ɞ. In the current IPA chart it is shown as standing for an open-mid central vowel, the rounded equivalent of ɜ. But rightly or wrongly it is simply not among the sounds we drill advanced students on. (Rightly, I think: when did you last see this symbol in use, as opposed to sitting in a chart?)

The same applies to ɘ, the symbol for an unrounded close-mid central vowel.

You will indeed be tested on the cardinal vowels i e ɛ a ɑ ɔ o u y ø œ ɒ ʌ ɤ ɯ, though probably not on ɨ ʉ ɵ and certainly not on ɶ. (Although there are some quite well-known languages for which one or other of these symbols is needed.) Among the non-cardinal vowels the only ones you must know are the ɪ ʊ æ ɜ ə that you need for RP English, plus the ɐ that you may know from the phonetics of German or Portuguese.

As with vowels, so with consonants. You can ignore the 'other symbols' ɭ ɧ ʜ ʢ ʔ. Concentrate on mastering the recognition and production of the consonants shown in the main table at the top of the chart, plus clicks, implosives and ejectives.

Even in the main table I think you could probably ignore ʟ, the velar lateral.

3.20   alveolopalatals

The IPA chart includes ɕ and ʑ, the 'alveolopalatal' fricatives. Listed under 'other symbols' on the chart, these are nevertheless two sounds that the examination candidate needs to be familiar with.

There seems to be some confusion over the terms 'postalveolar', 'alveolopalatal' and 'palatoalveolar'. I came across a claim that most (if not all) Australian accents of English have alveolopalatals, whereas RP has postalveolars; and some American textbooks call AmE tʃ and dʒ 'alveolopalatal'.

I suspect that this may be just a difference of terminology, without any significant difference in the sounds referred to. I can't say I have ever noticed much of a difference between Australian or American tʃ dʒ and my own.

Like many other phoneticians, I do not follow the post-Kiel IPA chart in classifying tʃ dʒ as 'postalveolar'. For me, the English affricates that are post-alveolar are the ones in *trace* and *drab*, while those in *chase* and *jab* are palatoalveolar.

How do alveolopalatals and palatoalveolars differ?

One important difference between ɕ ʑ tɕ dʑ and ʃ ʒ tʃ dʒ is that the fricatives and affricates in the latter of these two sets of four sound 'darker' than those in the former.

One of the exercises I used to do with students was to make them slide back and forth along the continuum ɕ – ʃ – ʂ.

I think the important thing is the auditory/acoustic effect rather than the precise configuration of the articulators (since speakers differ so much in the anatomy of the mouth). For alveolopalatals you can also imitate those of Japanese, Chinese or Polish.

We must also bear in mind that the symbols ɕ ʑ are only needed in languages that have a phonemic contrast between them and a darker type of ʃ ʒ (e.g. Polish, Mandarin Chinese). For languages where this is not the case (e.g. Japanese) people often use just the symbols ʃ ʒ whatever the exact phonetic quality. This is in line with the principle of simplicity in transcription.

Equally, you could write the postalveolars as ʃ ʒ tʃ dʒ in Polish and Chinese. I usually do this for Polish *sz rz (ż) cz dż*, but for Chinese *sh r ch zh* it seems better to write ʂ ʐ tʂʰ tʂ.

Indeed, the ʃ ʒ symbols can be used very flexibly. If you compare the Japanese *s(i)*, the English *sh*, the French *ch* and the Russian ш, you notice a gradual change in the friction noise from clear (very palatal) to dark (not at all palatal).

Yet they can all reasonably be written ʃ in simple transcription of those languages. For comparative work you can choose as appropriate from ɕ ʃ ʂ or even, following Ladefoged, ṣ.

I could add that in my experience Poles are not really happy about accepting Chinese *x q j* as exact equivalents of Polish ɕ tɕ dz, while the Chinese in turn are not sure about accepting the *ś ć dź* of Polish as the exact equivalents of their own sounds. But the difference (perhaps mainly one of degree of voicing and aspiration) is below the radar of what IPA oral examiners, for example, are on the lookout for.

A Polish word including both types is *cześć* tʃeɕtɕ 'hello', for which you can easily find audio clips on the web. For comparison, listen to Chinese *xi* ɕi and *shi* ʂʅ.

3.21   BrE or AmE for TEFL?

A Dutch correspondent writes:

> The Dutch have always been at the forefront as foreign learners of English and RP has been the standard accent for EFL in the Netherlands for many years. This is now coming under pressure from GA [General American] (among others) and we are slowly being faced with the fact that we shall have to let RP go, that is if we want any of our students to graduate.

This is a difficult issue, and one people often ask me about. Is RP ('BrE') still the right pronunciation model for EFL, or ought it to be replaced by some form of American or Lingua Franca English?

The first thing I usually say is that it is much more important to concentrate on the common phonetic core of all kinds of English than to worry about the minute details of this or that model. First any learner has to get a good grasp of such matters as:

- syllable structure – final consonants, consonant clusters;
- word stress placement;
- tonicity (nucleus placement) in intonation;
- vowel weakening;
- important phonemic oppositions that all native speakers make – particularly those with a high functional load, such as **p – f, r – l, iː – ɪ, ɔː – əʊ/oʊ** (*pin – fin, write – light, seat – sit, law – low*);
- spelling-to-sound rules and the most important exceptions to them.

Only when those are all thoroughly under control should you start worrying about whether to take British or American or some other kind of English as your model. And let's face it, for most learners of EFL they are not all thoroughly under control.

Second, the ideal circumstances for learning to pronounce English are when the learner has a close relationship with a single native speaker or a group of native speakers. If you are lucky enough to be in that position, imitate what you hear. Your native speaker friend or colleague can operate in any kind of native-English-speaking environment, so if you are like them you will be able to too. (In my time I have met a German who sounded as if he came from Essex, a Japanese who sounded as if he was Texan and a Korean who sounded like an upper-class Indian. I consider all three to be highly successful learners of English pronunciation, even though none of them pronounced in exactly the way any textbook prescribed.)

However, that does not altogether address the question put.

From Germany, Petr Rösel reports:

> My experience with German students of English who come to my phonetics classes at university is that they have [typically] been taught English at secondary school for seven to nine years by different teachers; for example, during the first two or three years their teacher spoke British English (with or without a German accent), for the next three years their instructor favoured American English and the rest of the time at secondary school they heard British English again.

> When they come to my diagnostic sessions I'm confronted with a hodge-podge of accents: British English with patches of Americanisms and a strong tinge of German spoken by one and the same student. And I am not speaking of errors that consist in pronouncing some isolated word in the accent they are not aiming at. On the contrary! They pronounce the non-prevocalic **r** in some words and leave it out in others. They pronounce *stop* with an open **ɑ**, but *dog* with an **ɒ**. They flap the **t** in *city*, but not in *letter* etc., etc. If I were sarcastic I would call it International English. No, those poor souls are to be pitied. They should not have been confronted with this diversity during their first steps into the world of English and they should have been warned and encouraged by their teachers not to mix varieties. This is not to say that they should not be able to understand different varieties!

> Mainz University, where I teach English phonetics (among other things), accepts both standard varieties, which is a double-edged thing (see above). This is the main reason why I split my phonetics classes when it comes to practising pronunciation. I hired a native speaker of American English as a tutor. She takes care of those students aspiring to speak AmE and I look after those who want to speak BrE. But, alas, this is just a drop in the ocean.

...while another Dutch correspondent wrote:

> Although BrE is still the norm taught at school, I think the average Dutch student of English is exposed far more to AmE (in all varieties) than BrE, as a result of American movies, TV series, pop music, etc. being predominant.

EFL learners should be exposed (passively) to a wide variety of types of English even if their teachers, dictionaries and textbooks offer a single standardized model for imitation. As native speakers we do admittedly sometimes have difficulty in understanding an accent we haven't encountered before, or even one we have. We need time to 'tune in'. And it's interesting that New Zealanders – with less than two centuries to create their own variety – should be right up there with Ulstermen and American southerners in presenting a challenge to the rest of us.

3.22   spot the mistake

I'd been doing some exam marking. It was a phonetics written exam in which candidates, among other tasks, had to convert a short English passage in orthography into phonetic transcription.

Some candidates were native speakers, some were not (and none of them were from north Wales). The examiners are extremely liberal in allowing all sorts of, shall we say, less usual pronunciations. Native speakers, in particular, are encouraged to transcribe their own accent (but must say what it is). Non-native speakers normally attempt RP, but there too the examiners are very flexible.

Here, however, are some transcriptions offered by candidates but penalized by the examiners. These must be wrong, and candidates ought to know that they are wrong. Readers might like to check that they can see where and why they're wrong.

Each is a single word, extracted from the passage in which it was embedded.

James **dʒeɪms**
laws **lɔːwz**
wrong **wrɒŋ**
talking **ˈtaʊkɪŋ**
magazine **mæɡˈzɪŋ, mæɡˈzɪn, məɡəˈziːn**
managed **ˈmænɪʒd, ˈmænɪdʒɪd**
dangerous **ˈdæŋɡərəs, ˈdeɪŋɡrəz, ˈdeɪŋdʒərəs**
think **ðɪŋk**
news **njuːs**
ignoring **ˈɪɡnɔːrɪŋ**
conservative **cənˈsəvətɪv**

3.23   excuse my excuse

For an examiner, marking phonetic transcriptions of English from dictation can be rather depressing.

In one test passage the first two words were *excuse me*, which I dictated in a perfectly ordinary way, as ɪkˈskjuːz mi. Among the versions I was offered by the examinees were ɪˈkjus me, ɪˈkjʊz ˈmiː, ˈɪkskjuz mi and several cases of ɪkˈskjuːs mi. Now these were proficient speakers of English, often professional teachers of the language, students of phonetics. And this was from my very clear, slow, repetitious dictation, so all they had to do was listen and transcribe. Those who were not native speakers didn't have to work out that *excuse* is a verb here, not a noun, and therefore has final **z**, not **s**.

That's assuming they actually knew about the **s ~ z** noun~verb alternation in *use, abuse, excuse, refuse, house*. And that it doesn't apply in *ease, tease, phase, pause, bruise, cruise, surprise* (always **z**) or in *base, case, promise* (always **s**). And that in *advice~advise* we have the same alternation but change the spelling. And that in *practice~practise* both noun and verb have **s**, but we Brits change the spelling. In *choice~choose* there is a vowel change in addition to the consonantal alternation, reflected in spelling. And in *close* it's mainly an adjective~verb alternation **kləʊs ~ kləʊz**, as it is in *diffuse* and *loose~lose* **luːs ~ luːz**, this latter pair with a spelling change. And *used* is **juːzd** when it means 'employed' but **juːst** when it means 'accustomed'. Ah, English!

In these dictation exams candidates tend to regard the nonsense words as a big challenge, while assuming the English will be easy to do. In practice, almost everyone does better on the nonsense than on the English.

Are you ready to be a phonetics examiner?

3.24   miscellanea

Here are some jokes for your EFL class (or your seven-year-old).

How do you weigh a whale?
– You go to a whale-weigh station!
What do you call a deer with no eyes?
– No idea!
And a deer with no eyes and no legs?
– Still no idea!

***

And here's a nice mispronunciation recently heard from a BBC Radio 4 newsreader. He wanted to refer to the newspaper *City AM*, given away free every weekday morning to London commuters. Its name derives from *City* (= financial centre) and *AM* (a.m. = morning). But the newsreader didn't realize this. He called it ˌsɪti ˈæm.

4   Intonation

Assorted comments on English intonation

4.1	introduction

Intonation is best seen, in my opinion, as reflecting three types of decision that speakers repeatedly make as they speak. They are how to break up the material (chunking, the signalling of syntactic boundaries); what tones to use (e.g. fall vs. rise, signalling certain grammatical functions as well as such things as the speaker's attitude to what they are saying); and where to place sentence accents (particularly nuclear accents, mainly used to signal focus). We call these systems *tonality*, *tone* and *tonicity* respectively. Informally, they are the three Ts.

In tonality the speaker has to decide how to break the stream of speech into successive intonation phrases (IPs). By default, each clause will be made a separate IP; but the speaker is free to make the IPs longer or shorter than this. I think that the principles of chunking are probably pretty universal. No EFL learner needs to be taught to make or hear the difference between (1) and (2) in speech:

(1)   I don't know.   (one IP)
(2)   I don't, | no.   (two IPs)

Where it is relevant, I show IP boundaries with the mark '|', as in example (2).

Clearly, tone varies wildly across languages and dialects, at least at the superficial level. The question is what underlying regularities there may be. We can dismiss obviously untrue claims such as that statements always have a fall, while questions always have a rise. (Just think of Belfast and the west of Scotland.) But there are other candidates for the status of universal that are worth considering. How general is it that, as in English, wh-questions tend to have the same pattern as statements, while yes-no questions are different? Pretty widespread, I think.

When discussing tone in English, it is enough at the basic level to distinguish only three types of nuclear tone: fall ('\'), rise ('/') and fall-rise ('V'). I write the tone mark immediately before the syllable that bears it, and underline that syllable.

(3)   Do you want /coffee | or /tea | or \cola?
(4)   \Marvellous!

(5)   What lovely \flowers!
(6)   A: I've just \spifflicated them.
           – B: You've just /what? | /Spifflicated them?

Note that the syllable with the tone mark is where the falling, rising or falling-rising pitch movement begins; particularly in the case of non-falls, it may not be completed until the end of the IP. In (6), the fall in A's utterance is manifested as a high pitch on *spiff* followed by an immediate drop to a low pitch for the rest of the utterance: typically, *-licated them* will be on a low level pitch. In B's response, the rise in the second IP starts on the syllable *spiff* and continues steadily to the end of the utterance: the unaccented *them*, paradoxically as it may seem, has the highest pitch in the IP.

(7)   I Vthink it's true | (...but I could be wrong.)

In (7) the pitch starts high on *think*, drops abruptly down, and then rises on *true*.

If tone and/or tonicity are not relevant to the discussion, I leave them unshown, as in examples (1) and (2) above.

4.2   intonation notation

I hope you like the notation system used here. It is the system I use in my book *English Intonation* (Cambridge University Press 2008). My aim is a notation system that is intuitive for the reader to interpret, while being easy to type on a computer.

Given that I want to be able to combine it with ordinary phonetic transcription, it has to be based on adding to the orthographic or segmental text (text-decoration) rather than changing it (text-alteration). This means that although I approve of Brazil's principle of symbolizing the place of the nucleus (the tonic) separately from the choice of nuclear tone (see *Discourse Intonation and Language Teaching*, Longman 1980), I have rejected his device of using capitaliZAtion for this purpose, and have instead adopted Halliday's old idea of underlining the nucleus (see *On Language and Linguistics*, Continuum 2003).

In the notation of tone, I want to use marks that are iconic, i.e. that suggest by their shape the pitch characteristics involved, as do those of the O'Connor and Arnold system (see *Intonation of Colloquial English*, Prentice Hall 1973). But keeping the notation easily typable means rejecting some of their special marks, since some of them are not even Unicode symbols. In any case, I think that for most EFL purposes (and even for native speakers) the distinction between different kinds of fall (high fall, low fall, rise-fall) is relatively unimportant, and that for most purposes it is sufficient to symbolize them all with the backslash symbol [\]. Likewise with the various types of rise [/] and fall-rise [V]. So I operate with a basic three-tone system.

Where the choice of nuclear tone is irrelevant, I just put ['] as a place holder.

For non-nuclear accents I think it is generally adequate to use a simple straight apostrophe ['], or if available its phonetic equivalent the stress mark [ˈ]. In the basic markup I do not mark simple rhythmic stress at all, though the symbol [°] is available for those who want to show it.

V̌ðıs | ʃəʊz ˈhaʊ tə kəmV̌baın | fəˈnetık sımbl̩z ən ıntə\neıʃn̩ mɑːks ‖

In pedagogical applications, I think that ToBI-style notation (H*L-L% and the like) is a non-starter (see www.ling.ohio-state.edu/~tobi/). But I could be wrong.

4.3   idiomatic intonation

English has various tone idioms – words or phrases for which the choice of tone (rise, fall or fall-rise) is fixed rather than free. For example, the interjection *oops* or *whoops*, used when you've fallen, dropped something or made a mistake, can only have a rise. You can't say it with a fall.

/Oops!
× \Oops!

On the other hand the phrase *by the way*, used in spoken English to introduce a side issue not connected with the main subject you were talking about before, seems (at least for me) always to have some kind of fall (high fall, low fall, rise-fall), never a rise or fall-rise.

By the \way, | have you ˈseen my um/brella anywhere?
× By the /way, | have you ˈseen my um/brella anywhere?

This is despite the fact that (as Alan Cruttenden has shown us – see *Intonation*, Cambridge University Press 1997, second edition) most limiting adverbials tend to have a rise; it is reinforcing ones that usually take a fall.

You can say *hello!* with any tone. But its newer equivalent *hi!* seems to demand a fall.

Hel\lo!
Hel/lo!
HelV̌lo!
\Hi!
× /Hi!

(I suppose there is also a cutesy way of saying *hi* with a fall-rise, but I think that only a few speakers would use it. When I was young, people in my circle didn't say *hi* at all. We thought of it as an Americanism. But now you hear it everywhere. I think I started using it myself in the mid-1990s, on the principle that if you can't beat them join them.)

You can use any tone for *goodbye*, though probably the most usual one is a rise. But its informal equivalent *see you* sounds odd with a simple rise: it seems to need a fall-rise.

Good/<u>bye</u>! (also with a high head or prehead, 'Good/<u>bye</u>! or ⁻Good/<u>bye</u>!)
V<u>See</u> you!
?? /<u>See</u> you!

A rise seems OK if we add an adverbial. So is a fall.

'See you to/<u>morrow</u>!
'See you to\<u>morrow</u>!

There are also tonicity idioms – in which the place of the nucleus is fixed, though not necessarily the tone. Here are some examples involving personal pronouns which bear the nucleus despite seeming from a pragmatic point of view not to be in contrastive focus.

'Good for '<u>you</u>! (= congratulations!)
'Bully for '<u>you</u>! (= sarcastic congratulation)
'Blow '<u>me</u>! (= I am surprised or annoyed)
'Get '<u>her</u>! (= look at her putting on airs)
'Search '<u>me</u> (= I don't know, I've no idea)

The fixed tonicity is necessary for the idiomatic meaning. If, instead, you say:

'<u>Search</u> me!

– that's an invitation (perhaps to a policeman or immigration official) to do just that, rather than a confession of ignorance. And if you say:

'<u>Blow</u> me!

– then that's an invitation to perform a sexual act. The same tonicity-dependent interpretations apply if we replace *blow* by the f-word.

4.4   systems

A student from Argentina wanted to know how to account for the word 'system' in the expression 'the English intonation system'. 'I know Brazil talks about the system of English intonation,' she wrote, 'but why is it called a system?'

Intonation is systematic, or a system, in the technical sense of having a finite set of either/or options (e.g. a syllable either is, or is not, prominent). In linguistics, a system is a fixed set of choices. Nouns in many (but not all) languages exhibit a NUMBER system – every time we utter a noun we have to make it either singular or plural. Verbs usually display a TENSE system (present vs. past, etc.). Most people analyse English verbs as also displaying an ASPECT system (progressive vs. non-progressive, perfective vs. non-perfective).

Similarly, ever since Halliday's work in the 1960s, people analysing English intonation have identified three systems in operation (see 4.1 above):

- a tonality system, or 'chunking', whereby we divide the spoken material exhaustively into successive IPs (aka word groups, tone units, etc.);
- a tonicity system, or 'nucleus placement', whereby we select one lexical item to highlight by placing on its stressed syllable the nucleus (aka tonic) of the IP – in English this has the pragmatic function of marking the end of the focus domain;
- and a tone system, whereby we select fall, or rise, or fall-rise, each with a characteristic tone-meaning, as the tone for the IP (located physically on and after the nucleus but pragmatically characterizing the whole IP).

The claim here is that in these three respects we make a succession of choices all the time as we speak, as we decide how to structure our material, what to focus on and what attitude (etc.) to express towards what we are saying. Some would claim that this is all also part of a complicated battle with our interlocutor(s) for control of the conversation.

4.5   politeness

As I was jogging in a local park, a man coming the other way asked me:

You 'haven't got the /time on you, have you mate?

Since I was indeed wearing a watch, I duly answered him:

E'leven fifty-\seven.

The wording and intonation of his question was appropriate for the situation of an English person addressing a stranger. But an EFL student would probably have cast the question differently:

'What's the \time?

– which in this context would have sounded rude.

Why is this? We use the simple wording and the fall when we wish to be businesslike with someone we are already talking to. We would also use this pattern if repeating the question to someone who seemed not to have heard it, or who was refusing to answer, or if we were otherwise annoyed at their non-cooperation. But when starting a conversation, particularly with a stranger, we prefer to be indirect. The negative statement followed by a reverse-polarity tag question in the same IP does the job nicely.

You 'haven't got the /time on you, have you mate?

Alternative polite formulae in BrE would be:

> 'Have you got the /time on you by any chance?
> ExVcuse me, | d'you 'happen to know what /time it is?
> VSorry, | d'you 'have the /time?
> 'Got the /time, mate?
> ExVcuse me, | I was \wondering, | 'what /time d'you make it?

Some speakers (particularly younger ones?) might alternatively use a highish fall-rise instead of the rise.

Americans would probably not be so indirect. And they would not use the BrE working-class non-deferential male-to-male vocative *mate*, but probably *bud(dy)*.

The formulae you sometimes hear from speakers of Russian, involving a negative question:

'Haven't you got the /time on you?
'Don't you know the /time?

sound like accusations and are therefore very inappropriate ways to ask the question. They would be heard as reproaches to someone who is late.

4.6   fall-rise or fall plus rise?

As I breasted the brow of a rather steep hill during my running club's Sunday morning social run, a fellow runner sweetly enquired, 'Did you run up that hill?'

My answer was:

> \No, | I'm a'fraid I \didn't. || I 'have to admit I \walked up.

However, what interests me here is the intonation used by my interlocutor. She had a wide falling pitch on *run* and then a wide rising pitch on *hill*. The problem is to decide whether she was using (a) a fall tone followed by a rise tone, or (b) a fall-rise tone:

(a)   Did you \run up | that /hill?
(b)   Did you Vrun up that hill?

I think the answer is (b), for three reasons.

First, we both knew we'd just got to the top of a hill. So from the pragmatics of the situation, *that hill* was old information (given). Accordingly, we would not expect focus on those words: we would not expect them to be accented. Analysis (a) places not just an accent but a nuclear accent on *hill*; analysis (b) treats it as unaccented.

If, introspecting, I change the tone on *run* into a rise, but otherwise keep the pragmatics the same, I find myself saying not (a') but (b'):

(a′)   Did you /run up | that /hill?
(b′)   Did you /run up that hill?

And if I had not heard clearly and had asked her to repeat the question, I think she would have then said not (a″) but (b″):

(a″)   Did you \run up | that \hill?
(b″)   Did you \run up that hill?

Thirdly, if – introspecting again – I ask myself how she would have said the same thing without the last three words, but keeping the pragmatics the same, I feel pretty sure she would have said not (a‴) but (b‴):

(a‴)   Did you \run?
(b‴)   Did you Vrun?

Conclusion: she used a single IP, with a fall-rise tone on *run*. I have noticed that a fall-rise tone on a yes-no question is heard increasingly frequently.

I think that phoneticians, or at least intonologists, have to be ready to perform mental speculations like this to elucidate structures, just as syntacticians do.

4.7   empty things

In English intonation there are certain types of word and phrase that tend not to receive the nucleus, even though they may be the last lexical item in an IP. They include various nouns that have very little meaning of their own, particularly vague general nouns such as *things*, *people* – often known as 'empty words'.

I 'keep 'seeing things.
'What are you going to 'tell people?

A correspondent, having read the section in my book *English Intonation* that deals with this point, mentions the greeting expression *How are things?* 'Where would the nucleus occur?' he asks. 'Probably on the question word *how*? Yet don't some native speakers put the nucleus on the empty word *things*?'

The problem is that the nucleus has to go Vsomewhere, and if all the other words in the IP are function words then it will even go on a weak ('empty') content word. In fact, this is the usual tonicity for this question.

'How are \things?

Actually, for reasons I cannot explain, people like me usually violate number concord here, and say:

'How's \things?

– though that is not relevant to the intonation.

A nucleus on *how* would constitute marked tonicity, and might be, for example, a disbelieving echo question.

A: 'How's \things?
B: \Oh, | \otiose.
A: /What did you say?! | /How are things?

My correspondent then offered the following counter-examples, in which *things* receives the nucleus.

(1)   A: Mary, I'm sorry to hear about your father.
         B: Thank you, John. | It was 'one of those \things.
         A: When did he pass away?
         B: He was buried on December 20th.

(2)   A: What does your father do for a living?
         B: He's into 'many \things. (= jobs)
         A: Does he have a major line of work or. . .?
         B: Yes, he's a waste material dealer.

(3)   'Get your \things. (= belongings) You'll be leaving with the police!

(4)   We'll drive out right after dinner | and 'get your \things.

Numbers (1), (3) and (4) are clear: we have to accent *things*. You could consider *just one of those things* an idiom, and exempt *things* 'belongings' from the category of empty words. It seems to me that (2), though, could go either way: the nucleus can go on *things* or, alternatively, on *many*, given that the speaker can imply that *jobs* is given (= predictable from the context).

There are similar difficulties with *people*. Although we say:

(5)   I 'want to \meet people.

(6)   I 'want to com\municate with people.

(because a nucleus on *people* might suggest a contrast with, say, *machines* or even *animals*), we nevertheless say:

(7)   There were a 'lot of \people in the room.

4.8   counterpresuppositional insists

One area of English intonation that is really difficult to explain is found in exchanges like this:

A: Have you /eaten?
B: \No, | there was 'nothing \to eat.

Why does B put the nuclear accent on *to*, a function word that appears to have virtually no meaning of its own?

This is an example of a class of utterances known as counterpresuppositionals. Here, A says something that *presupposes* that there was something available for B to eat. That is, A treats the availability of food as something that is shared ground (mutual knowledge) for the two participants in the conversation. B's reply involves a rejection of this presupposition: it counters it. The supposed fact of the availability of food was not in fact shared ground: B denies that it was the case.

We know that in English it is usual to avoid putting the nucleus on a repeated item. So we don't expect a nucleus on *eat*. Logically, we might expect a nucleus on *nothing*. But that's not where native speakers put it. They usually put it on *to* (above), or sometimes, less commonly, on *was*, or indeed on *eat*:

B: There \was nothing to eat.
B: There was 'nothing to \eat.

In my book *English Intonation* (p. 183), I give various other examples of this, including:

A: They 'want you to a\pologize.
B: But I've 'no reason \to apologize.
A: 'Never /mind. | 'Worse things happen at /sea.
B: We're 'not \at sea.

Alan Cruttenden, in his book *Intonation* (Cambridge University Press 1997, second edition, p. 85), calls this kind of answer an 'insist'. He says that in these 'the nucleus is only rarely on a final noun, may fall on the main verb, but may also fall on classes of word not usually accented at all, in particular on auxiliary verbs, on a negator, and on a preposition immediately following copula "be"'.

Among his examples are the following.

(1)   A: Did you meet the Ripper when you were in prison?
         B: But I haven't been in prison.
(2)   A: I put my bag in your study because there was nowhere else to
         put it.

A correspondent asks, 'Is that always the case? I mean, cannot the verb *been* be stressed instead of the preposition? Would that imply a change of meaning of the sentence?' My answer is that it Vis possible to put the nuclear accent on *been*. But it's also possible to put it on *in*, and that's the mysterious fact that Cruttenden is discussing at this point of his chapter. As to whether there is any difference in (pragmatic) meaning, I confess I find it very difficult to put my finger on what, if anything, it is.

With regard to (2), my correspondent says, 'I myself would have placed the nucleus on *else* instead'. I think that it is indeed possible to put it on *else*, but that I myself might well, like Cruttenden, have put it on *to*. I can't really explain why.

In reply to the above, Alan Cruttenden writes as follows.

> I used the term 'insists' in my book because I deliberately wanted a fairly vague term which covered many types of preposition and auxiliary verb accenting. These include presuppositionals but many other uses which are only presuppositionals by a considerable extension of the meaning of 'presuppositional'. David Faber and I published an article some years ago in the *Journal of Pragmatics* (1991, 15: 265–86) called 'The accentuation of prepositions' in which we discussed examples like:
>
> (a)   This poem describes London and the journey <u>to</u> London
> (b)   The rules and the interpretation <u>of</u> those rules
> (c)   A woman shouldn't be a politician; she should be the wife <u>of</u> a politician
> (d)   I like children; what I don't like is looking <u>after</u> children
> (e)   You keep on going on about Guyana but have you ever met anyone <u>from</u> Guyana?
> (f)   They're not particularly good but there are masses <u>of</u> the brutes.
>
> In all these cases there are alternative nucleus placements which more easily fit the general rules and non-stressing of function and 'given' words, e.g on <u>jour</u>ney, interpret<u>a</u>tion . . . etc. (though this is not always true). The prepositional placement does a variety of things like contrasting two noun phrases 'London' and 'to London', suggesting that the preposition should be considered as a lexical item rather than just a function word, and suggesting the newness of the preposition as opposed to the givenness of the following noun. But a characteristic of them all is that the impression is given that the user is somehow showing off his sophisticated use of language; as such they are used by articulate middle-class speakers (frequently by journalists and reporters). I cannot imagine a road sweeper saying 'I hate litter and the leavers <u>of</u> that litter'.

The last point, linking this usage to social class, is a very acute one and I think probably correct. Unlike the road sweeper, I think that Alan and I could well say:

> I 'hate \/<u>lit</u>ter | and the 'leavers \<u>of</u> that litter.

Touché.

4.9   that's funny

Quite a common idiomatic intonation pattern in English consists of a fall on the word *That* with the verb *to be*, followed by a rise on the complement.

\<u>That's</u> | /<u>funny</u>.
\<u>That</u> was | /<u>good</u>.
\<u>That's</u> | a re/<u>lief</u>.
\<u>That's</u> | a /<u>pity</u>.
\<u>That'll</u> be | the /<u>day</u>!

A: Your 'keys aren't \here.
B: Well \that's | rather /odd. ||
(I could have \sworn | I 'left them here Vsomewhere.)
A: I'm 'going to start going to the \gym.
B: \That'll be | the /day!

This pattern is rather difficult to explain. The word *that* is merely anaphoric – it refers to some situation or thing already mentioned, rather as a pronoun does. But if we replace *that* by *it*, we cannot use the same tone pattern.

* \It's | /funny.
* \It was | /good.

Obviously, this is connected to the fact that the default for demonstratives is to be accented, whereas the default for pronouns is to be unaccented. But why is *that* so important that it is not merely accented, but carries a nuclear tone?

We might wonder whether this pattern is not a fall plus rise but a fall-rise.

? VThat's funny.
? VThat was good.

But in this analysis, if the single nucleus is on the demonstrative, the words *funny* and *good* are deaccented, postnuclear – which would normally imply that they must be given (old), or repetitious, or predictable in the context, none of which is the case here. So that can't be right. And in any case we would still be left with a difficult-to-explain nucleus on the demonstrative.

Compare contrastive focus on *that*, with a genuine fall-rise:

A: They're 'both pretty \good.
B: Well Vthat one is | but Vthis one isn't.

Unfortunately, I don't think I discussed this intonational idiom in my *English Intonation* book. Your appropriate response, reader, is

\That's | a /pity.

4.10   where? wohin?

I had been invited to Berlin to give a lecture on intonation. I mentioned an example I have used several times before: an exchange that is ambiguous in writing but probably not in speech:

A: I'm off to England tomorrow.
B: Where?

My claim was that with a fall on *Where* B's response means 'What part of England? Where in England?' But if the intended meaning is 'I didn't quite catch what you said. Please repeat' then *Where?* must have a rise (or a high fall-rise).

Carefully worded like that, I think the claim is correct. However, it doesn't necessarily follow that a rise on *Where?* must always signal a pardon-question. It could just be a friendly way of asking for more precise details (as with the fall). Although the default/neutral/unmarked tone for a wh-question is a fall, we can also use a rise or (low) fall-rise. Hence a rise on *Where?* might be ambiguous as between the two possible readings.

One of the audience pointed out that the German equivalent is not open to ambiguity in this way. In German you can't use *Wo?* (the word for 'where?') in this context. You have to say *Wohin?* 'where to? whither? where hence?'. And the word will be stressed differently depending on the intended meaning.

(1)   A: Morgen fahre ich nach England.
             B: Wo<u>hin</u>? (Also nach London, oder. . .?)

(2)   A. Morgen fahre ich nach England.
             B: <u>Wo</u>hin? (Das kann ich kaum glauben!)

No matter whether the nucleus on *-hin* in (1) has a fall or a rise, the meaning must be a request for further details. With a (rising) nucleus on *wo-*, as in (2), it must be a pardon-question, 'I didn't quite catch what you said. Please repeat', or 'I can't really believe that'.

I then realized that the same applies to the alternative way of framing the question in English, *Where to?*

(1)   A: I'm off to England tomorrow.
             B: Where <u>to</u>? (Liverpool, Norwich, Southampton?)

(2)   A: I'm off to England tomorrow.
             B: <u>Where</u> to? (<u>Where</u> did you say you were going?)

(1) asks for amplification; (2) is a pardon-question.

It's fun giving lectures. Sometimes even the lecturer learns something.

4.11   examining intonation

When we ran an undergraduate course on English intonation at UCL, mainly for native speakers, how did we conduct the practical part of the exam?

The candidates were set three tasks: a prepared reading, an unseen reading and the description of their own and the examiner's intonation of a given sentence.

For the prepared reading, candidates were given in advance a short piece of conversational English marked up with intonation marks. The candidate had to read the passage out loud, using the intonation patterns indicated.

Here's part of a sample passage. The further intonation marks are those I use in *English Intonation: an introduction.* `\` = falling head; `/` = rising head; `¯` = high level prehead; ° = rhythmical stress. For nuclear tones, we distinguish ˈhigh fall from ˌlow fall, ʹhigh rise from ˌlow rise.

- He ˌseems to be enˈ°joying the °job imˈmensely
- though I must Vsay | it ʹwouldn't suit ˌme very well.
- ˈAll that ˈtravelling aVbout | sounds exΛhausting.
- ˌStill | ¯I supˌpose some ˌpeople ˈthrive on °that sort of °thing.

This is a much more complicated pattern than one would usually recommend to EFL students. But as a performance exercise it certainly tests the abilities of native speakers and foreign learners alike. (Candidates lost one mark per symbol incorrectly realized.)

If I were setting this as a test for EFL teachers and learners, I would treat as unimportant everything except the three Ts: tone (candidates should make rises, falls and fall-rises as required, but without worrying about such distinctions as low fall vs. high fall), tonicity (put the nuclear tones in the right places as required: preferably get the other accents in the right places too) and tonality (break the material into chunks as required).

So I might mark it up in this simpler way.

- He ʹseems to be enʹjoying the ʹjob imˌmensely
- though I must Vsay | it ʹwouldn't suit ˌme very well.
- ʹAll that ʹtravelling aVbout | sounds exˌhausting.
- /Still | I supʹpose some ʹpeople ˌthrive on that sort of thing.

This is still a good test of performance ability, since not all the tones and tonicities are those that would first come to mind in the given situation. Accordingly, even those with a good feeling for English intonation might be misled into producing a different intonation pattern if it seemed to make more sense. For example, I think that in real life I would be more likely to say the following rather than the patterns asked for in the exam:

- . . .it ʹwouldn't suit Vme very well

(with a fall-rise to show the implicit contrast between me and others) and

- . . .I suppose ʹsome people ˌthrive on that sort of thing

(some people do, some don't).

4.12   the importance of being accented

In my intonation book there's a very brief discussion of the possible relationship between accent and pronoun reference (anaphora):

In the following examples, the reference of the pronoun *he* depends on whether or not it is accented:

> Bill threatened Jim, | and then he 'hit him. (=Bill hit Jim.)
> Bill threatened Jim | and then 'he 'hit him. (=Jim hit Bill.)
> Bill threatened Jim | and then 'he hit 'him. (=Jim hit Bill.)   *English*
> *Intonation*, p. 239

The point is that an ordinary unaccented subject pronoun (here, the *he* that is the subject of *hit*) has the same referent as the subject of the previous verb (here, *threatened*). But by accenting the subject pronoun we signal that its referent is not the same as the subject of the previous verb. Accenting *he* means that there is a change of subject, in this case from *Bill* to *Jim*. Likewise, accenting *him* indicates that the object of *hit* is different from the object of *threatened*; though since in this case logic means that a change of subject must also imply a change of object, it is not actually necessary to spell this out by accenting *him* as well as *he*.

So accent on a subject pronoun means that there is a change of grammatical subject. Lack of accent means that there isn't. Now comes an interesting example taken from a newspaper report (American, as you can tell from the spelling), the subject of an item in Language Log.

> *If leadership never takes time off, people will be skeptical whether they can.*

Does the pronoun *they* to refer to the company's leadership? In that case, *they* will be unaccented when you say it aloud. Or is the intended referent of this pronoun actually *people*? If so, there will have to be a contrastive accent on *they*.

The difficulty is that the distinction is not normally shown in writing. Hence the newspaper report was ambiguous. If the writer of the report had realized this, and had wished to avoid the ambiguity, he might have chosen one of various ways of resolving it: for example, he could have emboldened *they*, or changed it to *they themselves*.

Take the written sentence *A third of the women surveyed thought that their husbands were better cooks than they were*. As it stands, it is ambiguous. But in speech it would be disambiguated by intonation.

1.   . . . thought that their husbands were better cooks than <u>they</u> were
          = than the women
2.   . . . thought that their husbands were better cooks than they <u>were</u>
          = than in reality

In (1) the accenting of *they* signals the change of grammatical subject. In (2) I suppose we have to call the accented modal a 'marked positive'.

4.13   accented *be*

The general rule for whether or not the verb *to be* is accented – which applies to all auxiliary verbs, too – is that we accent it only if it shows contrastive polarity (= positive vs. negative) or contrastive tense.

You 'thought he wasn't 'ready, | but 'actually he 'was.
(Why didn't they 'make you 'manager?) – Well I 'am manager, | 'actually.
Well I 'was happy, | but 'now I'm 'not.
I 'used to be at the top, | and I 'still 'am at the top.

There is a further case where *to be* is accented, a case which seems to be illogical and so is perhaps best regarded as idiomatic: in the pattern wh-word plus *be* plus pronoun, or syntactic manipulations thereof. I devote a separate section (3.18) to this in my intonation book.

'What 'is it?
'Where 'are you?
'How would it 'be | if we 'met for 'lunch?
'Who do you think you 'are?

However, none of these explanations fit two sentences I have heard recently.

('Welcome 'back!) – We're 'happy to 'be back! (at the end of a TV programme about the history of East Anglia)
. . .and 'so we 'see | what a 'honeypot East Anglia 'was.

(In the second example I picked up no contrast of tense or polarity.)

I think these fall under the heading of 'Difficult cases of tonicity' (pp. 182–4 in my *English Intonation*). As I comment there, there is always a strong pressure not to accent repeated words. Yet the nucleus has to go \somewhere. This may lead to its being placed on a function word, even one that may appear to be utterly lacking in semantic content.

4.14   O lift: your voice

At the dental surgery where I have my teeth done there are five floors, or six counting the ground floor. There is a lift with an automated recorded voice telling you what the lift is doing and where it has got to.

I was struck by the intonation patterns of the recorded voice as I went up to the top.

'Doors \closing.
'Going /up. . .
'Floor \/four.
'Doors \/opening. . .
'Going /up. . .
'Floor \five.

These patterns are just what a human operator might use, which is perhaps only to be expected given that they were recorded by a living human being. We have a fall on a declarative statement, followed by a non-final rise (because there is more to come), followed by another non-final tone, this time a fall-rise (because there's still another floor to go), then another fall-rise (a warning), a repeat of the second line, and finally a fall proclaiming that we've reached our destination.

This was followed of course by a repeat of the warning:

>'Doors Vopening.

What is interesting is the difference of tone between *four* and *five*. Although this fitted in excellently with my progress upwards, presumably it arose by accident, since the voice-over actress probably recorded:

>ground floor ‖ floor one ‖ floor two ‖ floor three ‖ floor four ‖ floor five

– with the usual listing sequence comprising a rise or fall-rise on the non-final list items and a fall on the final one. Then the speech engineer chopped them up into separate sound files for the onboard computer to use.

Coming down again I had the lift to myself.

'Doors \closing.
'Going \down...
'Ground /floor.

With a fall instead of a rise on *floor* here it would have been perfect.

I have to congratulate the anonymous speaker on saying *going up* with an iconic rising tone and *going down* with an iconic falling tone. Not all would-be students of intonation, let alone members of the general public, can identify and reproduce the difference between rises and falls.

4.15   stating the bleeding obvious

I saw what is described as a 'terrible Essex joke' in the *Guardian*.

NURSE, IN CASUALTY, TO INJURED PATIENT: Where are you bleeding from?
PATIENT: I'm from bleedin' Romford!

(Explanatory note for non-Brits: the patient wrongly interprets *bleeding* as an expletive. See the *Concise Oxford Dictionary*: bleeding *adj. & adv. Brit. coarse slang* expressing annoyance or antipathy. Casualty = the E.R. The inhabitants of Romford, a suburb in Essex out beyond London's East End, are stereotypically white working-class Londoners and thus supposedly likely to swear a lot.)

The trouble is that as a spoken joke this doesn't actually work. The reason is that the two readings of the ambiguous question differ in tonicity (= nucleus placement).

The nurse's question asks what part of his body is the source of the blood:

(1)   'Where are you 'bleeding from?

But the patient's answer is an answer to a different question, one about the patient's origins:

(2)   'Where are you bleeding 'from?

Version (1) is parallel to other examples such as:

'What are you 'looking at?
'Who were you 'thinking of?
'Where do you 'come from?

Version (2) is just an expansion of the expletive-free

'Where are you 'from?

The way I explain this point in *English Intonation* (section 3.17) is that the nucleus goes on the last lexical item (= the last content word) if there is one. That accounts for (1). If there is no lexical material – no content words – it goes on the preposition. That accounts for (2).

   And what the tonicity difference seems to demonstrate is that *bleeding* and its more forceful variants do not count as content words. So a nuclear accent on *bleeding*, as in (1), is a signal that the word is to be interpreted literally, lexically.

4.16   chunking

          Here are two nice examples I have recently come across which are ambiguous in writing but normally distinguished by tonality (or 'chunking') in speech.

People who do this often get bored.
Subscribing now means you will receive all three issues promptly.

In speech we could have either:

People who do this | often get bored, or
People who do this often | get bored.

And either

Subscribing now | means... or
Subscribing | now means...

The adverb of time can go either way. So there is no ambiguity in speech.

4.17   des accents enfantins

          The other day I overheard a snatch of conversation.
   A father has just got onto a bus with his two children, a girl aged about five and a boy aged about seven. They sit right at the front of the upper deck of

the bus, so they all have a good panoramic window view. The boy takes the seat next to the side window. The girl protests.

> *Girl*: \VDaddy, | 'I want to sit on the \window side.
> *Boy*: But you're \on the window side!

My first reaction was to think that if it were me I would probably have said:

> But you \are on the window side!

General principles lead us to say that accenting *on* would be avoided, since it is a repeated item (it has just featured in the girl's utterance). Hence, I assume, my immediate reaction that the boy's command of English intonation was not yet quite adult-like, and that the proper place for the nucleus is somewhere else, namely on *are*.

This is the word that carries the polarity (positive as against negative). We have what Halliday calls a 'marked positive' (see my *English Intonation*, p. 135).

But on reflection I think this is not the whole story, and that adult native speakers could after all put the nucleus on *on*, just as the boy did. (/Couldn't they?)

I find it very difficult to put into words what difference, if any, there is between a nucleus on the preposition *on* and a nucleus on the verb *are*.

We are dealing here with a counterpresuppositional. The girl's utterance implies that she is not sitting by the window. The boy (deviously, perhaps) challenges this presupposition. So it's comparable to:

A: Never 'mind. | Worse things happen at 'sea.
B: But we're not 'at sea.

(p. 183 in my *English Intonation*). And the intonation patterns of counter-presuppositionals are notoriously difficult to explain (4.8 above).

Perhaps someone who knows more pragmatics than I do can shed some light.

Christopher Bergmann points out there that in German you cannot put the nucleus on the preposition in such cases.

A: Ich möchte auf der 'Fensterseite sitzen.
B: Aber du 'sitzt doch auf der Fensterseite!

and not

B: *Aber du sitzt doch 'auf der Fensterseite!

The only reason you would put the nucleus on the preposition would be for contrast. That would be pretty impossible to contextualize here: not on the window side but ??? below/beyond/outside it.

4.18   intonation idioms in the Germanic languages

There are some arbitrary or illogical intonation patterns in English that are also found in German and Swedish.

One concerns the grammatical structure *Wh – be – pronoun*. My Japanese colleagues tell me that their advanced students of English are surprised at the usual English tonicity in questions like *What 'is it? Where 'am I?* Logically, they feel, the focus ought to be not on the verb *to be* but on the interrogative, the wh-word.

But in English that would happen only in a pardon-question: (*What 'is it? – It's a 'slurge.*) – /*What is it?* or, more likely, – *It's a /what?*

My only explanation of the pattern *What 'is it?* is that it is idiomatic, and something we can't really explain logically.

It is, however, found also in German: *Was 'ist es? Wo 'bin ich?* (but as pardon-questions /*Was ist das? Das ist /was?*).

And in Swedish: *Vad 'är det? Var 'är jag?*

In each language, however, if this kind of sentence ends in a demonstrative rather than a personal pronoun, the nucleus may go in the expected place, namely on the demonstrative: *What's 'that? Was ist 'das?* Or it can stay on the verb: *What 'is that? Was 'ist das?*

The other pattern concerns apparently predictable words. The nucleus, we know, goes on the last item that adds new information. That's where the focus domain ends.

If we're in England and you ask me how much, say, a computer costs, you know that the answer will involve *pounds*: the name of the currency is part of our shared knowledge rather than truly new information. So it is rather illogical that by default we nevertheless accent *pounds*. You would expect that the name of the currency, being already known, would be out of focus. Yet in a broad-focus answer we use the pattern *It costs four hundred 'pounds*, rather than the apparently more logical *It costs four 'hundred pounds*. (The latter is of course also available if we want to narrow-focus on the exact number).

It's the same in German: *Es kostet sechshundert 'Euro*. And it's the same in Swedish: *Den kostar tjugo 'kronor*.

Other examples of the same sort of thing include *It's a lovely 'day* = *Es ist ein wunderschöner 'Tag* = *Vilken härlig 'dag!* (but we both know that it's daytime); *She's a beautiful 'girl* = *Sie ist ein schönes 'Mädchen* (but we know she's a girl); *It's seven o' 'clock* = *Es ist sieben 'Uhr*.

I suspect that these patterns are common to all the Germanic languages, and would accordingly expect that they are also found in Dutch, Danish, Norwegian, Icelandic and Faroese. They may well also extend further afield.

One difficulty about doing comparative intonation studies is that we are interested (or at least I am) not so much in the surface differences in tune shape, but in the deeper differences, if any. Do the two languages differ in such matters as:

- the principles of chunking;
- the nuclear tones available;
- and, most importantly, the principles governing the location of the nucleus (focus)?

That is, are there differences in the three Ts: tone, tonality and tonicity? And to discover whether such deeper differences exist, you need to have access to native speakers who have insight into what is going on. You won't get very far by just sitting in a phonetics lab analysing the pitch patterns of random utterances in a spoken corpus.

I think it's clear that English and German have a good deal in common, not just in vocabulary, syntax and morphology, but also in intonation, if seen in this light. The same is probably true for all the Germanic languages.

There are differences, of course. We have already discussed one. Another concerns sentences consisting of a major part with a minor part, for instance some adverbial or other subordinate material. English has two favourite intonation patterns for these. If the minor part comes first, it tends to have a fall-rise, followed by a fall on the major part. If the major part comes first, it has a fall, usually followed by a rise on the minor part. Thus, depending on the order we choose for the two parts, we might have either of the following.

This \/evening | I'm re'turning to \London.
I'm re'turning to \London | this /evening.

In German there is a strong preference for a rise on the minor part and then a fall on the major part. (The other option, with the adverbial at the end, so-called Ausklammerung, is apparently now becoming commoner than it once was but is still very restricted.) There are two straightforward possibilities for the word order.

Ich 'komme heute /Abend | nach \London zurück.
Heute /Abend | 'komme ich nach \London zurück.

It would be awkward or impossible to say, as in the second English pattern:

?* Ich 'komme nach \London zurück | heute /Abend.

Though of course it would be OK with a change of speaker and with *heute Abend* as a question.

A. Ich 'komme nach \London zurück.
B: Heute /Abend?

(Thanks to Petr Rösel and Christopher Bergmann for the German and to Gunnel Melchers for the Swedish.)

4.19   compound stress in English and German

Although German and English share the general principle of putting primary lexical stress on the first element of a compound, English has a rather large number of exceptions where German does not. These include cases where the first element names a material, ingredient, time or place. English usually stresses the second element, German the first.

ham 'sandwich'	Schinkenbrötchen
evening 'paper'	Abendblatt
summer 'holidays'	Sommerferien
kitchen 'table'	Küchentisch
leather 'jacket'	Lederjacke

(A 'leatherjacket, on the other hand, is a kind of grub.)
Assorted other cases:

town 'hall	'Rathaus
Leicester 'Square	Ale'xanderplatz
capital 'city	'Hauptstadt

There are exceptions in English where the first element names an ingredient (etc.) but we nevertheless have regular compound stress on the first element.

'fruit cake
'soda water
'orange juice
'breadcrumbs

And there are certain place names where German nevertheless has stress on the second element.

Kurfürsten'damm
Friedrichs'hagen
Heiligen'hafen

Just as English is hopelessly inconsistent in '*Christmas cake/card/tree/present* but *Christmas* '*Day/*'*Eve/*'*pudding/*'*crackers*, so German is inconsistent in '*Heiligenberg/-haus/-stadt/-wald* but *Heiligen* '*beil/-* '*blut/-* '*damm/-* '*hafen/-* '*kreuz*. (German data from the Duden Aussprachewörterbuch.)

My impression is that the other Germanic languages (Dutch, Danish, Swedish, Norwegian, Icelandic, Faroese) mostly have fairly regular compound stress. In Norwegian and Swedish it involves a special word tone, in Danish their *stød* (glottalization).

4.20   accenting phrasal verbs

If you manoeuvre an English phrasal verb into a position where it bears the intonation nucleus, the nucleus will be placed either on the verb word or on the particle. Generally speaking, the nucleus goes (i) on the verb word if the particle is prepositional, but (ii) on the particle if it is adverbial. Usually, prepositional (= pseudo) phrasal verbs are lexically single-stressed, but adverbial (= true) phrasal verbs are lexically double-stressed.

(i), prepositional	'What are you 'look<u>ing</u> at?
	'Tell me what you're 'look<u>ing</u> for.
(ii), adverbial	'Don't (')look '<u>back</u>!
	'Look a'<u>way</u>!
	They 'all (')look '<u>up</u> to him.

Accents shown in the examples as (') are likely to be downgraded for rhythmical reasons ('Rule of Three', *English Intonation*, p. 229; and 4.22 below).

There are a few phrasal verbs which rather rarely bear the nucleus. With a transitive verb, where there is an object following, the nucleus naturally tends to go on the object. In the resultant string Verb + Particle + Object, it can be difficult to tell whether the lack of an accent on the particle is because the particle is lexically unstressed (type (i)), or because it is rhythmically downgraded by the rule of three (type (ii)).

'Look up the '<u>ans</u>wer.

You can usually resolve the uncertainty:

- by replacing the object noun phrase with a pronoun (and extraposing the particle if appropriate);
- by switching to a wh-question;
- or by switching to a passive construction.

This forces the nucleus onto the phrasal verb.

'Look it '<u>up</u>.
'What did you (')look '<u>up</u>?
The answer I was 'duly (')looked '<u>up</u>.

Hence *look up* 'find in a list' is type (ii), adverbial.

For most phrasal verbs I have no hesitation with this classification. My native-speaker intuition, supported by observation, readily tells me whether they are type (i) or type (ii). However, there are cases where I find myself hesitating. One such is *to look after*. Applying the techniques mentioned resolves the uncertainty. (This is a verb in which the particle cannot be extraposed.)

What about Mary? I We must 'look '<u>af</u>ter her.
'Who do you want me to (')look '<u>af</u>ter?
She's 'being (')looked '<u>af</u>ter.

Hence *look after*, despite seeming to be prepositional, is actually double-stressed.

Michael Ashby thinks that these are fixed focus patterns rather than matters of lexical stress. For EFL purposes it comes to the same thing.

4.21   train times

'The 'train at platform ∨three | ...', says the automated train announcement at the railway station, 'is the four/<u>teen</u> | forty-/<u>two</u> | to \Woking.' (In Britain we use the 24-hour clock for travel announcements.)

What's wrong with that?

Well, it's not how a live native speaker of English would actually say those words. The announcement was obviously based on recordings of individual words or phrases spoken by a human being but concatenated on the fly by a computer.

The announcer or actor being recorded must have gone through all the numbers that were needed, probably using a rising tone until he got to the end of the list.

/<u>One</u>, | /<u>two</u>, | /<u>three</u>, | ... e/<u>leven</u>, | /<u>twelve</u> ...

Being a trained speaker, he must have drilled himself to say each numeral as if it were in isolation. Because he seems to have continued:

thir/<u>teen</u>, | four/<u>teen</u>, | fif/<u>teen</u> ...

where a person counting would ordinarily use contrastive stress among the teen numerals:

/<u>thirteen</u>, | /<u>fourteen</u>, | /<u>fifteen</u> ...

The result is that the computer putting the message together could draw on recorded instances of *four/<u>teen</u>* and *forty /<u>two</u>* but was not programmed to apply 'stress shift' (perhaps better termed 'accent shift'), in the way that native speakers do when a teen numeral (or any other double-stressed item) is followed by another accented word:

'fourteen forty-'<u>two</u>

The irony is that if he'd let himself follow his instinct and had recorded:

/<u>thirteen</u>, | /<u>fourteen</u>, | /<u>fifteen</u> ...

then everything would have come out fine.

The 'train at platform ∨three | is the /<u>fourteen</u> | forty-/<u>two</u> | to \Woking.

But there'd still have been a problem, because the version of each number above *eleven* suitable for the hours would not have been suitable for the minutes:

(hours) /<u>thirteen</u>, | /<u>fourteen</u>, | ... /<u>twenty-one</u> ...
(minutes) thir/<u>teen</u>, | four/<u>teen</u>, | ... twenty-/<u>one</u> ...

The only satisfactory solution would be to have made two recordings of each item, and to have built in to the software the equivalent of the stress-shift rule. But unfortunately speech engineers tend not to consult phoneticians.

4.22   the rule of three

There are plenty of words in English that seem to change their stress depending on the phonetic context. Typical examples are *afternoon, unknown, sixteen*. We say *the 'late after'noon* but *an 'afternoon 'nap*, *'quite un'known* but *an 'unknown as'sailant*, *'just six'teen* but *'sixteen 'people*.

The usual explanation of this is that the words in question are lexically double-stressed. Dictionaries show them with a secondary stress on the early syllable, a primary stress on the later one, thus for example ˌɑːftə'nuːn or *àfternóon*.

I think that really the two stresses are of equal lexical status. The supposed difference between secondary and primary merely reflects the fact that when we say one of these words aloud, in isolation, the intonation nucleus necessarily goes on the last lexical stress, making it more prominent than the first.

The alternation goes by various names, including 'stress shift' and 'iambic reversal', but I call the general principle involved the 'rule of three'. This means that when there are three successive potential accents (= syllables that could be realized with pitch prominence plus a rhythmic beat), the middle one can be, and often is, downgraded, losing its pitch prominence and possibly its rhythmic beat too.

Thus *a 'nice 'old 'dog* becomes *a 'nice old 'dog*, and *'very 'well de'signed* becomes *'very well de'signed*. *The 'B'B'C* becomes *the 'BB'C*, and our *'after 'noon 'nap* becomes *an 'afternoon 'nap*. Likewise *an 'un(')known as'sailant*, *'six(')teen 'people*.

Anyhow, the point of all this is that in Italy some years ago I got caught out through applying the same principle, wrongly, to Italian. My room number in my hotel was 202, which in English is *'two 'hundred and 'two*, which by the rule of three becomes *'two hundred and 'two*. In Italian it's *duecento due*, which I discovered does <u>not</u> become ** 'duecento 'due*. It has to be *due'cento 'due*. That's because (most) Italian words can have only a single lexical stress. So 'two hundred' is *due'cento*, not *'due'cento*.

The consequence is that English people sometimes put accents in the wrong place in Italian, as I did; and conversely that Italians find it difficult to apply the rule of three to English double-stressed words.

4.23   Are you asking me or telling me?

English intonation is not very good at making clear whether an utterance is a statement or a question.

(1)   So he's 'right.
(2)   So he's 'right?

The statement, (1), is typically said with a fall.

(1')   So he's \right.

But it can also have a rise, to show truculence or mere non-finality (not to mention the new fashion of uptalk).

(1″)   So he's /right, | what\ever you say.

The yes-no question, (2), 'so do you mean he's right?' is said by default with a rise.

(2')   So he's /right? | Is /that what you mean?

But it can also have a fall, if presented as a kind of challenge to the interlocutor.

(2″)   So he's \right!? | Is \that what you mean!?

You could also use a fall-rise, in either meaning...
     A correspondent writes:

> I heard an interesting example of contrastive intonations at the pub tonight. Someone asked 'What wines do you serve by the glass?' and the barman asked 'White or red?', but the customer misheard it as an uninformative answer 'White or red'.
>
> At first I thought it was obvious: the answer has falling intonation but the question has rising. But it doesn't. The clarifying question 'White or red?' had a fall-rise on both 'white' and 'red'. So it's rather more subtle than sentence-question intonation, and I'm less surprised that the customer misunderstood.

4.24   accent on a VP subordinator

     I continue to fret about anomalous tonicity. Consider the accenting of the word *to* in exchanges like this, heard recently.

A: 'What are you going to 'do?
B: There's 'nothing 'to do.

Logically, you would think, B's intonation nucleus ought to go on *nothing*. But it doesn't. It goes on the function word *to*. Why?
     (We ought not to call this *to* a preposition. In its role as part of an English infinitive, as here, Huddleston and Pullum call it a 'VP subordinator' in their *Cambridge Grammar of the English Language*.)
     Other ways for B to say the same thing in his answer include these.

B: There's 'nothing I 'can do.
B: There's 'nothing I 'could do.

Or the idea can be lexicalized.

B: There's 'nothing 'left.
B: There's 'nothing 'possible.

Or, going back to the first version, we can change *nothing* to *not anything*.

B: There 'isn't anything 'to do.

This is another of those counterpresuppositionals (4.8 above), and one explanation that has been offered is that the accented *to* signals marked polarity. The speaker emphasizes the absence of anything that is doable, as against what is not. So we have a marked positive.

However, there is a difficulty here. Taking the sentence as a whole, the speaker is saying that nothing is possible. The polarity is negative, so it seems perverse to talk of a marked positive.

A marked positive would be expected to be the dubiously acceptable:

B: ?There 'is nothing to do.

Compare what happens if B gives an answer with negative polarity for *do*. The nuclear accent goes on the negator.

B: There's 'one thing 'not to do. (And 'that's re'sign.)
B: There's 'one thing I will 'not do.
B: There's 'one thing I 'can't do.

Notice that it is impossible with negated *do* to accent *to*.

B: *There's 'one thing not 'to do.
B: *There's 'one thing 'to not do.

I feel confused.

I gather that in German things are somewhat more straightforward. You don't accent *zu* where you would English *to*.

B: *Da 'gibt's nichts 'zu tun.

Instead, you accent the word corresponding to English *is*.

A: 'Was wirst du 'tun?
B: Es 'gibt (aber) nichts zu tun.

or

B: Da 'gibt's nichts zu tun.

Apparently, though, while you cannot have accented *zu* to show marked polarity, you can have it to show marked tense. So the following might be OK.

B: Es 'gibt nichts 'zu tun, | es hätte schon 'längst ge'tan werden müssen.

'There's nothing to do (now), it ought to have been done long ago'.

How difficult it all is!
What happens with a slightly different wording?

A: What are you going to do?
B: There's nothing to be done.

I think I could then accent *be* or *to*.

B: There's 'nothing to 'be done.
B: There's 'nothing 'to be done.

4.25   on the train

Masaki Taniguchi has sent me a recording made aboard a train from Canterbury to London. Here is a fragment of the announcement made by the train manager to the customers (or, as we used to say, by the guard to the passengers).

Good afternoon, ladies and gentlemen, and welcome.

We are interested not so much in the segmental details – the extreme reduction of *and gentlemen and* – but in the intonation.

Clearly, the fragment ends with a falling nuclear tone on *welcome*. But what about the earlier part, the first IP up to *gentlemen*?

Hearing a high level pitch on *good* and a low, gradually rising pitch extending from *aft-* to *-men*, Masaki wondered whether to analyse this as a high head accent on *good* followed by a low-rise nuclear accent on *af-*.

'Good ͵afternoon ladies and gentlemen

The difficulty with this analysis, as he realized, is the unexplained stress (accent) shift on *afternoon*. We expect to lose the accent on *-noon* before a following accented syllable, but not otherwise.

We've come for 'afternoon 'tea.
It's a 'nice after'noon.
*It's a 'nice 'afternoon.

So what's going on? After all, we don't expect any accents at all in a routine trailing vocative such as *ladies and gentlemen*. What causes the stress shift in this case?

In my opinion, there isn't one. The correct analysis is:

⁻Good ͵after͵noon, ladies and gentlemen

– the high pitch on *good* is a prehead, not a head (the word is not accented); the low pitch on *after-* is a low level head; and the rising nucleus starts at its expected place, *-noon*. That seems to be the only analysis that corresponds (i) to the perceived pitches, and (ii) to what we know linguistically about English intonation. Here's a spectrogram of the utterance with a tracing of the fundamental frequency.

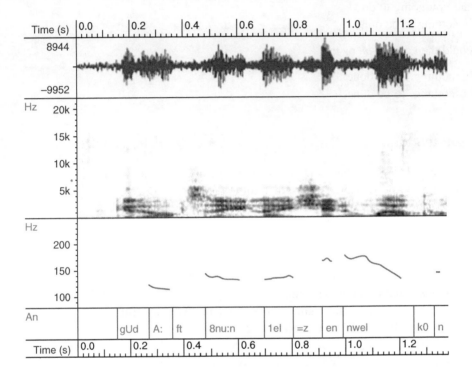

As is so often the case, a physical analysis of the speech signal doesn't help us resolve the issue. The high pitch we perceive on *good* doesn't show up at all on the frequency tracing, perhaps because I didn't adjust the levels properly. *Af-* is indeed physically lower than *-ternoon*, as Masaki perceived, and the whole of *-ternoon la-* is pretty level.

Not only is the articulatory detail very reduced as compared to the underlying linguistic facts, so is the fundamental frequency detail too. How marvellous it is that the human perceptual mechanism can nevertheless reconstruct it all. And how difficult for non-native speakers.

4.26   idiomatic nucleus on a pronoun

A few English intonation idioms involve a falling tone on a nuclear-accented pronoun (*English Intonation*, p. 126).

'Good for \you!
'Get \her!
'Search \me!

There are more.

They're 'not going to fool Vme.
You 'certainly told Vhim where to get off!
I 'don't think we'll be hearing from Vthem again!
I 'don't expect any more trouble from Vyou lot.
You 'certainly left Vher in no doubt.
I'll 'soon show Vhim what's what.

I have shown these all with a fall-rise tone, though I think they can also, less
usually, have a simple fall.
   The unspoken corollary of the fall-rise is something like the following.

They're 'not going to fool Vme again (I though they 'may still fool Vyou).
You 'certainly told Vhim where to get off (I 'even if you didn't say anything
   to the \others)!

and similarly with the remaining examples.
   Perhaps these are not exactly idioms. But they're certainly cases in which the
location of the nucleus is unexpected I 'even for the ad\vanced EFL learner.

4.27   not a drop

'Petrol is expensive', warns the newspaper, 'don't waste a drop'.
   If you say this aloud, the intonation nucleus goes on *drop*.

'Don't waste a 'drop.

You would think the most important word would be *waste*, or even *don't*. Yet we
place the main accent on neither of those items, but on the apparently rather
unimportant *drop*.
   There's no kind of contrast involved. We're not contrasting *drop* with *bucket-
ful* or *litre*. So what's going on?
   Not ... a drop is a more complicated way of saying *nothing*. *Don't waste a
drop* is an idiomatic way of saying *Waste nothing*. It parallels other similar
expressions.

I 'can't see a 'thing. (= I can see nothing.)
I 'won't tell a 'soul. (= I'll tell no one.)
(Have you 'heard from them?) – 'No, I 'not a 'dickybird. (= nothing)
(Have you 'heard from 'Tom?) – 'No, I 'not a 'sausage.
I 'haven't got a 'dime. (= I have no money.)

The nucleus that would otherwise be located on *nothing* or *no one* is retained on the dummy word that is left behind after the negative has been fronted.

This is different from what happens with the dummy words I call 'empty words' (4.7 above). They do not get an accent.

I keep 'seeing things.
I 'promise I won't 'tell people.
Hurry up!! | 'Don't waste a 'minute.

4.28   a little while

My Japanese colleague Masaki Taniguchi has been reading the Bible, and asked me about the likely intonation of John 16:16.

> In a little while you will see me no more, and then after a little while you will see me.

His suggestion, which he asked me to comment on, was:

> In a 'little Vwhile | you will 'see me no /more, | and then Vafter a little while | you \will see me.

I told him that this was fine, except that I think I would use a fall rather than a rise on *more*, since that is the end of Christ's first declaration.

> In a 'little Vwhile | you will 'see me no \more, | and then Vafter a little while | you \will see me.

The reason for the choice of nucleus placement in the second half is that *a little while* and *see me* are repeated (old, given) material, which in English means they are likely to get deaccented.

I noted that the wording he quoted from was the New International Version. In the Authorized Version (known to some as the King James version) that I was brought up on it reads:

> A little while, and ye shall not see me: and again, a little while, and ye shall see me.

I then found an American audio clip of the chapter from which this verse is taken. The reader chose the intonation pattern:

> A 'little Vwhile | and you will 'not \see me. ‖ AVgain a little while | and you \will see me.

– which nicely vindicates Masaki's suggestion, as amended by me.

Interestingly, in the Greek original there are two different words translated into English as 'see'.

μικρὸν καὶ οὐκέτι θεωρεῖτέ με, καὶ πάλιν μικρὸν καὶ ὄψεσθέ με.
mikron kai ouketi theōreite me, kai palin mikron kai opsesthe me.
'little and no-longer you(pl.)-look-at me, and again little and
you(pl.)-will-see me.'

The first word, θεωρεῖτε *theōreite*, means 'look (at)' rather than 'see', and
is in the present tense. The second, ὄψεσθε *opsesthe*, is the ordinary verb 'see',
and is in the future tense. The first verb is from the stem that underlies our
modern word *theory*, the second from the stem that underlies *(syn)opsis*. These
subtleties are lost in the English versions. They are also lost in the Latin vulgate:

Modicum, et jam non videbitis me; et iterum modicum, et videbitis me.

– with *videbitis* (you will see) in both places.
A literal English translation would indeed be awkward.

A little, and you no longer look at me; and again a little, and you will see me.

I think it might affect the intonation, too.

4.29   international intonation

Most learners of English as an additional language (the latest expression for EFL/ESL) are not taught intonation and do not study intonation. Yet they
do not speak English on a monotone. A few may be gifted mimics who succeed
in imitating intonation along with everything else in the phonetics of the target
language. For most, though, their intonation patterns are presumably those of
their first language, transferred to English.

The same applies to English learners of foreign languages.

On the whole, even though this may make the speaker sound strange, typical
of their origin, boring or annoying, it seems not to cause much of an actual
breakdown in communication. How can this be?

It must be because the principles of intonation in language are sufficiently
universal for us to be able to rely on them even in a foreign-language situation.

However, it may also be the case that many of the nuances of meaning carried
by intonation in the speech of native speakers are overlooked or misinterpreted
by some or most non-native speakers. But this may also apply between different
native varieties of the same language: think only of Ulstermen interacting with
Londoners.

This leads me to ask which parts of intonation are universal and which are
language-specific. I am referring only to the linguistic (systemic) use of the pitch
of the voice, not the paralinguistic (presumably non-systemic) factors such
as pitch range, speech rate and voice quality.

Analysing intonation in terms of the three systems discussed above (4.1, 4.4),
we can say that the principles of chunking are probably pretty universal. Those of
tonicity (accentuation) clearly are not. Is choice of tone universal in any way? In

English, when we pronounce lists we signal that the list is incomplete by using a rise, and that it is complete by using a fall.

(3)   /One, | /two, | \three.

(4)   Do you want /coffee | or /tea | or \cola?

Is it a universal that the signal for list completion (if there is one) is always a falling tone?

Is it a universal that exclamations have a fall, pardon-questions a rise?

(5)   \Marvellous!

(6)   /What was that again?

How general is it that, as in English, wh-questions tend to have the same tone as statements, while yes-no questions are different? Lastly, there is the matter of tonicity (accentuation). By this I mean the location of sentence accents, and particularly their use to signal focus. Two principles that apply in English and seemingly in many languages are (i) that the last sentence accent within a given stretch (the IP) is particularly important – which is why we call it the nucleus or tonic – and (ii) that it signals the material on which the speaker chooses to focus, i.e. mark as foreground as against background, new as against given, comment as against topic, rheme as against theme.

What is not clear is that either of these principles is actually universal. Unless contrastive focus is involved, it is not clear that all languages impose a focus at all (it's been claimed that Danish is like that, not to mention French). And intonation is not the only way to signal focus, you can also do it syntactically.

This presumably is why nucleus placement is arguably the most complicated part of English intonation, and the hardest to learn.

It is not difficult, in simple cases, to understand the different meanings associated with switching narrow focus around.

A: What did you see? A red car?
B: (i) No, | a red bus.
B: (ii) No, | a green car.

But here the focus is obvious from the wording.

In core English we readily exploit tonicity to mark focus in examples like this:

A: I want to buy a comb.
B: But you've already got a comb!

Yet this doesn't seem to happen, or not as much, in African English.

In English we are so anxious to avoid accenting repeated items that we say:

Would you like your coffee with milk | or without milk?

But in Spanish, I gather, this would be:

...con leche | o sin leche?

In languages with a freer word order than English you can often use a change of word order to show focus instead of, or as well as, using intonation.

In an interesting unpublished experiment an MA student at UCL tested English people and speakers of Cantonese on whether they could correctly match up question and answer in pairs such as this (quoted from memory, to the best of my recall):

Q1. Have you any special dietary requirements?
Q2. Would you prefer beef or pork?

A1. I don't eat <u>meat</u>.
A2. I don't <u>eat</u> meat.

(A1 goes with Q1, A2 with Q2.)

The English score was near perfect, the Chinese no better than random. So no universal here.

Daniel Hirst and Albert di Cristo contributed an introductory article 'A survey of intonation systems' to the book they edited, *Intonation Systems* (Cambridge University Press 1998). Their first sentence ends: '. . . intonation is paradoxically one of the most universal and one of the most language specific features of human language'. We can all agree with that.

These points about intonation in EFL apply equally to intonation in Esperanto: somehow speakers manage to understand one another in the language very well despite the lack of any agreed, taught or described intonation system.

5   Symbol shapes, fonts and spelling

Topics in the design of the International Phonetic Alphabet and in English orthography

5.1   labiodental flap

In 2005 the International Phonetic Association approved a new phonetic symbol, to represent a voiced labiodental flap. It is like a letter *v*, but with a hook on the right-hand side, thus ⱱ. It is at U+2C71 LATIN SMALL LETTER V WITH RIGHT HOOK.

It was adopted by the IPA too late to make it to the most recent printed Unicode standard, 5.0. However, it was added for the Unicode 5.1 revision, and you'll find it in the online Unicode charts at www.unicode.org/charts. It may not yet be found in the Microsoft fonts routinely supplied with new PCs, nor in the Lucida Grande that comes with Mac computers. So to use it you may need to download and install a specialist font. Try the SIL fonts Charis SIL and Doulos SIL at www.sil.org/computing, which you can download free. (You will then need to unzip the files and install them.)

Tiresomely, Unicode did not add it to one of the blocks where phonetic symbols are usually found (IPA Extensions, U+0250–U+02AF; Phonetic Extensions, U+1D00–U+1DBF). Instead, it is in a small block called Latin Extended-C (U+2C60–U+2C7F), nestling unobtrusively between Glagolitic and Coptic. Within that block it lies among the 'miscellaneous additions' located between 'Additions for Uighur' and 'Claudian letters' (Latin letters invented by the emperor Claudius but soon dropped).

Early versions of Doulos SIL did not contain the symbol. Nor does Lucida Sans Unicode. Nor, of course, did any of the old single-byte fonts such as SIL Doulos or the ipa-sam fonts that I developed many years ago.

SIL also offers Mac users a keyboard facility called Ukulele that will enable them to insert all the Unicode symbols they need. Users of Word/Windows don't really need any such extra software, since they can immediately 'see' all installed Unicode characters with Insert Symbol, and quickly create macros using AutoCorrect. However, for those who like a keyboard facility, SIL offers one called Keyman. My colleague Mark Huckvale has made a rather simpler one called simply Unicode Phonetic Keyboard, which you can download from www. phon.ucl.ac.uk/resource/phonetics.

5.2   similar symbols

The IPA symbol for the vowel of English *foot*, *put*, *good*, ʊ, sometimes gives trouble to authors, printers and publishers. It tends to get confused with the symbol for the labiodental approximant, ʋ.

So it is important that font designers (and the rest of us) differentiate clearly between the two symbols. The *foot* symbol, known to Unicode as U+028A LATIN SMALL LETTER UPSILON, is symmetrical about the vertical axis. Despite the name, it is not so much a Greek upsilon (υ) as an inverted small capital omega (Ω).

The labiodental approximant symbol, on the other hand, is asymmetrical, with the right side having a leftward-pointing lip or hook. In Unicode it is U+028B LATIN SMALL LETTER V WITH HOOK.

There are other IPA symbols which authors and printers often confuse with other letters or symbols:

- θ and o voiceless dental fricative (U+03B8); rounded schwa (U+0275);
- ɣ and ɤ voiced velar fricative (U+0263); close-mid back unrounded vowel, cardinal 15 (U+0264);
- ɑ and a back open vowel, cardinal 5 (U+0251); front open vowel, cardinal 4;
- ə and ɘ schwa (U+0259); close-mid central unrounded vowel (U+0258);
- ɫ and ɬ voiced velarized alveolar lateral, dark l (U+026B); voiceless alveolar lateral fricative (U+026C);
- ŋ and ɧ voiced velar nasal (U+014B); voiceless postalveolar-velar fricative (U+0267).

It is also important not to confuse IPA symbols, which are all lower-case, with the upper-case versions used in the orthographies of certain languages:

- ɪ not I lax close front unrounded vowel (U+026A); and upper-case I;
- ʊ not Ʊ lax close back rounded vowel (U+028A); and U+01B1;
- ɛ not Ɛ open-mid front unrounded vowel, cardinal 3 (U+025B); and U+0190;
- ɔ not Ɔ open-mid back rounded vowel, cardinal 6 (U+0254); and U+0186;
- ə not Ə schwa (U+0259); and U+018F;
- ʒ not Ʒ voiced postalveolar fricative (U+0292); and U+01B7;
- θ not Θ or Ɵ voiceless dental fricative (U+03B8); and U+0398 or U+019F.

Lastly, be careful to write:

- ɑ not α unrounded back open vowel (U+0251); Greek alpha (U+03B1);

- ɣ not γ voiced velar fricative (U+0263); Greek gamma (U+03B3);
- ð not δ voiced dental fricative (U+00F0); Greek delta (U+03B4);
- ɛ not ε unrounded open-mid front vowel (U+025B); Greek epsilon (U+03B5);
- ŋ not η voiced velar nasal (U+014B); Greek eta (U+03B7);
- ʃ not ʅ voiceless postalveolar fricative (U+0283); retroflex apical vowel (U+0285).

5.3   clicks

Clicks are sounds articulated with an ingressive velaric (oral) airstream mechanism. As such, they necessarily have a simultaneous velar closure. When we write ‖, say, to symbolize a voiceless alveolar lateral click (former IPA symbol ʎ), we imply a simultaneous **k**. The click articulation is produced during the hold stage of a voiceless velar plosive.

In the case of a voiced click, e.g. g‖, or a nasalized click, e.g. ŋ‖, we symbolize the velar component explicitly. (Many people show the simultaneity explicitly, too, by linking the two symbols with a tie: g͜‖, ŋ͜‖.)

Treating the voiceless clicks as symbolically unmarked and the voiced or nasalized ones as marked has its parallel in the orthographies of the click languages. Zulu ‖ is written as *x*, g‖ is written as *gx*, and ŋ‖ is written as *nx*. There are also the voiceless aspirated ‖ʰ, written *xh*, and the breathy-voiced (depressor) nasalized ŋ̤‖, written *ngx*.

Some phoneticians symbolize all clicks by a double symbol, always making the nature of the velar component explicit. They write the voiceless alveolar lateral click as k‖, and likewise for the other places of click articulation. This makes the treatment of all classes of click parallel, at the expense of necessitating an extra letter for each voiceless click. So is it better to transcribe the Zulu for 'no', *cha*, as kᵐʘa or just as ‖ʰa? Do we transcribe Zulu *xoxa* 'narrate!' as k‖ɔk‖a, or is ‖ɔ‖a sufficient?

In click languages there are no click consonant clusters. So it doesn't matter that the symbol for an alveolar lateral click, [‖], is barely distinguishable from two successive instances of the dental/alveolar click, [ǀ]. Unfortunately the English non-speech interjection sometimes written 'tut-tut' (to show disapproval) may consist of just that: two successive central coronal clicks. To show it you must be careful to use good spacing between the two click symbols … or write each with its non-click component, thus k͜ǀk͜ǀ.

Or, like some reference books, you may think that the tut click is properly symbolized [!s]. But it sounds to me not like Nama !, which always has an abrupt release and is apical, but more like Nama ǀ, which is laminal and somewhat affricated.

5.4   IPA capitals

Kera is a language spoken by some 50,000 people in Chad. It is a tonal language, with three tones (high, mid, low). It has no voicing contrast in consonants, but VOT (voice onset time) varies depending on the tone of the following vowel: so a velar plosive before a high or mid tone sounds like **k**, but before a low tone like **g**.

The SIL organization (sil.org) is involved in both Bible translation and a literacy project, and has produced both the New Testament in Kera (*JAA TƏMARWAD*) and a reading primer (*Aŋ aŋkə ku keera la*). As you can see, Kera orthography uses the Latin alphabet supplemented by IPA symbols: not only *ə* and *ŋ* but also *ɓ* and *ɗ*. Following the conventions of Latin-based orthographies, each letter requires an upper-case as well as a lower-case form: hence *Ə Ŋ Ɓ Ɗ*. So although phonetic symbols are normally lower-case, and not subject to the usual capitalization rules for proper names or the start of a sentence, we do need capitals when we use IPA symbols outside a phonetic context.

Some Kera proper names have clearly passed through French. The names of the four evangelists are Matiye, Markə, Liki and Zaŋ.

5.5   dashes

What do you call the punctuation mark '-', as in *re-enter*?

I have always called it a hyphen. So I was surprised when I heard native-English-speaking undergraduates refer to it as a 'dash'. My reaction was that this was a simple error, and if they did it in writing I corrected them. A dash, for me, is the similar but longer sign '–'.

This was the terminology I was taught at school—and this is the usage of professional typographers and indeed phoneticians. After all, Daniel Jones's 1955 article (*Zeitschrift für Phonetik* 9) was entitled 'The hyphen as a phonetic sign', not 'The dash as a phonetic sign'. MS Word's AutoCorrect options include 'Replace hyphens (-) with dash (–)'. This and other word-processing software usually includes a *hyphen*ation function that can be toggled on or off. The distinction between 'hyphen' and 'dash' is a useful one.

Recently I have come across the dash-for-hyphen solecism even in serious printed works.

I see that the Unicode reference materials use 'dash' as a general term for horizontal line punctuation of various widths: 'Unicode Dash Characters' include:

- hyphen (-);
- en dash (–), the same width as the letter n;
- em dash (—), the same width as the letter m, and others.

Another problematic question is whether the dash ought to be surrounded by spaces – like this – or not (as a few lines above), when used to make a break in the flow of a sentence. I'm happy to go either way on that one.

5.6   linguolabial trill

(I posted this note online on the first day in April 2006.)

I hear from my colleague Olaf Lipor that the International Phonetic Asssociation is considering recognizing a further new symbol, in order to cater for the *voiced linguolabial trill*, a sound-type recently discovered to be used contrastively in Caslon and Ki-Flong, languages spoken on the island of San Serriffe.

Linguolabials, articulated by the tongue tip against the upper lip, are very rare in the languages of the world. Nevertheless linguolabial plosives, fricatives and a nasal are known to occur in a cluster of languages in the island state of Vanuatu. Among these languages are Tangoa and Vao. But until now there had been no report of a linguolabial trill.

The way in which the IPA is expected to symbolize the new sound is with the 'combining seagull below' diacritic, U+033C, thus r̼.

We are hoping to have the Serriffean phonetician Dr Charis Doulos, a native speaker of Caslon and the person who first described the linguolabial trill, come to UCL Phonetics & Linguistics as an academic visitor at this time next year. She will no doubt be willing to act as a language consultant for our practical phonetics class, so that the students can have the opportunity of observing the sound first-hand and of learning to perform it to the native speaker's satisfaction.

San Serriffe sprang to world fame as a consequence of a feature article in the *Guardian* newspaper, published on 1 April 1977, the tenth anniversary of its independence. But at that time its native languages had not been thoroughly investigated.

(Subsequently there appeared a report of an Amerindian language, Santo Domingo Coatlán Zapotec, in which this sound is now, excitingly, further attested, though disappointingly not as part of the phonemic inventor, but only in an 'onomatopoeic word' denoting the 'sound of a child's fart'.)

5.7   the symbol ɮ

In 1938 the Council of the IPA took a decision concerning the symbol for the voiced alveolar lateral fricative. It read as follows (m.f. 61, p. 15):

la prɔpozisjɔ̃ d rãplase ɮ par ɧ ɛ dɔ̃:k apruve. nu pãsɔ̃ spãdã
k la fɔrm prɔpoze par Chatterji pura ɛ:tr ãplwaje sãz ɛ̃kɔ̃venjã
par sø ki prefɛ:r œ̃ sɛ̃bɔl mwɛ̃z elwaɲe d l ãsjɛ̃ ɮ.

Bear in mind that in those days the official language of the Association was French, and that its journal *Le Maître Phonétique* was printed entirely in phonetic transcription. So this decision is expressed in phonetically transcribed French. Translated, it reads as follows:

> The proposal to replace ɮ by [the second symbol shown] is therefore approved. We think nevertheless that the form proposed by Chatterji can be employed without disadvantage by those who prefer a symbol less remote from the old ɮ.

Chatterji's suggestion was a compromise between the ʒ-shaped right-hand side of the 'old' symbol and the straight side of the 'new'. The compromise shape is what Daniel Jones adopted for the symbol in the 1949 *Principles* booklet (p. 11, also p. 50):

ɮ. Zulu *dhl* as in *dhla* (eat).

However, this decision by the IPA seems subsequently to have been overturned as we moved from hot metal typography to software fonts. After the 1989 Kiel Convention of the IPA both printed and on-screen usage reverted in practice to the older shape. The *IPA Handbook* presents the symbol as an 'L-Ezh ligature' and our current chart shows the form ɮ. Unicode calls it LATIN SMALL LETTER LEZH (U+026E). All available computer phonetic fonts show this same ɮ shape.

By the way, the Unicode documentation (www.unicode.org) also repeats the *Principles* booklet's assertion that ɮ is *dhl* in Zulu orthography. But Zulu has had a spelling reform, and (as rightly recognized in the *IPA Handbook*) the current spelling is *dl*. The site of the famous battle that used to be spelt *Isandhlwana* is now *Isandlwana*. It's still pronounced ísanˈdɮwáːna. (After **n** you get a laterally released affricate rather than a lateral fricative.)

5.8   scenes from IPA history

Here, extracted from back issues of *Le Maître Phonétique*, is a list of the changes to the IPA Alphabet agreed during the 1940s.

- 1943: the symbols ɪ and ω were introduced as alternatives to ɪ and ʊ respectively, which nevertheless remained 'authorized alternatives' and 'could be used instead of the new symbols, except in the official publications of the IPA'. This ban was not maintained in practice after Jones's retirement. Recognition of ɪ and ω was withdrawn in 1989.
- 1945: the symbol ɾ (voiced dental/alveolar fricative trill) was approved as the replacement of ř. Recognition of the new symbol was withdrawn in 1989.

- 1945–7: vowel symbols with a retroflex hook were introduced, to represent r-coloured vowels: a̗ ɑ̗ e̗ ɛ̗ ɝ ə̗ i̗ ɔ̗. Recognition was withdrawn in 1989.
- 1947: the alveolar affricate symbols ƚ and ƻ were approved, 'but only by a small majority'. Recognition was withdrawn in 1976.
- 1947: the symbols ʃ and ʒ were introduced for palatalized versions of ʃ, ʒ. They were considered necessary for Russian, which Daniel Jones was then working on. Recognition was withdrawn in 1989.
- 1947: the diacritic _ , or a serifed variant, was approved to denote retraction, including use with **t**, **d**, **n** (thus **t̠ d̠ n̠**) to denote alveolars in languages where they were distinct from, and rarer than, dentals.
- 1947: the symbol **ŋ** was approved for the Japanese 'syllabic' (i.e. moraic) nasal. 'It will nevertheless be desirable to consult Japanese phoneticians [...] and if necessary to revise our decision when we know what they think of it.' Withdrawn 1976.
- 1947: the symbol **ɧ** was approved for the 'combination of **x** and **ʃ** (one variety of Swedish *tj*, *kj*, etc.)'. (See 3.5 above.)
- 1948: the symbol shape **g** (spectacles) was approved as an alternative to **ɡ** (nine). 'They will be considered as typographic variants of the same letter', except in Russian, where the former could symbolize the non-palatalized voiced velar plosive, the latter the palatalized. Where separate letters were needed for ordinary and advanced **g**, as in the narrow transcription of Russian, **g** (spectacles) was recommended for the ordinary and **ɡ** (nine) for the advanced, i.e. palatalized. I don't think anyone ever applied this distinction in practice. Certainly Jones himself didn't: see below what the symbols look like in his *The Phonetics of Russian* (co-authored with Dennis Ward, Cambridge University Press 1969).

17.128   The palatalized allophone of g, which may when necessary be represented by the phonetic symbol ɡ̘, may be acquired by adding voice to Russian ḵ, or by approaching it from English sounds.
17.129   Russian ɡ̘ has a slightly more forward place of articu-

Judging by the comments I received on the publication of LPD, where I use **g** (spectacles) for the voiced velar plosive, some phoneticians are unaware that the decision to treat the two shapes of that letter as glyph variants, equally valid, was ever taken.

In fact, we see that most of the decisions taken during that period of fiddling around with the Alphabet were subsequently either overturned or ignored.

5.9   affricates

A correspondent was worried that the IPA allows for the representation of the palatoalveolar affricates as **c, ɟ** instead of what s/he considers to be the correct way of writing them, namely **t͡ʃ, d͡ʒ**.

Why does this provision exist? It is because there are some languages in which it doesn't seem very satisfactory to write affricates with the plosive-plus-fricative notation. A speaker of Italian, for example, reports that he is very conscious of the difference in tongue configuration between the ordinary Italian plosive **t** and the first element of the Italian affricate spelt *c(i)*, *c(e)*, usually represented in IPA as **tʃ**. He would be happier with a notation that does not imply their equivalence. That is what the use of **c, ɟ** for the affricates provides, as was implicitly recommended in the 1949 *Principles of the IPA* booklet, similarly to that of the then official **ṭ** and **2**. You can only do this, of course, in a language in which you do not need to symbolize a voiceless palatal plosive, which is the default general-phonetic meaning of **c**.

Another such language is Hindi, in which the affricates very obviously pattern as single units, not as sequences.

Many linguists use the symbols **č, ǰ** for these affricates, although they do not have the approval of the IPA.

In ordinary orthography, although the Latin alphabet offers no way to write affricates without using diacritics or digraphs, other alphabets do: for example, in Cyrillic the voiceless palatoalveolar affricate is written Ч ч and the voiced one (in Serbian) as Џ џ. There is clearly a perceived need for a unitary way of writing these affricates.

Returning to the two-symbol notation, my correspondent also assumed that the correct way to write them is with a tie bar: **t͡ʃ, d͡ʒ**. Personally, I normally omit the tie bar, and write just **tʃ, dʒ**. That is what you find in most pronunciation dictionaries and textbooks, too. It does involve the convention that a sequence of plosive plus fricative that does NOT form an affricate must be written some other way. Daniel Jones does this with a hyphen (see his article 'The hyphen as a phonetic sign', *Zeitschrift für Phonetik* 1955, 9), thus **t-ʃ, d-ʒ**. This enables us to show the difference in the Polish minimal pair *trzy* **t-ʃi** vs. *czy* **tʃi** (though the former is perhaps better analysed as **tʃʃi**, i.e. affricate plus fricative). In English any such sequence must straddle a syllable boundary, so you can show it using a full stop, as in *Wiltshire* **ˈwɪlt.ʃə** vs. *vulture* **ˈvʌltʃ.ə** (if you think I am right about English syllabification) or **ˈvʌl.tʃə** (if you don't).

Another way is to use the ligatured symbols **ʧ, ʤ** for the affricates, leaving the separated **tʃ, dʒ** for the non-affricate plosive-plus-fricative sequences.

5.10   orthographic schwa

Which language makes use of the schwa symbol, **ə**, in its everyday orthography?

There may be various such languages only relatively recently reduced to writing by missionaries or linguists. It is difficult to find information about how many they might be, or what they are called. I do know that it is used in the Latin Chechen alphabet, though this language is more usually written in Cyrillic.

However, there is one well-established language, spoken by tens of millions of people, that uses the schwa symbol: namely the Turkic language of Azerbaijan, Azeri, also known as (North) Azerbaijani. You can see plenty of examples on the web if you go to the Azərbaycan (sic) version of Wikipedia.

The schwa letter comes in upper-case as well as lower-case. However, the sound denoted by Azeri Ə, ə is not the IPA's mid central vowel but a front open vowel, æ.

Strangely, Unicode includes three identical-looking versions of the schwa symbol. One is, as expected, in the IPA Extensions block at U+0259. Another is in the Cyrillic block, at U+04D9, with an upper-case version at U+04D8 – this is fair enough, given that schwa is also a Cyrillic letter, used when writing Azeri (and some other languages) in Cyrillic. The third, however, is at U+01DD, and belongs to the Pan-Nigerian alphabet; it is called 'turned e' and is distinguished from the ordinary schwa inasmuch as it has a different upper-case form (Ǝ). This is also used in the transliteration of Avestan. 'All other usages of schwa are 0259 ə', says the Unicode standard; and this basic schwa has a similar but larger upper-case form, U+018F Ə.

Although the current official orthography in Azerbaijan is Latin-based, during Soviet times it was Cyrillic, and before that Arabic. There are also millions of Azeris living in Iran, but their Southern Azerbaijani has its own distinctive phonology, lexicon, morphology, syntax and loanwords. They mostly use Arabic script.

5.11   placing the suprasegmental symbols

Where should phonetic symbols for suprasegmental features (tone, stress, etc.) go?

One of the things in LPD that people knowing Chinese have commented on is the fact that in transcriptions of Chinese words I decided to place the tone mark at the beginning of the syllable in question, rather than over the vowel or at the end.

The sinologist tradition is to use a trailing tone numeral, thus *ma2* ('hemp', with tone 2, a rise). This is also how you input tones in the Chinese version of Word (the word processor). In printed Hanyu Pinyin, however, the tone mark, if used, goes over the vowel, thus *má*. If I had wanted to include this word in LPD, I would have transcribed it as [2]**ma**, with the tone number superscript and leading.

So: is the best place for the tone mark trailing (at the end), central (in the middle, superscript), or leading (at the beginning)?

My motivation in choosing to write tone marks as leading was for consistency with the IPA placement of stress marks in stress languages. For the same reason, I place the pitch accent marks for Japanese at the beginning, not the end, of the mora concerned.

The IPA, too, used to place tone marks at the beginning, thus ´**ma**. The tone symbols were iconic, i.e. their shape suggested the relevant pitch movement.

This was changed at the 1989 Kiel Convention to the current IPA rule, which is to place a non-iconic mark over the vowel, thus **mǎ**, or to use an iconic Chao tone letter, presumably trailing, thus **ma⌐**.

I am convinced that the best place for all such prosodic marks is at the beginning of the syllable, before the symbols for the segments. In order to pronounce a syllable with the appropriate tone, you have to know what the tone is before you start. You can't wait until you've finished making the vowels and consonants and then add the tone as an afterthought. Logically, the tone is the first thing you need to know about a syllable. Articulatorily, for the Chinese word for 'hemp', **ma** with a rising tone, you have to get low pitch in place right at the beginning, so that the **m** is low-pitched, ready to start the rise. Acoustic-ally, the F_0 in this word is lowest at the beginning of the initial nasal. You're too late if you start to think about the tone only when you get to the vowel (Hanyu Pinyin) or when you reach the end of the syllable (Sinologist practice).

The same applies to stress marking. You need to know whether a syllable is stressed before uttering it, not afterwards. That's the justification for the IPA practice, revolutionary in its day, of placing the stress mark at the beginning of the stressed syllable, as against the traditional English practice, still found in some dictionaries, of placing it at the end.

In my view the IPA's Kiel change in tone notation was a misguided concession to the Africanist and Sinologist traditions. (They disagree with one another, anyhow. In the Africanist tradition, for a rising tone – Low, High – we have to write **mǎ**.)

5.12   why Hawai'i?

The name of the American state Hawaii is often written *Hawai'i*. Why?

Phoneticians will not be surprised to learn that the apostrophe reflects a glottal stop in the Hawaiian (or Hawai'ian) pronunciation of the name: **ha'waiʔi, haˈvaiʔi.**

However, they may be surprised – I certainly was – to be told that the preferred way of writing this is as a LEFT apostrophe (an OPENING quote), i.e. *Hawai'i*, not *Hawai'i*. The Hawaiians call this letter the *'okina*.

Its shape is surprising, given that the IPA symbol for the glottal stop was chosen for its resemblance to a RIGHT apostrophe (a CLOSING quote): the top of <ʔ> has the same shape as <'>. Correspondingly, the top of the symbol for the so-called voiced pharyngeal fricative, the Arabic *'ayn* <>ع, namely <ʕ>, has the same shape as <'>. This reflects scholarly usage of <'> and <'> in the romanization of Arabic and other Semitic languages.

The spelling <'> for the glottal stop is part of the official orthography not only of Hawaiian but also of the related Polynesian language Tongan.

Hawaiian is well known for having very few consonant phonemes and no consonant clusters. There are just eight consonants: **p, k, ʔ, h, m, n, l, w**. Notice that the glottal stop is one of them, and the difference between it and zero can distinguish words. Here are some minimal pairs taken from Pukui and Elbert's *New Pocket Hawaiian Dictionary*, which I bought when I visited the islands some years ago.

pau 'finished'	*pa'u* 'soot'
kau 'to place'	*ka'u* 'mine'
koi 'to urge'	*ko'i* 'adze'

On the other hand, **t** and **k** are in free variation.

The paucity of consonants and absence of consonant clusters makes for some interesting adaptations of European names. My name, *John*, can become *Keoni*, *Ioane* (in the Bible), or... *Keanu* (which latter is also a Hawaiian word meaning 'coolness'). Now you know where Keanu Reeves gets his name from.

Towards the end of December, Hawaiians say *Meli Kalikimaka*.

5.13   funny letters

In the village outside Birmingham where my brother lives there is a dress shop. The name board on the fascia reads MAΨA.

My schooling was unusual in that I started to learn (Classical) Greek at the age of twelve. I went on to read Classics at university. So I have been very familiar with the Greek alphabet ever since childhood. Naturally, therefore, I read this name as ˈmæpsə. After all, the letter between the two As is a Greek psi.

But no, this is just a fancy way of writing MAYA. The name of the dressmaker is Maya, ˈmaɪə, like the Central American Indians.

Maya is following the same path as people who invite you to visit GRΣΣCΣ, where the Greek capital sigma does duty for E. Indeed, there is a well-known chain of toyshops called TOYS 'Я' US, whose logo exploits the similarity between the Cyrillic capital Ya and the Latin R.

And phoneticians who ought to know better sometimes use a Greek eta, η, instead of the velar nasal symbol ŋ.

5.14   anomalous *g*

We all know about the spelling-to-sound oddity of:

- *gaol* **dʒeɪl**, alternatively (and more logically) spelt *jail*;
- and *margarine* ˌmɑːdʒəˈriːn.

Their oddity consists in the fact that the letter *g* normally corresponds to **dʒ** (rather than to **g**) only when followed by *e*, *i* or *y*. Even that applies mostly to words of Romance rather than Germanic origin: compare *gem* and *get*. In *gaol* and *margarine*, though, we have *g* = **dʒ** even when followed by something else.

Ted Carney, in his comprehensive *Survey of English Spelling* (Routledge 1994, p. 327) also mentions:

- *veg* **vedʒ**, the colloquial abbreviation of *vegetable* – compare the abbreviation of *refrigerator*, usually now spelt *fridge*;
- and (rather strangely) *syringa*, which nevertheless for me and all other reference books I can lay my hands on has **g**, not **dʒ**.

But now I have a number of further candidates for this category – words that I have noticed native speakers pronouncing with **dʒ** even though the spelling would suggest **g**.

- *Meningococcal*: here it is clearly the influence of *meningitis* with regular **dʒ** that leads people to say **meˌnɪndʒəˈkɒkl̩**. The word frequently occurs in the phrase *meningococcal meningitis*.
- *Digoxin*: similarly, it must be the influence of *digitalis* and *digit* that leads people to call this heart drug **dɪˈdʒɒksɪn**. (That's what everyone at my cardiac support group calls it.)
- *Purgative*, which I heard on the radio the other day as **ˈpɜːdʒətɪv** rather than the usual **ˈpɜːgətɪv**: it must be the influence of *purge*.
- *Analogous*: I have quite often heard it pronounced with **dʒ**, no doubt because of analogy with *analogy*.

What we have in each case here is morphological regularization. The morpheme in question (*mening-*, *dig-*, *purg-*, *analog-*) keeps the same phonetic shape (with **dʒ**) despite suffixation. Chomsky and Halle's rule of Velar Softening clearly does not work quite as regularly as some would have us believe.

5.15   the spelling *wor*

We have a number of words spelt *worC*, where *C* is a consonant letter. Some of them are of quite high frequency. In almost all, the vowel is **ɜː** (NURSE) rather than the vowel that usually corresponds to *or*, namely **ɔː** (FORCE). They include *word*, *work*, *worth*, *worm*, *worse*, *worst* and *worship*.

We find **ɔː**, on the other hand, in the verb forms *wore*, *worn*, *swore*, *sworn*. The noun *sword* **sɔːd** is clearly orthographically irregular, as is *Worcester* **ˈwʊstə**. These are exceptions to the general rule above.

Overall, you'd think that the equivalence *worC* = **wɜːC** was pretty strong, and that speakers would apply it to new words of unknown pronunciation. Strangely, though, that does not happen.

In Wimbledon where I live there is a road called Worple Road. Everyone calls it **ˈwɔːpl̩**.

And now there is the newly popular herbal remedy *St John's wort*. I have known this plant since boyhood, when my mother taught me the names of the wildflowers around us. She called it **sn̩ ˈdʒɒnz wɜːt**, as I do in turn. But the herbal remedy enthusiasts all seem to call it **seɪnt ˌdʒɒnz ˈwɔːt**. I wonder if they would do the same for the many other compounds of *-wort* that I remember from my childhood, all pronounced **-wɜːt**: *glasswort*, *woundwort*, *sneezewort*, *ragwort*, *mugwort*, *bladderwort*, *liverwort* and so on. They've probably never heard of them.

This new form **wɔːt** is presumably a spelling pronunciation. Yet its rise is mysterious: you would think that the large number of common words spelt with *wor-* and pronounced **wɜː** – *word*, *work*, *world*, *worm*, *worse*, *worth* – would rather reinforce the traditional pronunciation, the one my mother used.

5.16   practicing (sic) wot I preach

At a question-and-answer session on a UCL Summer Course in English Phonetics one of the students asked about the possibility of reforming the chaotic and inconsistent spelling of English. I expressed the view that this would be a Good Thing, though for social and political reasons difficult to achieve. Jack Windsor Lewis then challenged me – given that I, like Daniel Jones before me, was President of the English Spelling Society (formerly the Simplified Spelling Society) – to publish some of my writing in reformed spelling instead of in traditional orthography. He claimed that he himself always writes *re'd* for the past tense of the verb *to read*.

So heer goes. In my view, English spelling reform shoud be gradual rather than raddical. As Patricia Ashby suggested, we aut to be like the Dutch and hav a minor reform evry few yeers rather than a big bang awl at wunce.

The Society has a House Stile, wich probbably goes further than we woud wont to go in the first instance, tho not as far as we mite wish to go in the end.

The most important principals in this House Stile ar these.

- No chanje is compulsory. U can go on using the traditional orthografy if u prefer.
- Redundant letters ar cut: *giv, hav, det, thum, thaut.* We retain the use of *e* to sho that a preseeding vowel is long: *drive, shave.*
- Consonants are dubbled after stressed short vowels consistently rather than sporaddicly: *rappid, coppy, nevver, sitty, reddy* (just as in *happy, coffee,* etc.). Dubbling is also made consistent in *-ing* forms: *givving, driving.*

Few!

These proposals are probbably at leest too hundred yeers old.

5.17   why *ph?*

Why do we write *ph*, not *f*, in words of Greek origin?

As usual with the oddities of English spelling, the reason is historical. Although the letter phi (φ) of Modern Greek is pronounced **f**, and usually transliterated into English as *f*, the phi of Classical (Ancient) Greek is transliterated as *ph*. This is because in classical times it was actually pronounced as an aspirated $\mathbf{p^h}$. The Romans represented this rather naturally as *ph*, e.g. *Philippus*, and we follow Latin despite the change in pronunciation that has occurred meanwhile. Hence *photograph*, etc.

The same applies to *th* for theta (θ), as in *Theocritus, theory* and *athletic*, classically an aspirated $\mathbf{t^h}$. In English, as in Modern Greek, this has become a fricative, **θ**.

However, *ch* for chi (χ), as in *Achilles, echo* and *Christ*, classically an aspirated **kh**, has reverted to being a plosive in English, since we don't have the fricative **x** in our modern English consonant system.

(The evidence in support of this claim is summarized in W. Sidney Allen's *Vox Graeca*, Cambridge University Press 1987, third edition, pp. 16–27.)

The voiced plosives of Ancient Greek have become fricatives, too, in Modern Greek, so that classical *Euboea* is now called *Evvia*, and as a modern placename *Delphi* (the home of the Delphic oracle) is sometimes transliterated *Dhelfi*.

Just occasionally, a classical education is really useful.

This does not cover all cases of the English spelling *ph*. It doesn't explain the *ph* in *caliph*, *nephew* or various other words.

Caliph comes from Arabic *khalīfah* via medieval Latin *calīpha*. Probably the Romans felt that not only Greek words but all foreign borrowings with **f** should have the spelling *ph*.

Nephew comes from Latin *nepos*, *nepōtem* via French *neveu*. For the first few centuries of its existence in English it was spelt with *v*; the spelling with *ph* is presumably a bit of erudite Latinizing (as with the *b* in *debt*). The pronunciation was also traditionally **v**, which is what I say myself; but most people nowadays say it with **f**, which must have originated as a spelling pronunciation.

Then there is *typhoon*, which has a complicated etymology involving the coming together of an Urdu-Persian-Arabic word of possible Greek origin (τῦφῶν) with a Chinese (Cantonese?) expression *tai fung* 'big wind' (Mandarin: *dà fēng*).

In *Macpherson* the explanation is quite different. In Scottish Gaelic, as in other Celtic languages, some consonants are subject to lenition (mutation) in certain positions. The spelling reflects this: **p** mutates to **f**, and the result is spelt *ph*. So the son of the *p*arson was *Mac an Phearsain*, or in English Mac*p*herson.

As for the *ph* in *Westphalia* (German *Westfalen*) or indeed in *Randolph* and *Humphrey* (which are names of Germanic origin) I have no idea. It's usually put down to 'classicizing'.

5.18   yogh and ezh

My colleague John Maidment says he's 'slightly annoyed' at the pronunciation of *Beijing* with ʒ instead of **dʒ**, and similarly in *raj*, *adagio* and several other borrowed words that have an affricate in their original language. 'This creeping *yoghism* should be stamped out', he says.

His neologism refers to yogh, not to yoga. However, *yogh* and *ezh* are different letters. And the Unicode name for ʒ is *ezh*. So perhaps he ought to be protesting against 'creeping *ezhism*'.

In Unicode, the phonetic symbol ʒ has the number U+0292 and the full name LATIN SMALL LETTER EZH. Yogh, on the other hand, i.e. the letter ȝ, has the Unicode number U+021D. This letter was used in Middle English and Middle Scots to stand for a velar fricative or palatal approximant. Norman scribes didn't like letters not found in the Latin alphabet, so yogh was phased out and replaced by *gh*. When it was retained, in a few Scottish words and names, it came to look just like *z*, which is why we have a spelling-to-sound mismatch in such names as *Dalziel* **diˈ(j)el** and *Menzies* ˈmɪŋɪs.

Ezh has an angled top, while yogh has a curly top.

The confusion between the two names is found, I am sorry to say, in the *Phonetic Symbol Guide* by Geoff Pullum and Bill Ladusaw (University of Chicago Press 1996, second edition), where the phonetic symbol is unfortunately labelled YOGH. But the *IPA Handbook* calls it Ezh or Tailed Z.

5.19   bevy, bevvy

One of the conventions of English spelling concerns consonant doubling. In derived and inflected forms we double a consonant letter between two vowel letters to show that the first vowel is short. So we have *shop, bat, swim* but *shopping, shopped, shopper*; *batting, batted*; *swimming, swimmer*. In morphologically simple words, however, consonant doubling is extremely erratic: *rabbit* but *robin, eddy* but *edit, stagger* but *dragon*.

The advantage of having (havving?) the rule is that in inflected forms it enables us to drop the silent *e* that (thanks to another convention) shows the vowel as long. So a single consonant letter signals a preceding long vowel in *hope, hoping, hoped*; *rate, rating, rated*; *time, timing, timed*. Given an understanding of our spelling-to-sound conventions, these spellings are unambiguous: *shopping* ˈʃɒpɪŋ, but *hoping* ˈhəʊpɪŋ.

With *v*, however, this breaks down. Alongside *give, giving, giver* gɪv, ˈgɪvɪŋ, ˈgɪvə and *have, having* hæv, ˈhævɪŋ consider *drive, driving, driver* draɪv, ˈdraɪvɪŋ, ˈdraɪvə and *rave, raving* reɪv, ˈreɪvɪŋ. Because *v* does not follow the two rules, these spellings are ambiguous.

Correspondingly, we write *clever, devil, cover* rather than *clevver, *devvil, *covver. The spelling is again ambiguous, as we see by comparing these examples with *fever, evil, over*.

The only cases that do have medial *vv* or final *v* are slang, humorous forms or abbreviations, e.g. *navvy, flivver, civvy, skivvy, revving, bovver*; *gov* or *guv, lav, rev, spiv*. There is also *bevvy*, meaning a drink, especially an alcoholic one. This noun is slang, originating as an abbreviation of *beverage*. It is an interesting case, because there is a homophone *bevy*, meaning a flock (of certain birds) or a group (of women).

In the advertising world, new product launches may involve both bevies and bevvies.

5.20   low and long

A correspondent wrote to me saying that for work on Hausa he needed to use a combination of macron and grave on all five (Hausa) long vowels, but on his computer could only find this combination on *e* (ȅ) and *o* (ȍ). What can he do about the other vowels?

It was not my correspondent who was missing something. It's Unicode that is missing something, namely precomposed characters for *a*, *i*, *u* with both a macron (ˉ) and a grave accent (ˋ).

Unicode 5.0 does indeed include provision for *e* and *o* with the desired combination of diacritics. But not for the other vowel letters.

This must mean that no one has yet made a case for these combinations to the Unicode Consortium committee that recommends the inclusion of new symbols. To succeed in such a case I think the applicant would have not only to demonstrate substantial existing printed usage of the symbol but also to show that a combination of base letter plus diacritic would not be workable.

The experts' advice in such cases is that we should use just such a combination. We should combine a-macron (ā, U+0101), i-macron (ī, U+012B) and u-macron (ū, U+016B) with the combining grave diacritic (ˋ, U+0300). If the results you get from doing this are not very good, then the problem lies with the fonts and/or the rendering software that you are using (word processor, browser), rather than with Unicode per se.

Or we could fall back on IPA and write length with an IPA length mark (ː, U+02D0) following the grave-bearing vowel (thus àː, ìː, ùː). Historically, it was because of the difficulties of multiple diacritics and multistorey symbols that the IPA adopted that mark for length rather than the macron.

5.21   palatoalveolars and the like

With reference to alveolopalatals, palatoalveolars and postalveolars (3.20 above), we might note some other phonetic symbols for this general type of sound – symbols at one time approved by the IPA but from which recognition has since been withdrawn.

In the early days of the IPA, the symbols σ ʑ ɭ ʒ were approved for labialized sibilants which we would nowadays probably write sʷ zʷ ʃʷ ʒʷ. The title of Daniel Jones's *Sechuana Reader* (1916) reads ɟipalɔ tsā-sɾɛ̰ɭ aːnɑ. Apart from this, I don't think they were ever used very much. By 1949, when the *Principles of the IPA* booklet was published, Jones recommended sf, sv or sɥ, zɥ instead of σ ʑ for the 'whistling fricatives' of Shona, which are adequately reflected in the orthography as *sv*, *zv*. (Coleman, though, regards the voiceless one as a simultaneous ɸ and s.) In the same booklet Jones wrote the Tswana sound he had formerly written ɭ ('a single sound having a peculiar type of lip-rounding involving an articulation by the inside of the lower lip against the upper teeth') as ʃw. Recognition of all these earlier symbols was finally withdrawn in 1976.

In 1947 the IPA approved two symbols to stand for palatalized ʃ, ʒ ('for use when these occur as phonemes separate from non-palatalised ʃ, ʒ'). They were ʃ and ʒ. Daniel Jones (posthumously) and Dennis Ward used these symbols in their book *The Phonetics of Russian* (Cambridge University Press 1969, p. 139).

The sound ʃ occurs in pronunciation where the letter щ occurs in spelling. Where this letter occurs some speakers pronounce ʃʃ, i.e. a long, palatalized ('soft') 'ʃ'.

As far as I can see the symbols ʃ and ʒ are more or less synonymous with ɕ, ʑ. In any case for Russian they could be written ʃʲ, ʒʲ. Recognition was withdrawn at the IPA Kiel Convention in 1989.

5.22   IPA reforms, 1976

In 1976 the IPA Council voted to add a number of symbols to the chart, notably ɵ, ɟ and ɥ, which we use to this day. At the same time it withdrew recognition from various symbols that had never been widely taken up, including the σ ɷ ʅ ʑ ʃ and ʒ discussed above.

The IPA has recommended various palatalization diacritics over the years. A dot above, as in ṫ, was used in the early days. Although impractical and hard to see, it was retained in 1928 as an optional alternative when the attached j-shaped hook, as in ƫ, was adopted. From 1976 to 1989 the hook was the only approved way of showing palatalization, other than possibly by a digraph (tj); but it in turn was superseded at the 1989 Kiel Convention by the raised j that we use now, as in tʲ.

Until 1976 the symbols ʦ and ƻ appeared in the chart, standing for the voiceless and voiced alveolar affricates. I have never seen them actually in use except in the 1949 booklet *The Principles of the IPA*, in the transcription of Georgian, where the first two lines have the words **ʦ'amosxmulma** and **ƻlieri**. Nowadays we write ͡ts and ͡dz, with a combining tie bar, or just **ts** and **dz**. (You may occasionally also see **ʦ** and **ʣ**, though these ligatures are not actually IPA-approved.)

Recognition was also withdrawn from the letter ƞ, which stood for the Japanese moraic nasal, a phonological unit with various possible nasal and nasalized realizations. In accordance with the principle of simplicity, it is usually sufficient to write this entity as ɴ or indeed **n** (provided you distinguish it from syllable-initial **n** in some way). If relevant we can also use various narrower symbols as appropriate, e.g. **m, n, ŋ, ũ**. (There is a Unicode number for this disused symbol, U+019E LATIN SMALL LETTER N WITH LONG RIGHT LEG, but not all fonts distinguish it properly from the Greek eta η.)

Lastly, the way of writing r-coloured vowels was changed. The symbols a̜, ɛ̜, ə̜ etc. were withdrawn; as the r-colouring modifier the IPA now recognizes a retroflex hook higher up, thus ɛ˞ a˞ ə˞. The symbols ɚ ɝ, which include this diacritic, were first introduced by Kenyon and Knott in their *Pronouncing Dictionary of American English*, 1944, and have been in widespread use since then.

5.23   Ortuguese

There is one column in the *Guardian* newspaper that is an unfailing source of delight: 'Corrections and clarifications'. Here's an apology I saw there.

> We wrongly reported that a proposed reform of the Portuguese language could mean that the letters c, p and h are removed from the alphabet.

After the original report appeared a Dublin reader wrote in to say:

> I fear on my next visit the atmospheric second city of Oorto, the ancient university centre of Oimbra and many other places I have loved in Ortugal will be, well, just not quite the same.

The *Guardian*'s correction continued,

> The Orthographic Accord signed by Portuguese-speaking countries seeks only to remove these letters from words where they are never pronounced, such as húmido (humid). The letters will remain in the alphabet for words where they are pronounced (World's Portuguese speakers in new attempt to unify language, page 16, March 26). In the same article we said one of the signatories to the accord is Western Timor when we meant Timor-Leste (formerly East Timor).

If the *Guardian* journalist were a student of mine I would also have pointed out to him that a minor change in spelling conventions is not a 'reform of the Portuguese language'. A language remains the same no matter how it is represented by marks on paper.

German remains German, no matter whether you write *daß* or *dass*. English would still be English if we were to reform its chaotic (cayottic) spelling. Portuguese remains Portuguese with the spelling *úmido* just as much as with the spelling *húmido*. On the other hand getting rid of gender, for instance, or regularizing irregular verbs like *fazer* – that would be language reform.

5.24   Panglish, or unintelligibility?

Oh, Jennifer Jenkins, what have you started? The *Daily Mail* reported 'How English as we know it is disappearing ... to be replaced by "Panglish"'. According to experts, it claimed, a new global tongue called 'Panglish' was expected to take over in the decades ahead.

Er, up to a point, Lord Copper.

'As English becomes more common, it will increasingly fragment into regional dialects, experts believe.' Braj Kachru, of Ohio State University, is credited with saying that non-native-English dialects were already becoming unintelligible to each other.

The *Mail* had lifted its story from the *New Scientist*.

> ... the 'great vowel shift' ... shortened some vowels – like *ee* to *aye*, as in
> *mice* – and pushed others to the front of the mouth, for example the Middle
> English vowel pronounced *oh*, which became *oo* as in *boot*.

Readers of this book hardly need to be told that the great vowel shift affected quality but not length, while **uː** is a back vowel, not a front one. I wonder if the *New Scientist* would allow crass errors of this kind in an article on, say, physics or biology.

The article goes on to mention various well-known linguists: as well as namechecks for Kachru, Al Marckwardt and Geoff Pullum, we also find the usual suspects Jennifer Jenkins and Barbara Seidlhofer.

> Jennifer Jenkins is credited with finding that the *th* sounds of *thus* and *thin*
> are often dropped and replaced with either *s* and *z*, or *t* and *d*.

No, the other way round. These foreigners' mispronunciations typically do not affect voicing, only place or manner. So the **ð** of *thus* might become **z** or **d**, but not **s** or **t**. The **θ** of *thin*, on the other hand, could indeed become **s** or **t**.

> Another consonant that causes problems is the *l* of *hotel* and *rail*, which is
> often replaced with a vowel or a longer *l* sound as in *lady*.

What? Replaced by a vowel, yes. But by a longer l-sound? (And anyhow the l is surely not longer in *lady* than in *hotel* and *rail*.) Perhaps originally, before garbling, this was a reference to the loss of l-allophony, i.e. to the neglect in foreigners' English of the clear-dark distinction.

The source of the *Mail*'s headline is the American author Suzette Elgin, who is reported as musing:

> I don't see any way we can know whether the ultimate result of what's going
> on now will be Panglish – a single English that would have dialects but
> would display at least a rough consensus about its grammar – or scores of
> wildly varying Englishes all around the globe, many or most of them
> heading towards mutual unintelligibility.

People think I'm eccentric for knowing and using Esperanto. One of the regular arguments deployed against the idea of Esperanto is that it would be at risk of *disdialektiĝo*, splitting into mutually incomprehensible dialects. But it seems that this may be precisely the danger threatening English, its more successful rival for the role of everyone's second language. And I don't find any unintelligibility Japlish-style on Esperanto websites based in Japan or Chinglish-style on those from China.

5.25   definitely

It has always surprised me how many people misspell *definitely* as *definately*.

On the web, authors get it wrong about one time in seven.

The difficulty, of course, stems from the fact that adjectival weak *-ate* and *-ite* are pronounced identically.

It's particularly surprising that students of phonetics and linguistics would get this wrong (which some of them do). You'd think they would be aware of orthographic and etymological relationships such as those between *definite(ly)* and *definition*, where the stressed ɪ vowel of *-ition* in the latter shows clearly how *-ite* in the former is to be spelt. Not to mention *definitive, finish, infinite* and the foreign but widely known *finis* and *finito*.

As *(in)considerate(ly)* is to *consideration*, so *(in)definite(ly)* is to *definition*. Why don't people get it?

Anyone who has learnt Latin should have no difficulty, since verbs belonging to the first conjugation give us *-ate -ation -ative*, while those belonging to the fourth conjugation give us *-ite -ition -itive*. (OK, since you ask, the second conjugation is exemplified by *complete completion expletive* and the third conjugation, in which the stem is consonantal, by *correct correction corrective*.)

I try not to be annoyed by spelling mistakes. After all, I do think it would be a good idea to reform English spelling so that we don't obsess so much about such ultimately trivial matters.

Nevertheless, as things stand educated people are supposed to get it right. Until we have a spelling reform. Deffo.

5.26   lexicographers and spelling

English lexicographers over the past four centuries have not in general been innovators in spelling, but rather have felt constrained to follow contemporary practice.

Samuel Johnson declared that it was necessary to 'sacrifice uniformity to custom' and thus for example to accept the difficult *inveigh* alongside the etymologically parallel and easier *convey, receipt* alongside *deceit*, and *phantom* alongside *fancy*.

Furthermore, by no means all of the spellings in Johnson's great dictionary (1755) met general acceptance. We do not nowadays write *persue, raindeer, spunge, villany* or *musick*.

By 1806 we were ready to agree with Noah Webster and drop the *k* from *musick*. Webster persuaded the Americans (but not the British) to write *favor, honor, color*, but failed to convince anyone that we should drop the final *e* from *determine* and *examine* and the final *b* from *thumb*. By 1828 he had retreated on these latter points.

Even some of the OED's preferred spellings have not succeeded in displacing deprecated alternatives: *ax* and *tire* (tyre) are the norm in the States but not in Britain, while the OED's preference for *rime* and *connexion* has not won out over *rhyme* and *connection*. And its preference for *-z-* in *organize* and *organization*, etc., has not persuaded the British to abandon the -s- spellings in these words as the Americans have.

5.27   respelling

Would-be dictionary users who are native speakers of English are often reluctant to get to grips with proper IPA transcription. The phonetic symbols are unfamiliar; you have to learn them. Anyhow, most dictionary users never read the front matter where such things are explained.

So, despite the widespread adoption of IPA in British-published monolingual dictionaries, others hold out for something perceived as more user-friendly. That means a respelling system.

In the US the IPA has made less headway than in Britain among dictionary publishers. In US-published dictionaries (as far as I am aware) there is no use of IPA, only of respelling.

In a respelling system we ideally use the familiar letters of English in their familiar meanings, as far as possible without diacritic marks.

This poses some difficult problems. How, for example, can we represent the 'long i' **aɪ** diphthong of *price*? We need to distinguish it clearly from the short ɪ of *kit*. Otherwise, how could we discuss the two competing pronunciations of *dissect*? Or distinguish the two words spelt *wind*? One traditional solution is to use a macron diacritic, as in *ī*, so that *aisle* **aɪl** is shown as *īl*. But people don't like diacritics. Another is to write *y*, thus *yl*. But this is in danger of being misinterpreted, since traditional spelling uses *y* in this meaning only when word-final (*cry*, *shy*). A third possible solution is *igh*, thus *ighl*, which is unambiguous but clumsy. Ordinary *iCe* would do for *ile* but not for *winde* (wind around, not the wind that blows). There is no ideal solution.

There is also no really unambiguous way to respell the diphthong **aʊ** of *cow*: both *ou* and *ow* are open to misinterpretation (*soul*, *mouth*, *soup*; *know*, *how*).

And what about schwa? The best solution, *ə*, requires a special letter. The alternative, *uh*, involves an arbitrary meaning for a digraph not used at all in traditional orthography. Non-rhotic speakers might be happy with *er*: but spellings such as *bernáhner* (banana) will shock rhotic speakers.

There is also sometimes a problem distinguishing clearly between **s** and **z**, since in non-initial position the letter *s* is commonly used for both: alongside *base* **beɪs** we have *rise* **raɪz**. In the respelling systems I designed first for the Reader's Digest *Great Illustrated Dictionary* (1984) and then later for the *Encarta World English Dictionary* (1999), with their spin-offs, I adopted the idea of making use of doubled consonant letters. The BBC has used this device in its respelling system since 1928; it is not only a familiar way to indicate that a preceding vowel is short (*rívvər*), but also means that *ss* will automatically be read as voiceless (*bayss* as against *rīz*).

So I respelt *rubber* as /rúbbər/, *petrol* as /péttrəl/, *travel* as /trávv'l/, *inward* as /ínnwərd/, *deputy* as /déppyəti/, *supposition* as /súppə zísh'n/, and *teakettle* as /tée kett'l/. To show that **s** was required, not **z**, I doubled /s/ in *face* /fayss/, *miscue* /miss kyóo/, and *mincer* /mínssər/; though there is no need to do that in *wasp* /wosp/, *first* /fúrst/, and *tax* /taks/.

5.28   pea's, plea's

From time to time I get invited to take part in a radio discussion on the topic of the apostrophe. Its use or misuse is something of an obsession of the kind of listener who likes to bemoan the deteriorating standards of the younger generation, in this case their failure to master the principles of English spelling and punctuation.

One question that arose was the correct spelling of expressions like *sports day / sport's day / sports' day*. On that occasion there were three of us 'experts' being interviewed. We all agreed that we need no apostrophe in *sports day*, since it is a day for sports, not a day of a sport or a day of sports. Going further, somewhat to my surprise, we all agreed that possessive apostrophes could well be entirely banished from English spelling. Since we do not distinguish *boys*, *boy's* and *boys'* in speech (all are **bɔɪz**), there should be no need to distinguish them in writing.

I pointed out various inconsistencies in current usage such as the adjacent stations in the London Underground officially spelt *Barons Court* and *Earl's Court* respectively.

When I was a boy people quite often still wrote *'bus* and *'phone*, to show that these were shortenings of longer words. No one does that any more. Well, hardly anyone.

It is clear that the rules for using the apostrophe are quite difficult for people to learn. Although they may seem quite straightforward to the linguistically sophisticated, you only have to observe public signs or internet postings to see that the rules are nevertheless problematic for many people. Other than confusion of *its* and *it's* or *your* and *you're* the commonest error is actually the overuse of the apostrophe – the 'greengrocer's apostrophe' as when *banana's* and *avocado's* are offered for sale.

The only apostrophes we really do need, I suggested, are those in the contractions *he'll*, *she'll*, *I'll*, *we'll*, since otherwise they could be misread as *hell*, *shell*, *ill*, *well*. Other than that, we can do without.

5.29   sibilant genitives

A correspondent has a query about apostrophes. She wants to know whether it is correct to write *Liz' diary*. Is *Liz's diary* better? In her dictionary, she finds the examples *St James' Palace* and *King Charles' crown*.

This topic is covered in LPD, under -'s. There are longer and more detailed discussions in the big grammars: Pullum and Huddleston *Cambridge Grammar of the English Language* (Cambridge University Press 2002, pp. 1595–6) or Quirk et al. *Comprehensive Grammar of the English Language* (Longman 1985 pp. 320–1).

Stems ending in sibilants (i.e. **s z ʃ ʒ tʃ dʒ**) form their plural by adding an extra syllable, namely **ɪz** (or for some speakers **əz**). They form the genitive (possessive) singular in the same way in speech, although we write this ending as *'s*, using an apostrophe.

So we have

spoken: ˈlɪzɪz ˈdaɪəri
written: *Liz's diary*

No one speaking standard BrE or AmE would say ˈlɪz ˈdaɪəri. Nor do we write *Liz' diary*. Similarly, it's *Liz Jones's diary*.

This is the general pattern applying to words and names ending in a sibilant.

maɪ ˈniːsɪz ˈwedɪŋ *my niece's wedding*
ˈrɒsɪz əˈdres *Ross's address*
sən ˈdʒɔːdʒɪz ˈhɒspɪtl *St George's Hospital*
ˈdʒəʊnzɪz səkˈsesəz *Jones's successors*
ˈdʒɒn ˈwelzɪz ˈblɒg *John Wells's blog*

But there are certain exceptions, most of them being classical, literary or religious names ending in the sound **z** (not necessarily the letter *z*). With these you can optionally pronounce zero and write just the apostrophe.

ˈdɪkɪnzɪz ˈraɪtɪŋ *Dickens's writing* OR
ˈdɪkɪnz ˈraɪtɪŋ *Dickens' writing*
ˈbɜːnzɪz ˈpəʊtri *Burns's poetry* OR
ˈbɜːnz ˈpəʊtri *Burns' poetry*

This explains *St James' Palace* and *King Charles' crown* above.

Personally I usually follow the regular rule with these names, i.e. I would say ˈbɜːnzɪz ˈpəʊtri and write *Burns's poetry*; I would say kɪŋ ˈtʃɑːlzɪz ˈkraʊn and write *King Charles's crown*. The only cases where I might go for the irregular version would be with Greek or Hebrew names.

juˈrɪpɪdiːz ˈpleɪz *Euripides' plays*
ˈsɒkrətiːz fɪˈlɒsəfi *Socrates' philosophy*
ˈməʊzɪz ˈlɔː *Moses' law*

There are also two special cases, which end in **s** rather than **z**. One is the fixed expression *for goodness' sake*, which never has a spoken extra syllable or a written extra *s*. The other is the name *Jesus*. For this, we can write either *Jesus's love* or *Jesus' love*, and pronounce correspondingly. Poets and hymnodists can also write *Jesu's* and pronounce ˈdʒiːz(j)uːz or even ˈjeɪzuːz.

5.30   greengrocers' spellings

I saw signs on a greengrocer's stall in a London street market offering
for sale *obo-jeans* and *monge-two*. Brits ought to be able to interpret them.
Non-Brits may find it more difficult.

Obo-jeans is straightforward. This is clearly a pronunciation spelling of
ˈəʊbədʒiːnz, or more elegantly ˈəʊbəʒiːnz, which is properly spelt *aubergines*.
Americans know these vegetables as eggplants.

Monge-two reads ˌmɒndʒ ˈtuː, or more elegantly ˌmɒ̃ʒ ˈtuː, properly spelt
mange-touts. These are peas of which you eat the whole pod with its contents.
Hence the name *mange-tout*, French for 'eat (it) all'. I think Americans call them
snow peas or sugar snap peas.

If nothing else, the mis-spellings prove the lively existence of these vegetable names in the spoken English of people who are not very literate. (Or, I suppose, it just might be a literate greengrocer having a laugh.) Despite their French origin, they are well known to the general public – they are not restricted to educated speech. They may not even be perceived as French by the ordinary user.

Educated people, though, recognize that they are French and therefore may well pronounce them in a more sophisticated, semi-French way.

In native-speaker French they'd be **obɛʁʒin**, and **mãʒ(ə)tu** or **mãʃtu**.

5.31   O tempora! O mores!

The previous section (5.30) was about what you might call pronunciation spellings. This one is about the more familiar territory of spelling pronunciations.

The word *mores*, meaning 'the customs, social behaviour, and moral values of a particular group' (LDOCE) is a word that only educated people know. And most of them know that it is disyllabic, pronounced **ˈmɔːreɪz** (or in a more old-fashioned way **ˈmɔːriːz**).

So it was quite a surprise to hear someone on BBC Radio 4 pronounce it monosyllabically as **mɔːz**, as if it were the plural of *more*.

It isn't, and it isn't etymologically related to *more*. It is the Latin plural of *mōs* 'custom', of which the stem is *mōr-*. The nominative plural ending is *-ēs*. The word *moral* is derived from the corresponding Latin adjective.

I expect that one day soon we shall hear *lares et penates* (household gods) pronounced **ˈleəz et peˈneɪts**. But the mayor of London, Boris Johnson, wouldn't commit such a solecism. He is a classicist. I have to admit, though, that I think he's being overoptimistic in suggesting (as reported in the press) that teaching unruly youths Latin would stop them knifing one another.

(Hey, it worked for me. I was taught Latin when young and I've never knifed anyone.)

5.32   the cost of spelling

In 2008 I attended a conference with the topic 'The cost of English spelling'. What is the cost to the British economy of having a difficult-to-learn spelling system?

The only presentation that really attempted to address this issue seriously was a paper by Zuzana Kotercová of the University of Coventry, 'The economic cost of current English spelling'. She started from the claim (how well based I do not know) that English schoolchildren take three years to reach the same level of literacy skills as Finnish schoolchildren achieve in three months.

In Finnish, learning to read and write requires no more than learning the letters of the alphabet and the sounds they correspond to: then you just sound out every word as it is written, and write down every word in the way it sounds. In English, this approach gives you a good start (and is now known by the buzzword 'synthetic phonics'). Children can also take in their stride conventions such as the effect of silent *e* (*hop* – *hope*, *rat* – *rate*). But all too soon the learner is then faced by hundeds of words whose pronunciation is not what you get by sounding out the spelling (*money*, *two*, *find*) or in which a rule that they've just learnt (such as the silent *e*) doesn't apply (*have*, *give*) – and words whose spelling you would not get right if you based it just on how you say them aloud (*friend*, *head*, *knife*, *climb*).

One of the other conference presenters claimed that approximately 25% of learners cope well with this extra learning burden, 50% manage but with a lot of extra time and effort, while 25% do not cope and end up disheartened and ultimately functionally illiterate.

To return to Kotercová's work: she started by estimating the cost of the extra teaching time required to achieve literacy in English. She investigated four Coventry primary schools and calculated the number of hours of additional teaching expended on spelling instruction as opposed to general literacy. The average annual cost per teacher came out at £556. Multiplying by the number of primary teachers in England, we arrive at a lowest estimate of just over a hundred million pounds per annum: the additional expense we incur in England through the inadequacies of our spelling system.

This figure does not include the additional cost of remedial literacy teaching in secondary schools, which must be substantial. Nor does it take into account the lower lifetime earnings expectations of the functionally illiterate when compared with the literate. Nor does it address the similar additional costs incurred in other English-speaking countries, still less the additional hours of teaching and learning required in the case of those millions who attempt to learn English as a foreign language.

It would be particularly difficult to quantify the adverse effects on the intelligibility of EFL learners – who naturally assume (unless taught otherwise) that *broad* must have the same vowel sound as *road* and that *son* must rhyme with *on*.

So her figures are not only based on a very small sample, they must also be pretty conservative. But I hope she will inspire some team of economists and educational researchers to attempt to get a robust answer to the question.

My sister-in-law, who has extensive experience in educational policy, commented as follows.

> Whilst I cannot categorically state that the spelling system in English is not a factor, what I can say is that the fundamental difference between the English educational system and that of Finland is definitely a factor. Finland, in common with most, if not all, Scandanavian countries, begins formal education at the age of 7 years, i.e. when children are developmentally ready to learn to read, write and spell (I'm thinking especially in terms of the fine motor control needed to control a pencil successfully), whilst here in England the Government persists in the notion that 'earlier is better' and insists on starting formal education at age 4/5 years.

5.33   capital eszett

Standard German spelling includes the special double-*s* letter *ß*, as in *Fuß* 'foot'. The spelling reform has removed it from some words, so that what used to be *daß* is now *dass*; but it remains in plenty of others. (That's in Germany proper and Austria. Not in Switzerland, where they write *ss* instead.)

This letter is known as *eszett* or *scharfes ss* ('sharp *s*'). It is now used only after long vowels and diphthongs, which means among other things that it is never used at the beginning of a word, only in the middle or at the end.

If it's never initial in a word, it will never be found at the beginning of a proper name or at the beginning of a sentence. Therefore, you might conclude, it is never capitalized. And traditional German printing in blackletter never used all-caps.

Thus *ß* is the only letter of the Latin alphabet that has no upper-case form. Or is it? In 2008, Unicode added a capital *ß* (*ẞ*) as U+1E9E LATIN CAPITAL LETTER SHARP S. Why? Because modern signage and product design does sometimes call for it.

The Unicode Standard (5.1) comments:

> In particular, capital sharp s is intended for typographical representations of signage and uppercase titles, and other environments where users require the sharp s to be preserved in uppercase. Overall, such usage is rare. In contrast, standard German orthography uses the string 'SS' as uppercase mapping for small sharp s. Thus, with the default Unicode casing operations, capital sharp s will lowercase to small sharp s, but not the reverse: small sharp s uppercases to 'SS'. In those instances where the reverse casing operation is needed, a tailored operation would be required.

Nevertheless, upper-case *ß* 'ist nicht Bestandteil der offiziellen deutschen Rechtschreibung' ('is not a component of official German orthography').

5.34   Jumieka

There has been a vigorous debate in Jamaica, sparked by the publication of a translation of part of the Bible into Jamaican Creole.

A web page devoted to 'Jumieka Langwij' explains:

> Di hiem a dis sait a fi bring tigeda haxpek ahn suos a Jumiekan langwij fi chrai prizaabi fi paasteriti ahn fi di huoliip we lib a farin wid Jumiekan kanekshan uu maita hinchres iina dehn linguistik eritij. hUoliip a dem kuda gat pierans ar grampierans uu kiahn kot di patwa, bot dem siem wan kiaahn piik di mada-tong, ar els piik wahn luokalaiz verjan, laik Landan patwa.

> 'The aim of this site is to bring together aspects and sources of Jamaican language in an effort to preserve it for posterity and for the many living abroad with Jamaican connections who may have an interest in their linguistic heritage. Many of these may have parents or grandparents who are or were patois speakers, but are themselves not fluent in the mother-tongue, or else speak a localized variant, such as London patois.'

This spelling you see here is more or less the one used in Cassidy and Le Page's *Dictionary of Jamaican English* (Cambridge University Press 1980, second edition). It differs by adding one or two more symbols: an optional italic *h* for the h that comes and goes before word-initial vowels, particularly after a final vowel in the preceding word, and *hn* to stand for what the web page author (not Cassidy and Le Page) calls a 'soft, breathy n' (actually nasalization of the preceding vowel), as *duohn* **duõ** 'don't'.

This spelling is phonemic ('ebri leta fi soun, aalwiez soun siem wie') and uses the ordinary alphabet with no diacritics. Its main disadvantage for those unfamiliar with it and with IPA is the use of *ai* for the vowel of PRICE and of *ie, uo* (phonetically spot on) for FACE-NEAR and GOAT-FORCE respectively.

Fred Cassidy (1907–2000), the deviser of this spelling, was an enthusiast for the spelling reform of Standard English, too. When I was much younger, and not then involved in the Spelling Society, he invited me to dinner and urged me to campaign for the cause. His co-author, Bob Le Page (1920–2006), was the external examiner for my PhD.

You can read about the serious academic side of language in Jamaica – the Jamaican Language Unit of the UWI – at www.mona.uwi.edu/dllp/jlu/about/.

5.35   fame at last!

Gosh, I've been denounced by David Cameron!
Here's what he said in his speech to the Conservative party conference yesterday:

> The election of a Conservative government will bring – and I mean this almost literally – a declaration of war against those parts of the educational establishment who still cling to the cruelty of the 'all must win prizes' philosophy...

> ...and the dangerous practice of dumbing down.

> Listen to this.

> It's the President of the Spelling Society.

> He said, and I quote, 'people should be able to use whichever spelling they prefer.'

> He's the President of the Spelling Society.

> I say that he's wrong. And by the way, that's spelt with a 'W'.

He is quoting me out of context. Here's what I actually said at the Spelling Society centenary dinner, as quoted in my press release:

> ... Let's return to a time when English spelling allowed greater variation ... Nowadays we often see *light* written *lite* and *through* as *thru*. Let's not hold up our hands in horror – people should be able to use whichever spelling they prefer.

I didn't mean that we should abandon all standards in spelling. I was referring to pairs such as those I mentioned. I added a few more, such as the text messaging *u* alongside *you*. And I suggested we get rid of the apostrophe.

I'm not calling for any dumbing down. I'm not calling for a free-for-all. I'm not suggesting we abandon all rules, just that we might relax some of them in a controlled way.

I'm in favour of consistency, logic and obeying the rules, in spelling as in other things. I just think the rules need to be modified.

6 English accents

Regional and social accents of English

On the quayside at St John's, Antigua, where the cruise ships dock, there used to be a painted hoarding inviting the cruise passengers to a casino offering various forms of gambling, including *stud porker* (sic).

In the English of Antigua, *pork* is a homophone of *poke* **poːk**, which explains this spelling mistake. It is not a matter of 'r-fulness on the march' or 'a sneaky little creeping /r/', as one linguist characterized it. It is not a matter of sounds at all, just of spelling. Neither the Antiguans nor most English people have an **r** in *pork*. The problem is not the sound **r** but the letter *r*. Just as with *larva* and *lava*, we speakers of non-rhotic English may have difficulty in knowing which words to spell with *r* and which not.

When we look at different accents of English, there are two sets of words spelt with *-or-*. In terms of the Standard Lexical Sets of chapter 2 of my *Accents of English*, some belong in the FORCE set and some in the NORTH set. It is the FORCE words that in Leeward Islands English fall in with the GOAT words, producing such homophones as *court-coat*, *porch-poach* and indeed *pork-poke*. The NORTH set, on the other hand, fall in with START in the local creole, producing homophones such as *form-farm*, *born-barn*, *lord-lard*. *North* **naːt** and *bath* **baːt** rhyme. But pairs such as *hoarse-horse* are distinct, **hoːs** vs. **haːs**.

Most Scots and Irish people preserve the distinction between the FORCE and NORTH sets. They, the Jamaicans and the Leeward Islanders are conservative in this aspect of their pronunciation. They retain a historical distinction that most of us have lost.

In *roll*, *cold*, *bolt* and other words where the vowel is followed by a morpheme-final or preconsonantal **l**, some English people use a special vowel quality **ɒʊ**, a quality so different from their usual **əʊ** (as in *grow*, *code*, *boat*) that they are reluctant to view it as an allophone of /əʊ/. You can hear the difference if you ask such speakers to pronounce, for example, *cold* and *code*, or *bolt* and *boat*. They may also not rhyme *goalie* and *slowly* and have different vowel qualities in *rolling* and *Roland*.

Unlike such speakers, I personally use pretty much the same əʊ quality in all these words, no matter what the following consonant might be. In support of this contention (which surprises some people), let me tell you how, when I was a small boy and couldn't sleep one night, my father told me the Bible story of Moses and the burning bush (Exodus 3). In the words of the Authorized Version, God spake unto Moses from out of the midst of the bush and said, 'Draw not nigh hither: put off thy shoes from off thy feet, for the place whereon thou standest is holy ground'.

But I heard this as *hole-y* ground, ground with holes in it. (If Moses kept his shoes on, I thought, perhaps he would get them caught in the holes.)

This implies that my late father pronounced ˈhəʊli *holy* 'sacred' and ˈhəʊli *hole-y* 'containing holes' identically – like me, and unlike the speakers mentioned above.

6.3   hair lair!

Rory Bremner's Foreword to Andrew Taylor's *A Plum in your Mouth* (HarperCollins 2006) starts with a little dialogue which English people will understand, but probably not many non-English people.

> MAN A: Try pronouncing the word 'a-i-r'.
> MAN B: Air.
> MAN A: Good. Now try pronouncing the word 'h-a-i-r'.
> MAN B: Hair.
> MAN A: Excellent. Now try the word 'l-a-i-r'.
> MAN B: Lair.
> MAN A: Splendid. Now put them together and what have you got?
> MAN B: Air, hair, lair.
> MAN A: Welcome to Sandhurst.

Explanation: this pokes fun at upper-class speech (U-RP). Sandhurst is the Royal Military Academy where army officers are trained. One of the stereotypical features of U-RP is a front starting quality to the GOAT vowel, roughly ɛʊ, but without much backing or rounding in the second element. Thus U-RP *oh* can be caricatured as *air*, and what Man B ends up saying is *Oh, hello*.

6.4   minor royalty

Like her mother, whom journalists once caricatured as Princess *Unne*, Zara Phillips (born 1981, daughter of Princess Anne and thus grand-daughter of the Queen) uses a very open, retracted-cardinal-four kind of æ. You should be able to find a video clip of her on YouTube, and observe several other striking characteristics of the pronunciation used by her and others of her age and general background.

The replacement of word-final **t** by sound-types other than a voiceless alveolar plosive proceeds apace. For post-sonorant word-final **t** Zara often uses a glottal stop, as in *i*[ʔ], *bu*[ʔ], *wen*[ʔ] *ou*[ʔ]. In this she is indeed probably representative of people of her age and class (though not of people of <u>my</u> age and class, and sharply different from her grandmother).

When she says *No* her lips are unrounded throughout.

It is fascinating to be able to observe the really rather substantial change of accent within three generations of one family as we proceed from mother to daughter to granddaughter.

6.5   Prince Harry

There are various TV and radio clips available of Prince Harry being interviewed. He provides excellent exemplifications of the RP (?) spoken by upper-class young men of his age (born 1984). On one such clip I noted extensive T glottalling (*quite a lot* **kwaɪʔ ə lɒʔ**) and l-vocalization (*well, people, April* **weo, ˈpiːpo, ˈeɪpro**), including remarkable pronunciations of *multi-tasking* and *pulled*, in which where I would have **ʌl, ʊl** he has something like **oː** for both.

6.6   fricative *t*

In Irish English when /t/ is intervocalic (= between vowels) and in coda position (= at the end of a syllable) it is often fricative rather than plosive. I am thinking of the /t/ in examples such as *atom, bottom, jetty, ditto*; *get off, shut up, quite easy, wait a second*; or, in utterance-final position *a lot, who's that, very late, all right*.

In all of these cases the usual southern Irish sound is a kind of alveolar slit fricative. It is an example of lenition (weakening), a characteristic feature of Irish consonants in certain positions.

In *Accents of English* (p. 429) I used the symbol [t̢] for this sound, employing what was then the official IPA diacritic for 'opener articulation', an ogonek (reversed subscript comma). At the 1989 Kiel Convention the IPA changed this to a down tack, which means that the proper symbol would now be [t̞].

The contrast between /t/, /s/ and /ts/ is maintained: *hit ≠ hiss ≠ hits*. (The first two end in fricatives, the last in an affricate.)

You get this kind of /t/ in Scouse (the accent of Liverpool) as well: it's one of the typical Irish characteristics of Scouse. But there in certain environments you get further lenition, all the way to [**h**].

6.7   hypercorrection

We non-rhotic speakers find it very difficult to avoid intrusive **r** while retaining linking **r** (should we wish to do so) – there just isn't time, in the flow of speech, to stop and think whether a given word is spelt with or without an *r*. To stop ourselves pronouncing an **r** at the end of *Malta* in *Tell me how far away Malta is* we usually also have to stop ourselves pronouncing an **r** at the end of *Gibraltar* in *Tell me how far away Gibraltar is*.

We have a corresponding difficulty in putting on a rhotic accent if we want to imitate American or Scottish speech. The rule is simple: if there's an *r* in the spelling, pronounce an **r**. But it can be quite difficult to apply this rule in real time. Hugh Laurie in *House* is unusually talented in this respect: he gets it right. Personally, if I try to talk American it is only with conscious self-monitoring that I can stop myself from saying things like ˈfɑːrðɚ instead of ˈfɑːðɚ *father*. In my own accent, of course, *father* is a homophone of *farther*, both ˈfɑːðə. My unconscious default stratagem to make my speech rhotic clearly does not refer to the spelling, but says 'add **r**-colouring to every ə or ɜː and insert **r** after every ɑː or ɔː'. That's why it gives quite a few wrong results.

6.8   Montserrat Creole

My partner and I were invited to sing a duet at the funeral in London of a young man from Montserrat in the West Indies. After the service, a Montserratian I have known for many years, who like the deceased was forced to evacuate to England by the volcanic eruption of 1997, congratulated me by saying **mi no mi no ju kudu siŋ so**.

This was in the local dialect of English, Montserrat Creole. I wonder how far people unfamiliar with the dialect would have understood.

mi	no	mi	no	ju	kudu	siŋ	so
I	NEG	PAST	know	you	could	sing	so
Me	*no*	*me*	*know*	*you*	*couldoo*	*sing*	*so!*

'I didn't know you could sing like that!'

Unlike in Jamaican Creole, in Montserrat the past tense marker is **mi**, homophonous with the first person singular pronoun **mi** 'I, me, my'. And the mark of negation, **no**, is, like standard *no*, homophonous with the verb *know*.

Montserratians speak something much closer to Standard English than this when talking to outsiders, so I felt complimented to be addressed in dialect: it meant I was being treated as a belonger, an insider.

On a different note, here's something I overheard in the playground of a primary school in Montserrat.

> **a no ˅miː**
> *is not me*
> 'It wasn't me!'

Although the grammar in this utterance is the local creole, the intonation is English. It is the same pattern as I would use myself, with the same pragmatic meaning: a fall-rise on a negative statement (*English Intonation*, p. 31). This is a distinctively English pattern, which does not seem to be used with this meaning in (most) other languages. It reinforces my view that Caribbean English creoles are best considered dialects of English, not separate languages.

6.9   television newsreaders' RP

Bente Hannisdal's PhD thesis (University of Bergen 2007) is entitled *Variability and Change in Received Pronunciation.*

For this brilliant piece of work she had collected a large number of recordings of British television newsreaders (thirty people; half of them men, half women; from the BBC, ITV and Sky channels; an hour of speech from each individual). This constitutes an extensive corpus of contemporary RP, and has enabled her to discover some interesting facts, not previously established, about this variety of English. Among them were the following.

GOAT allophony

In words such as *sold*, *roll*, where the GOAT vowel is followed by dark **l**, 24 of the 30 newsreaders use the **ɒʊ** allophone categorically, and a further four of them do so variably. Only two do not use it at all. We need to update our descriptions of RP to cover this.

CURE lowering

Despite reports of its imminent demise, it turns out that **ʊə** is alive and well, persisting particularly after **j** and before **r**, as in *Euro, Europe, European, security, secure, during*. The switch to **ɔː** is found principally in the complementary phonetic environments, e.g. in *poor, sure, tour*. The only important exceptions to this generalization are *your* and *you're*, which – despite the **j** preceding and the possible linking **r** following – the newsreaders pronounced 100% with **ɔː**.

T voicing

A remarkable 35% of final /t/s, prevocalic across a word boundary, were voiced, i.e. pronounced American-style as **ɾ**. Unlike in American English, this is not found in content words: Brits don't make *atom* sound like *Adam*. (There were one or two exceptions, including *British* and pre-adjectival *pretty*.) In Hannisdal's corpus it is mainly found only in function words, across a word boundary. It was particularly prevalent in such cases as *it is*, *that it's*, *but if*, *at a*, *what about*, *a lot of*, *a bit of*, *not exactly*, *get elected*. Yes, we do need to update our descriptions.

Yod coalescence

Words with traditional **tj**, **dj** before a stressed vowel (*tube*, *Tuesday*, *student*, *due*, *reduce*, *duty*, *during*) were pronounced instead with **tʃ**, **dʒ** in a massive 46% of cases. We can no longer consider these variants 'non-RP' (even though that's what they were for people of my own advanced age).

Smoothing

Pronunciation of **aɪə** (*fire*) and **aʊə** (*power*) as **aə**, **aː** proved to be 'very frequent in broadcast RP'. My native-English-speaking undergraduate students often used to refuse to believe that any such thing was possible: how wrong they were! Among the newsreaders, there was a highly significant statistical difference between the sexes, with men smoothing much more than women. As you might expect, smoothing was less common across a morpheme boundary (e.g. *high#er* as compared with its possible homophone *hire*), and less common before a pause.

R sandhi

There was a tendency for men to use more linking/intrusive **r** than women, but the difference was not significant. The /r/ was realized as [r] only in foreign names (*Igor Ivanov*); otherwise it was an ordinary [ɹ]. (Compare Daniel Jones's pronunciation, where the tap was the norm for all linking **r**.) The factors favouring **r** sandhi are exemplified, in descending order, by *for a*, *four o'clock*, *former economic*. It was least likely in proper names (*Doctor Austen*, *Sir Alex*). The main factor disfavouring it was another **r** adjacent (e.g. *terror alert*). Overall, the link was used in 60% of possible cases. Interestingly, intrusive **r** was more prevalent after ɑː, ɔː than after ə. That is, it was more likely that there would be an **r** in *Jack Straw_ is* than in *Nelson Mandela_ is*. However, the raw number of cases of intrusive **r** after ə was higher because of the greater frequency of schwa in word-final position.

6.10   accents change over time shock horror

The Times newspaper carried a story about the supposed disappearance of middle-class speech in England, 'Where are the gels who can talk proper and pirouette?'

Casting directors are lost for words because the next generation of British actors just cannot speak proper. The rise of 'Estuary English' has left children with the intonation patterns of Lily Allen and Jonathan Ross, regardless of their background.

The decline in Received Pronunciation has not just transformed the presentation of BBC News. Film and drama producers are struggling to fill period roles that require unrepentantly middle-class vowels. BBC One is holding an open casting session tomorrow to try to find two girls to star in a film-length adaptation of the classic children's novel Ballet Shoes. Victoria Wood and Marc Warren have signed up to star in the story, by Noel Streatfeild, set in 1930s London. But the challenge of finding two ballet-dancing leads who can act, twirl and – most importantly – speak in middle-class accents has defeated the producers.

Notice anything odd here? First, there is the headline. The spelling *gels* alludes to an obsolete ***upper***-class pronunciation of *girls* (**gelz** or perhaps **geəlz** for **gɜ:lz**), which is surely not relevant to the task of casting child actors to play parts requiring the ***middle***-class accents of the 1930s.

In my view, middle-class children today speak with middle-class accents. If the British social class system persists (and it does, though much less sharply stratified than was the case a hundred years ago), then by definition middle-class accents are what the middle classes continue to speak with. Middle-class and working-class accents have certainly converged over the last half-century, but accent differences haven't disappeared.

That middle-class accents have changed over time need not surprise anyone: language does change. Rare indeed are children who speak like their grandparents or great-grandparents.

What the producers are really looking for is child actors who can speak with a particular historical accent. It is like casting a play in which the actors must speak with Victorian, or indeed Shakespearian, accents. People usually can't do it without training. Unless you are particularly talented in that direction and can do it on your own, you have to study. You must go to drama tuition, elocution lessons or even, dare one say it, phonetics classes.

6.11   bad sociophonetics

Here is an email I received recently.

Dear Sir, my name is XXX and I am the bureau chief here in London for [...] Australia publications [...].

I am interested in doing a report on the British language since I read a piece in the newspapers recently about how the Australian accent is well and truly creeping into the everyday [sic] of Britons. Apparently Neighbours, Home and Away, Kylie etc have a lot to do with it as well as lower socio [sic] not wanting to sound as such and the upper class wanting to sound a little more middle class.

– to which I replied:

> You really mustn't believe everything you read in the papers. The Australian accent is not in fact 'well and truly creeping into the everyday [speech] of Britons'.

> There is one, just one, survey – dating from seven years ago! – that uncovered one apparently Australian-type variant pronunciation of one vowel in one place and speculated that it might be of Australian origin, only to reject this explanation in favour of a more plausible one. The co-author of that survey was Paul Kerswill, whom you could contact for further information.

I feel like Ben Goldacre with his 'Bad Science' column in the *Guardian*, who says his archives at www.badscience.net:

> are overflowing with just a small sample of the media's crimes: preposterous cherry-picking, outrageous overextrapolation, startling ignorance or white-washing of known methodological flaws and, worst of all, reporting the authors' speculative conclusions, from the discussion section of a paper, as if they were the experimental results themselves.

6.12   The Book of Dave

I have recently been reading Will Self's novel *The Book of Dave*. I found it brilliant but not exactly enjoyable. Do read it.

The action takes place partly at the present day and partly in the distant future, perhaps a thousand years hence, by which time England has been inundated by rising sea levels, leaving only scattered patches of former high ground to support human life.

This future is a despotic feudal-theocratic dystopia. Its ideology is a religion derived from the ravings of Dave, a taxi-driver of the present day, driven mad by his ex-wife's refusal to allow him access to their son. He wrote down his disturbed misogyny in a book which he then buried. Most of his book is a recitation of the Knowledge required of London cabbies, a detailed familiarity with all the streets and routes within six miles of Charing Cross. The rest is Dave's misogynistic proposals to reform society, with 'dads' and 'mummies' strictly segregated from one another, the children moving from one to the other every WED and SUN. Dug up centuries later, this book is the foundation of a new religion which becomes the established orthodoxy. In this dystopic future, prayer (addressed to Dave) takes the form of reciting the Knowledge, even though the places referred to have long been submerged.

As a middle-class dropout who has moved down-market to become a cab driver, Dave speaks to himself 'with Received Pronunciation', but to the world in general in 'Mockney' (which is the name we use for the variety in which people consciously and intentionally make their speech less standard, more demotic). For the latter, writes the author, 'he hadn't dropped his Hs – he'd flung them away from himself, ninja stars that stuck quivering in the smoky bacon Victorian woodwork'.

What kind of language does the author puts into the mouths of the followers of Dave? They have two varieties of speech. One is a formal variety known as Arpee, which is ordinary Standard English except for various cabbie-derived vocabulary innovations (*screenwash* for rain, the *headlight* for the moon, and so on). The other, informal, register is known as Mokni, and bears a remarkably close resemblance (given the passage of centuries) to contemporary cockney. As well as having vocabulary innovations and typical cockney slang and phraseology, this is represented in what people would no doubt call phonetic spelling, with some elements of txt conventions. Here is an example:

> *Eyem gonna go onna bí! C if vairs anyfing bettah ovah vair! – Yeah, orlrì, but nó 2 fa.*

– which being interpreted is 'I'm going to go on a bit! (I'll) see if there's anything better over there! Yes, all right, but not too far'.

So the convention is that an acute accent denotes a short vowel followed (today, at least) by a glottal stop, and a grave accent denotes a long vowel.

Much of this is simply eye dialect. That is to say, the spelling is changed in a way that doesn't imply any difference of pronunciation, as *eyem* for *I'm* or *onna* for *on a*.

Other examples of this include *slorta* for *slaughter* and *carn* for *can't* – the sort of thing that is transparent to non-rhotic readers but that may prove trickier for the rhotic.

This book will surely spawn a thousand PhD dissertations in English departments around the world as non-Brits struggle to make sense of it.

6.13   character, calendar

In Caribbean English certain words have what to me is an unusual word stress. The words *character* and *calendar* are generally pronounced there with penultimate stress, **kæˈræktə, kæˈlendə**.

As far as I know, this stressing is not found in other kinds of English. Our usual British/American initial stressing, **ˈkærəktə(r), ˈkæləndə(r)**, is at least as old as Shakespeare.

The Caribbean stress pattern is actually what Chomsky and Halle's stress rules in *The Sound Pattern of English* predict for words of this phonological structure. My paraphrase of part of their Main Stress Rule would be:

> In a morphologically simple noun, disregard the last vowel if it is short. If what now remains as the final syllable is 'heavy' (= if it has a long vowel or ends in two or more consonants), stress it (yielding penultimate word stress). If it is 'light', stress the preceding syllable (yielding antepenultimate word stress).

We see the operation of this double-consonant effect in such items as *philander, November, momentum, sequester, meniscus, colostrum, conundrum*, all stressed on the penultimate.

The ordinary British/American stress pattern of *character* and *calendar* violates the SPE rules – though, as usual, you can get round this by arbitrarily positing a particular underlying representation, in this case one with final vowelless **-ktr, -ndr**. The same applies to other everyday items, apparently exceptional, such as *cucumber, cylinder, canister, barrister*.

The mystery remains: why do West Indians stress *character* and *calendar* differently from the rest of us? Further research shows that they are not alone: the Irish, too, often have penultimate stress at least in *cylinder* and *cucumber*. And there are even English people who stress *cucumber* on the penultimate. And Singaporeans put the stress on the second syllable in various words in which it has first-syllable stress in other varieties: *abacus, faculty, penalty, abdomen, industry, precedent, Agatha, lavender, predator, cucumber, maintenance, prevalent*.

6.14   Grand Turk

These are notes based on informal observations of the speech of our taxi-driver-cum-tour-guide on Grand Turk island, part of the British Overseas Territory of Turks and Caicos, lying to the north of Hispaniola and to the southeast of the Bahamas. He told us he was a native of Grand Turk.

Our driver consistently pronounced *town* as **taːn**. I think this was probably the same vowel as he had in *pass* **paːs**, but I was unable to test this by eliciting for example *mouth* and *bath*. This monophthongal MOUTH vowel is not uncommon in the north of England, but I have never before heard it from a West Indian (though it has been reported by others writing on Bahamian).

He said *coffee* with a definitely back, mid, rounded vowel similar to RP *thought*: ˈkɔːfi. (Compare Jamaican speech, where *coffee* typically has the same vowel as *pass*.)

His PRICE vowel, at least before a voiceless consonant, was very narrow: *right* rəit, *like* ləik. Trudgill reports this for various remote islands in *New-dialect Formation: The Inevitability of Colonial Englishes* (Edinburgh University Press 2004, p. 52).

His accent was consistently non-rhotic. His NEAR vowel was wide, thus *here* hiɐ. His NURSE vowel was open, back and lightly rounded, thus *first* fɒːs(t), *Turk* tɒːk.

When he pointed out the *Anglican* church, it sounded like ˈɛ̃lɪkən.

But casual notes from a forty-five minute tour are no substitute for a proper analysis.

There are some general comments on Turks speech in Trudgill's 'The history of the lesser-known varieties of English', in R. Watts and P. Trudgill (eds.), *Alternative Histories of English* (Routledge 2002, p. 37).

> The speech of the islands is often described as being very close to Bahamian English.
>
> ... [John Holm] reports (personal communication) that certain students at the College of the Bahamas in Nassau where he taught in 1978–80 were said by other students to have 'Turks accents'.
>
> Turks Islanders claim that people in the Caicos Islands speak differently [from them] ...

I'm kicking myself that I did not notice or elicit the pronunciation of the only town, *Cockburn Town*. I bet it contains only one **k** and rhymes with *Oban*.

6.15   popular phonetics

The *Guardian*'s television critic was discussing a programme in which two people had the job of scouting the streets looking for new [fashion] models. He commented:

> 'Model' needs to be pronounced as it is in the industry, with no 'l' sound at the end, just a glottal stop instead.

I put a comment on the *Guardian* blog saying:

> No one pronounces this word with a glottal stop. What your critic means is 'with a vocalized **l**'.
>
> I will try and get a life (though my livelihood is phonetics).

Other readers chimed in:

> Yes, it would be strange to hear 'model' end with a glottal stop...
>
> And I was just practising saying it that way...
> I'll have to start all over again now.

What is interesting about the original comment is that *glottal stop* – perhaps the only one of our phonetic technical terms to have become truly popular in the wider world – seems to be being used as a catch-all term for any and every pronunciation feature the writer disapproves of.

6.16   changing London speech

A correspondent wrote to say he had read about the development of a 'multi-ethnic dialect' in London, seemingly independent of social origin and including patterns 'from Cockney, Jamaican creole, Bengali and other languages'. He wanted to know whether this was true – or was it 'more like a hype such as about Estuary English?'

My reply was that this research is highly respectable, being the work of well-known sociolinguists.

The research findings are described here.

Jenny Cheshire, Sue Fox, Paul Kerswill and Eivind Torgersen, 'Ethnicity, friendship network and social practices as the motor of dialect change: Linguistic innovation in London', *Sociolinguistica* 2008, 22: 1–23.

Susan Fox, 'The demise of Cockneys? Language change among adolescents in the 'traditional' East End of London', unpublished PhD dissertation, University of Essex 2007.

Paul Kerswill and Jenny Cheshire, 'Linguistics innovators: the English of adolescents in London. Project overview', 2007 www.lancs.ac.uk/fss/projects/linguistics/innovators/overview.htm.

Paul Kerswill, Eivind Torgersen and Susan Fox, 'Reversing "drift": Innovation and diffusion in the London diphthong system', *Language Variation and Change* 2008, 20: 451–91.

Prof Kerswill believes this new form of speech, which he and his associates refer to as Multicultural London English (MLE), arose as more recent immigrants learnt English with few English-speaking role models. He says:

> I think there has been a change in the last 30 years. The first generation of Afro-Caribbean children in London would have spoken Cockney, but they would have kept their own Caribbean patois and switched between the two. Now their descendants – and young people of other ethnicities – are inventing a new form of English.

The teenagers also used words like *blud* (blood, meaning mate), *creps* (trainers), *yard* (house) and *endz* (area or estate).

Here is a chart taken from the Cheshire et al. article. What particularly interests me is the change in vowel qualities among young inner-city speakers.

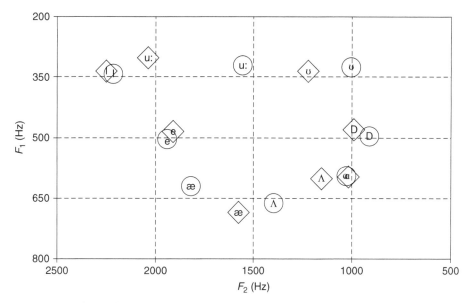

The southeastern short vowel shift in Hackney among elderly speakers (circles); young speakers (diamonds)

You can see in this formant plot the striking anticlockwise movement of TRAP, STRUT, FOOT and GOOSE (æ, ʌ, ʊ, uː). This makes *cat*, for example, into [kat], so pretty similar to older cockney *cut*, and leaves *cut* as [kɑt], with a very similar quality to that of *cart* [kɑːt]. Meanwhile FOOT and GOOSE lose their rounding and are no longer back but central or even front: /ʊ/ becomes more schwa-like and /uː/ turns into a sort of [iː] that can sound alarmingly similar to RP /iː/.

The authors say this confirms what they had already observed in other southeastern localities. In London, however, they find that the changes in STRUT and GOOSE are led by young non-Anglos (of African, West Indian, etc. heritage) and by Anglos (white English) with non-Anglo friends rather than by Anglos who socialize mainly with other Anglos. It makes the new London STRUT similar to Jamaican STRUT but makes GOOSE very different from Jamaican GOOSE, which is firmly back and rounded.

The authors go on to describe the 'reversal' of the London diphthong shift, leading to the restoration of RP-like qualities for FACE, GOAT, PRICE and MOUTH. Furthermore, they report, the young speakers drop **h** very much less than the older people; and they have an innovation called K-backing, involving [q] or something similar before non-high back vowels, as in *cousin, car, cot, caught.*

6.17   **American T voicing and *sentence***

A Japanese correspondent asked for an 'expert opinion' on American voiced **t**, shown in some dictionaries as ţ. He thought it would be used:

1.   After the stressed vowel, and followed by another vowel, e.g. *city*

...providing the following vowel, if within the same word, is weak (which it usually is). So although we get T voicing (aka 'flapping') in *city*, *better*, we don't get it in *latex* 'leɪteks. Strangely enough, this restriction doesn't apply across word boundaries, so we do get T voicing despite a following strong vowel in *put up*, *get over*, *quite obviously*.

2.   After the stressed vowel plus **n** or **r**, and then followed by another vowel, e.g. *party*, *twenty*

Yes, but the same rule about the next vowel being weak applies: so there is no T voicing in *syntax* 'sɪntæks. Again, across a word boundary a strong vowel is as good as a weak one, so there is T voicing in *start off*, *count up*.

3.   After the stressed vowel, and followed by syllabic **l**, e.g. *little*

Yes, and even after an unstressed vowel: *capital*.

He asked why we don't have any T voicing or elision for the pronunciation of *sentence*. This falls under the same heading as words such as *button*. Before **n** Americans typically pronounce **t** as a glottal stop, **ʔ**, which is not susceptible to voicing.

Although we British say *sentence* as 'sentəns, Americans have different rules about syllabic consonant formation (ən → ŋ). Americans typically use a syllabic **n** after the **t** in *sentence*. So the **t** is immediately followed by a nasal, which triggers **t** → **ʔ** (the **t** becomes glottal). You can get 'sentəns in very careful speech, but mostly Americans say 'senʔns. Since the **t** is pronounced as a glottal stop, it is not voiced. There can also be an epenthetic **t** (i.e. **ʔ**) between the last two segments, giving 'senʔnʔs. And the vowel can coalesce with the nasal, so that we end up with something like 'sẽʔnʔs.

We get the same thing in the American pronunciation of words such as *accountant* ə'kaʊnʔnt, *mountain* 'maʊnʔn, *Clinton* 'klɪnʔn. (Using a glottal stop is not the same thing as eliding **t**. People who claim they elide the **t** in these words are mistaken.)

So the crucial thing is the set of environments in which the speaker applies syllabic consonant formation. In the word *sentence*, Americans do form a syllabic nasal, the English don't (though people from northern Ireland do).

Tricky, isn't it?

6.18   sexy accents

'He speaks in a seductively French accent'. Just why a French accent in English is considered sexy I'm not sure. Like other stereotyped reactions to accents it presumably cannot be taken literally: there can hardly be any objective phonetic correlates of sexiness that are found in French voices and absent from English ones.

Presumably it is a relic of the late-Victorian and early-twentieth-century British attitude to France as the home of uninhibited sexuality. Dirty weekends took place in Deauville or Nice. Aristocrats or other public figures implicated in sex scandals would seek refuge in Paris. Condoms, condemned for encouraging immorality, were known as 'French letters'. We borrowed the word *risqué* (first use in English 1867).

Which country has now replaced France in this stereotypical role? Thailand? Perhaps. But a Thai accent is not considered particularly sexy.

6.19   Maori names

Some years ago I went on a cruise around New Zealand. Our ship sailed from Auckland, and the first port of call was *Tauranga*. I heard several different pronunciations of this name.

The chap on the ship's public address system called it **təˈræŋə** – but he was an Australian, so not reliable as a source of information about the pronunciation of NZ place names. The *Oxford BBC Guide to Pronunciation* gives the pronunciation **taʊˈræŋə**, and this is indeed one of the versions I heard locally.

However, the guide on our shore excursion bus, who was a Maori, stressed the name on the first syllable. On the whole he seemed to be saying **ˈtaʊræŋə**. But sometimes the first syllable seemed to be **ˈtɔː-** and/or the last part **-rəŋə**. His MOUTH vowel in this word (if that was what he was using) sounded rather un-NZ. Most Kiwis have a quality in the **æʊ** region, but our guide's diphthong started further back. Then I realized that I had been a bit slow on the uptake. Although most of the time he spoke with what sounded like an ordinary Kiwi accent, when he came to a Maori name he used not Kiwi English phonetics but Maori phonetics. Very probably what I heard was (in terms of the Maori phonetic system) **ˈtauraŋa**.

He also seemed to pronounce the word *Maori* itself as **ˈmɑːɾi**, with a tapped **r** perhaps preceded by some sort of central onglide. I find that the Maori form is actually *Māori*, i.e. with a long first vowel.

In Rotorua I bought a booklet entitled *Pronounce Māori with Confidence*, by Hoati Miwa (Auckland: Reed, 2003). Aimed at the general public, it isn't really too bad at all. The material in it is clearly set out, though I wish it wasn't presented entirely in the form of reading rules. It tells us that the letters are such and such, and that they are pronounced (= read aloud) like so and so. When serious phonetic description is called for, the author gets a bit lost. Fortunately there is a CD attached, so where the written word falters we can just listen to what it sounds like.

The phonemic system of Māori seems to be very straightforward. Like other Polynesian languages, it has a five-vowel system **i u e o a** (short and long), a very small consonant system and strictly (C)V(V) syllable structure. The Māori consonants are **p t k f m n ŋ ɾ w h**.

For the consonant written *wh*, Niwa tells us that:

> *Wh* is most commonly pronounced **f**, though the pronunciation varies from region to region. In the north, for example, you will hear **h** or **hw**. In Taranaki and Whanganui, they say **w**.

He recommends **f**. According to Wikipedia, generally it is more precisely a bilabial fricative **ɸ**.

When we come to the letter *r*, Niwa struggles.

> [It] is never rolled or trilled. Its sound is very close to **d** or **l**. When you make these two sounds, notice how you flick your tongue against your palate. To say **r** correctly on Māori, you flick just the tip of your tongue in the same way.

The examples on the CD show very clearly that the sound is a voiced alveolar tap **ɾ** (or occasionally even a trill). So Niwa's first sentence is way off-beam.

He struggles again when we come to **t**.

> Listen closely and you'll notice that it sometimes sounds like the **t** in English. This is before an *i* or a *u*. But when it comes before an *a*, *e* or *o*, the sound is softer – almost like a *d* in English.

What he is trying to say is that before high vowels the consonant is aspirated (and to my ear sometimes a bit affricated). But before non-high vowels it is unaspirated (though still voiceless).

> As with the letter *r*, it's to do with how you place your tongue against the palate.

(Oh no it isn't. It's to do with glottal timing, aka VOT.)

Trying to describe pronunciation without a knowledge of phonetics is like fighting with one arm tied behind your back. You just don't have the terminology or the theoretical framework that you need.

A correspondent comments:

> It was interesting reading your take on how Maori words are pronounced in New Zealand English. It's been a mess, really, as long as I can remember (I'm in my mid-thirties). Everyone would like to pronounce things right, but hardly anyone speaks the language, so hardly anyone gets it right. When I was a kid, *au* was usually pronounced to rhyme with *cow*. Now it seems to be supposed to rhyme with *flow*.

That's probably what I was commenting on for the first syllable of *Tauranga*, when I said the guide's MOUTH vowel sounded rather un-NZ. He was using the GOAT vowel.

I gather that since about 1980 there has been a drive to pronounce Māori names in an authentically Māori way, rather than in anglicized form. As a result there is a lot of variability in what people say. Another complication is that only a minority of Maoris can actually speak Māori, and fewer still are native speakers.

We passed through the townships of *Te Puke* and *Mount Maunganui*, which our guide pronounced **tə ˈpʊki** and **ˌmɔːŋəˈnuːi** (note anglicizing treatment of *au* in the latter).

When I saw a road sign saying we had reached *Ngongotaha* I listened out eagerly for an initial velar nasal. Disappointingly, our guide called it ˌnɒŋɒ ˈtaːhaː with an ordinary alveolar nasal at the beginning. (But then I read in Wikipedia that 'in Tu-hoe and the Eastern Bay of Plenty some speakers merge *ng* into *n*'.)

6.20   rich man, poor man

One of the upmarket areas in pre-volcano Montserrat, just outside the capital Plymouth, was called Richmond Hill. Now, after the 1997 destruction of Plymouth by pyroclastic flows, it is uninhabitable. So the locals wittily now call it Poorman Hill. Why? Because in the local creole and creole-flavoured English two characteristic processes apply: (1) cluster reduction means that **d** is lost from final **nd**, and (2) the distinction between schwa and the TRAP vowel is lost.

Hence the antonym of ˈrɪtʃman is obviously ˈpuoman.

7   Phonetics around the world

Languages other than English

7.1   Scottish Gaelic

Scottish Gaelic is a language with remarkable phonetics and a remarkable orthography. The name of the language, in Gaelic, is *Gàidhlig*, pronounced ǧaːlıǧʲ. The consonant system includes dental and palatal plosives, palatal and velar fricatives, three laterals and three r-sounds. There are no voiced plosives, but fortis consonants are distinguished from lenis by being aspirated or (in non-initial position) preaspirated. Consonants are divided into 'slender' (palatalized) and 'broad' (non-palatalized), and come in slender-broad pairs.

The vowel system includes back unrounded vowels ɯː and ɤː, as in *caol* 'narrow' and *ladhran* 'sandpiper' respectively.

Like the other Celtic languages, Gaelic has initial mutation (lenition) of consonants in various grammatical or positional environments. In the vocative case, masculine names undergo both lenition of the initial consonant and 'slenderization' of the final consonant. Hence *Seumas* ʃeːməs, the Gaelic for 'James', becomes *a Sheumais* ə heːmɪʃ. Now I understand why it has come into English as *Hamish*.

7.2   tangnefedd a thragwyddoldeb

The thing that first attracted me to the Welsh language was an LP of community hymn-singing (*cymanfa ganu*) that I borrowed from a colleague. As a serious linguist, I am of course disposed to set aside all aesthetic considerations when discussing language – but I would be being less than honest if I did not admit that words such as *tangnefedd* taŋˈneveð 'peace' and *tragwyddoldeb* tragwiˈðoldeb 'eternity' seemed to have a wonderful ring to them. And I have always enjoyed singing hymns.

When I was on one of my visits to Montserrat the local church choir had chosen to do a hymn set to the tune of *All through the night*. Since this is actually a Welsh melody, *Ar hyd y nos*, they asked me to sing a solo verse in Welsh between the two verses in English.

> *Holl amrantau'r sêr ddywedant*
> *Ar hyd y nos,*
> *Dyma'r ffordd i fro gogoniant*

Ar hyd y nos.
Golau arall yw tywyllwch,
I arddangos gwir brydferthwch,
Teulu'r nefoedd mewn tawelwch
Ar hyd y nos.

ˈhoːɬ amˈrantajr ˈseːr ðəˈwedant
ar ˈhiːd ə ˈnoːs
ˈdəmar ˈfɔrð i ˈvroː goˈgonjant
ar ˈhiːd ə ˈnoːs
ˈgolaj ˈaraɬ iw təˈwəɬux
i arˈðaŋgos ˈgwiːr brədˈvɛrθux
ˈtəjlir ˈnevojð mewn taˈwelux
ar ˈhiːd ə ˈnoːs

'All the twinkling stars proclaim
Throughout the night,
This is the way to the vale of glory
Throughout the night.
Other light is darkness
To reveal true beauty;
The family of the heavens in quietness
All through the night.'

Note on the phonetic transcription: Some speakers say **i** rather than **ɨ**, **ej** rather than **əj**. In the first syllable of the words *brydferthwch* and *tywyllwch*, some sing **ɨ** rather than **ə**. I have analysed the falling diphthongs as vowel plus **j** or **w**.

Look for the recording of this by Bryn Terfel (on YouTube).

In the Welsh text you may have noticed the rhymes *dywedant – gogoniant*, *tywyllwch – brydferthwch – tawelwch*.

These are acceptable rhymes within the Welsh literary tradition. But they wouldn't do in English, for two separate reasons.

1.   The stressed syllables don't rhyme (stress in Welsh is always on the penultimate), only the unstressed syllables (*-ant*, *-wch*). This would be like rhyming *lemon* and *bacon* in English, or *window* and *yellow*.

2.   In the second set of words, the rhymed element is actually a suffix, a morpheme like English *-ness*. *Tywyll-wch* = dark-ness; *prydferth-wch* = beautiful-ness; *tawel-wch* = quiet-ness. So this would be like making rhymes in English such as *gladly*, *brightly*, *surely*, or indeed *darkness*, *fairness*, *quietness*. You might get near-rhymes like these in non-traditional verse forms, but not in a hymn. (In Esperanto poetry, suffix rhyming is a well-known no-no, so much so that it has its own name, *adasismo*.)

Just as in Old English and Old Norse poets used alliteration rather than rhyme, so in the Welsh literary tradition the important thing is not rhyme but *cynghanedd* kəŋˈhaneð, in which patterns of consonants are repeated. (But there's no cynghanedd in *Ar hyd y nos*.)

Here's an example of cynghanedd from the poem composed by R. Williams Parry in memory of Hedd Wynn, killed in the First World War when about to be crowned bard at the eisteddfod.

> *Y bardd trwm dan bridd tramor, – y dwylo*
> *Na ddidolir rhagor:*
> *Y llygaid dwys dan ddwys ddôr,*
> *Y llygaid na all agor.*

> 'The poet heavy under foreign earth, – the hands
> that will never part again:
> the eyes thick beneath a thick door,
> the eyes that cannot open.'

The first line up to the dash repeats the pattern **b – r – ð – tr – m** twice, then across the first two lines we have **d – l – d – l**, then in the third line **d – d – ð – ð** and in the fourth **l – g – l – g**. There is a straightforward rhyme, too, between the second and fourth lines.

Parry continues this linguistic virtuosity for seven more verses. As with the sonnet, the ghazal or the haiku, truly beautiful poetry somehow combines memorable words with severe formal constraints.

7.3   Welsh letter names

The letters of the alphabet have their own names in Welsh. In the case of vowel letters, it is the corresponding vowel sound; in the case of consonant letters, some have the same name as in English, others have a distinctively Welsh name.

The learner of Welsh needs to know these names in order to talk about Welsh spelling and to play word games.

A problem arises with the name of the letters I and U. In northern Welsh the letter I is called iː and the letter U is called ɨː. But in the south there is no ɨ in the vowel system, and speakers use i in words where northerners would have ɨ. This makes the names of the two letters homophonous unless we can find a way to distinguish them.

How can we do that? Rather as the French call the letter Y *i grec* i ɡʁɛk to distinguish it from I i, so the solution for the southern Welsh is to call I *i dot* and U *u bedol*. The reason for the first is obvious: *dot* means 'dot', seen in the lower-case *i*. The reason for the second is that *pedol* means 'horseshoe'. (It gets soft-mutated to *bedol*.) And with a little imagination you will agree that U is shaped like a horseshoe.

An alternative name is *u gwpan* (*cwpan* 'cup').

I haven't seen these names in any textbook. I learnt them by listening to the teacher when I was going to Welsh evening classes and by watching

Welsh-language game shows on television – on S4C, the name of which is spoken aloud as *es pedwar ec*.

Like the newly popular English *haitch*, for H, the name *ec* for C includes an instance of the sound associated with the letter.

7.4   Welsh *ll*

The BBC has a web page where you can hear audio files of the pronunciation of various Welsh place names. Trying it out, I was immediately struck by the way the speaker pronounces the Welsh *ll* (e.g. in *Llandeilo*, *Llangwm*, *Llanddewi Brefi*, *Benllech*). Instead of the standard voiceless alveolar lateral fricative ɬ, he uses a voiceless palatal fricative ç. (It was Jack Windsor Lewis who first pointed this out, and Amy Stoller who drew it to my attention.)

I wrote to the BBC about this, and was delighted to receive a reply from BBC Cymru Wales, whose Ceri Davies wrote:

> Thank you for your comments about the Welsh pronunciation guides on bbc. co.uk/wales. I am not a specialist in the Welsh language, but happen to be a native Welsh speaker. To my ear, and to the ears of my Welsh-speaking colleagues here at BBC Wales Education & Learning, we cannot discern a problem with the pronunciation of the letter 'll' on BBC Wales' pronunciation guide. We have listened carefully, concentrating on 'Machynlleth' and 'Benllech' in particular. The audio . . . sounds good to us.
>
> It's interesting to consider the different ways in which 'll' might be pronounced, but (unless someone is actually saying a soft 'ch' in error) all techniques sound acceptable to us. I wonder however whether in future we should bear in mind a particular nuance of pronouncing 'll' when recording audio intended for Welsh learners?

Martha Figueroa-Clark of the BBC Pronunciation Unit (who holds an MA in Phonetics from UCL) comments:

> Following my conversation with Ceri . . . I have listened to many of the soundfiles repeatedly and, to my ear, there are still clear instances of realisations with the unexpected palatal fricative as well as the alveolar lateral fricative (*Llanwrtyd Wells*, *Llanelli* and *Machynlleth* in particular sound palatal to me). I find it very intriguing that these differences do not seem to be discernible to native Welsh speakers' ears.

So there we have it. The use of a palatal fricative rather than an alveolar lateral fricative, which is immediately obvious to us four phoneticians (Amy, Jack, Martha and me), is beneath the radar as far as (some) native Welsh speakers are concerned.

I wonder if there is a sound change in progress, and that ɬ is indeed giving way to ç. If so, and the palatal succeeds in driving out the alveolar lateral, speakers of Welsh will no longer be able to boast of having a really exotic sound in their consonant system. They'll be no more able to lay claim to exclusivity than the Germans, and the use of the true alveolar lateral fricative will be left to Zulu and Xhosa.

In the words of the Zulu farewell, ꞌhámba̱ ꞌga̱ːɬé *hamba kahle!* Go well!

7.5   c what I mean

I recently watched some ski-jumping on the digital television channel British Eurosport. The anonymous commentator coped pretty well on the whole with the many non-English names that inevitably came up. In particular, he knew the spelling-to-sound value of the letter *j* – the same value as in IPA – in the whole swathe of central European languages from Norwegian through Finnish and Polish to Croatian. He didn't, for example, make the mistake of calling the Czech competitor *Janda* ꞌdʒændə or ꞌʒændə instead of ꞌjændə.

Foreign sounds were mostly mapped onto English sounds, which is fair enough. But the commentator was also sufficiently familiar with German phonetics to supplement the English consonant system with not only **x** but also **ç**, and in the correct German distribution to boot.

He even produced a very creditable ꞌmaʊʃ for the Polish ski-jumper *Małysz*.

Where he really fell down – and he is not the only one – was over the letters *c* and *z*. Given his apparent familiarity with German, it was disappointing that he referred to *Schlierenzauer* as ꞌʃlɪərənzaʊə, treating the *z* as if it were English. (In German the last part is pronounced -tsaʊɐ.)

Then, oh dear oh dear, we heard that the next meeting would be in ꞌlɪbərek. But the Czech city of *Liberec* is pronounced with final **ts**, not **k**.

Why this reluctance to use an alveolar affricate? Heavens to Be[ts]y, it's as bad as when we used to hear about *Vá*[k]*lav Havel*. English people seem to have a complete blind spot about the letter *c* having the value **ts** in eastern European languages.

As the 2008 Wimbledon fortnight was in full swing, I watched a tennis match on the television in which one of the players bore the name Troicki. The Eurosport commentator called him ꞌtrɔɪki.

But he's Serbian, and in Cyrillic his name is written Троицки. It ought to be pronounced, in anglicized form, as ꞌtrɔɪtski. (I think it would be unreasonable for him to insist on our retaining the Serbian stress, troꞌitski.)

On the other hand, the final *-ić* in the names of various Serbian, Croatian and Bosnian players does not offer a problem to the commentators. The diacritic may be omitted in newspaper reports, on the scoreboards and in television captions, but there is no hesitation in giving Ančić, Bogdanović, Djoković, Ivanović, Jugić-Salkić, Karlović, Ljubičić and Tipsarević a final **tʃ**. (Ljubičić gets his medial **tʃ** in English, too, although Ivanišević, like the late Milošević, usually misses out on his **ʃ**.)

'Djokovic' is properly Djoković or Đoković, or in Cyrillic Ђоковић.

In one tournament there was a match between Aleksandra Wozniak and Caroline Wozniacki. The commentators had an amusing time trying to make sure we knew the difference between ˈwɒzniæk and ˌwɒzniˈæki. In Polish these surnames are respectively *Woźniak* ˈvozɲak and *Woźniacki* vozˌˈɲatski. So they are quite a lot more different from one another in Polish than in English. But Aleksandra is Canadian and Caroline Danish. Although both are native speakers of Polish, in their adopted countries they have to be content with the foreigner's version of their names, which doesn't include (in Caroline's case) any awareness that *c* might denote **ts**.

With Turkish names there's a different problem with the letter *c*, namely that in Turkish it stands for the voiced affricate **dʒ**. Most foreigners don't know this. So *Incirlik* air base (in Turkish spelling, *İncirlik*) gets mispronounced as ˈɪntʃ- and former prime minister *Ecevit* as ˈetʃ-. In Turkish they are inˈdʒirlik and ˈedʒevit.

There's a different problem for the commentators with the Slovak player Hrbatý. In Slovak he's stressed on his syllabic **r**, thus ˈfr̩batiː. In English they call him hɜːˈbɑːti or hɜːˈbæti.

Turning from sport to food, at one time a television advertisement enticed us to eat a particular brand of pizza by telling us that it was topped with tʃəˈrɪtsəʊ (a kind of sausage). That's *chorizo*.

So our confusion about the letter Z continues. OK, the ad is indeed about *pizza*, in which – as everyone knows – the letter *z*, or rather double *zz*, is pronounced **ts**.

But *pizza* is Italian, *chorizo* is Spanish.

If there were an Italian word pronounced tʃoˈritso it would probably be spelt *ciorizzo*. The sequence *cho-* would not be found in an Italian word.

However, as I say, *chorizo* is actually a Spanish word. And in Spanish the letter *z* corresponds to **θ** or **s**, depending on the kind of Spanish involved. Hence the Spanish pronunciation of *chorizo* is tʃoˈriθo (or in Andalucia and the Americas tʃoˈriso).

In English, though, *z* always means **z**. We don't generally know about Spanish phonetics. Anglicized, *chorizo* becomes tʃəˈriːzəʊ. Usually, at least.

7.6   Leewards, ABCs and Virgins

In the Caribbean, one of the Leeward Islands, St Martin (Sint Maarten, Saint-Martin), is divided into a Dutch part and a French part. The official languages are Dutch, English and French. (By the way, the islands we call the Leeward Islands are called the Windward Islands by the Dutch. It depends on where you are standing.) However, virtually the only Dutch to be seen in public signage is in street names.

Otherwise, the language in the Dutch part is English, and what you mostly hear on the street from the locals is a form of Caribbean English creole. In the French part of the island, as you might expect, everything is in French.

A cash machine (ATM) I looked at in the Dutch part is trilingual, but French is not one of the languages. Papiamento, on the other hand, is – no doubt for the benefit of Netherlands Antilles citizens from the ABC islands off the coast of Venezuela, whose language it is. (The other two languages were English and Dutch.)

> APRESIABEL CLIENTE, DESPENSA; E MASHIN AKI TA TEMPOR-
> ALMENTE FOR DI SERVISIO POR FABOR HUSA UN DI NOS OTRO
> BANKOMATIKONAN

Papiamento or Papiamentu is the everyday spoken language in Aruba, Bonaire and Curaçao. It is a Spanish/Portuguese-based creole. (The spelling of the name of the language depends on which island is concerned.)

The plural ending in Papiamentu is -*nan*, pronounced **naŋ** (with the final nasal being velar, as in Venezuelan Spanish). So in the bank ATM screen the last part of the word *bankomatikonan* is the plural ending. *Nan* is also the third person plural pronoun, 'they, them'. What its etymology is, I don't know, though it looks African.

The word for 'street' is *kaya*, from Spanish *calle* ˈkaʎe or ˈkaje.

In St Thomas (American Virgin Islands) the only official language is naturally enough English. However, the local dialect is a Caribbean English creole comparable to that of the other Leewards, which means it sounds more British than American. Other matters unusual for an American territory are that they drive on the left and that many of the street names are Danish. This is because the US Virgin Islands were Danish until purchased by the Americans in 1917.

7.7   clicks demonstrated

YouTube is a marvellous resource for everyone interested in sound and voices. One of the things I found there is a very clear demonstration of clicks. They are among the speech sounds of the Namibian language that the speakers in the video clip call *KhoeKhoegowab*. If you do a search on that term in YouTube you will find a set of language lessons. The clicks are demonstrated in 'Lesson No: 1'.

KhoeKhoegowab is an alternative name for the language otherwise known as Nama or Nàmá, and formerly known as Hottentot. It is a national language in Namibia, with a quarter of a million speakers.

The video brings out the differences between the four click types very clearly.

First there is the dental affricated click, Nama spelling /. This is the same as the click spelt *c* in Zulu and Xhosa, and in IPA written ǀ (formerly ʇ). Then there is the retroflex or (post)alveolar click, with an abrupt release, Nama !, Zulu-Xhosa *q*, IPA ! (ɡ). It has a lower-pitched resonance than the alveolar (so-called 'palatoalveolar') click, also with abrupt release, Nama #, IPA ǂ, which is not found in Zulu-Xhosa. Lastly we have the alveolar lateral affricated click, Nama //, Zulu-Xhosa *x*, IPA ǁ (ʖ).

For #, printed books often write ≠ (the doesn't-equal sign).
From the example sentence in the clip of Lesson 1 –

/khim !nu #hab //ga

– it seems that the language has not only plain clicks (voiceless, unaspirated, probably with an accompanying glottal stop) but also aspirated (/kh), nasalized (!n) and voiced (//g) – though the last-named doesn't always sound very voiced here. The click in the third word, #hab, sounds to me breathy-voiced and nasal, as if it were Zulu ng# (i.e. the pulmonic-air part sounds like that of the Zulu breathy-voiced nasalized clicks ngc, ngq, ngx – Zulu doesn't have #); however it is also described as involving a 'voiceless nasal with delayed aspiration'.

7.8   an impossible sound

In the 1949 edition of *The Principles of the International Phonetic Association* one of the IPA symbols listed is ʞ, defined as standing for a velar click.

This definition is repeated in the current Unicode standard, where ʞ, code point U+029E, LATIN SMALL LETTER TURNED K, is glossed as 'proposed for velar click'. The Unicode standard continues, 'withdrawn by IPA in 1970'.

Correct, though I suspect the date is wrong. In fact ʞ had disappeared from the IPA chart by 1951, though not from the *Principles* booklet.

And why was this symbol dropped? One answer is that no language had been found to have the velar click as one of its sounds. But the real reason is that a velar click is anatomically impossible.

By the 1960s we understood non-pulmonic airstreams better than our predecessors did. We knew that clicks are made with an ingressive velaric airstream mechanism, involving a closure between the back of the tongue and the velum (as in k). Since this closure is used to separate off the mouth cavity from the pharynx ready for initiation of the air flow, it cannot simultaneously be used for a velar velaric articulation. As well as the velar closure, clicks must have some closure forward of the velar place, involving therefore the front/blade/tip/side of the tongue or the lips. Muscular expansion of the cavity between the two closures provides the suction needed to make a click on release.

What you can have simultaneously with a click is a velar articulation involving a non-velaric airstream mechanism, typically a pulmonic one. That is why clicks can be nasal (simultaneous ŋ rather than k), voiced (simultaneous g), etc. Indeed, one way of checking that a sound is a click is to see whether you can do ŋ simultaneously with it: if you can, it's a click.

As Pullum and Ladusaw put it in their discussion of ʞ (*Phonetic Symbol Guide*, University of Chicago Press 1996, second edition, p. 101):

> The IPA's recommendation was simply a mistake, and the symbol could never be validly used. It was dropped from the IPA chart with the 1979 revision.

7.9   fricative trill, trill fricative

It's one of the rarest sounds in the world's languages. There may well be no language other than Czech that has it. I'm referring, of course, to the fricative trill, orthographically ř, which we all know through the name of the composer *Dvořák* (go to Wikipedia to listen to a sound file with the pronunciation of this name.)

In 1945 the IPA adopted the symbol ɼ to represent this sound, a voiced alveolar fricative trill. The composer's name could then be transcribed ˈdvoɼaːk.

One of the decisions made at the IPA's Kiel Convention in 1989 was to withdraw recognition from this symbol. The IPA members voting at the Convention took the view that it was adequate to use the ordinary symbol **r** (voiced alveolar trill) together with the 'raised' diacritic to show the closer, hence fricative, articulation.

So in the *Handbook of the IPA* (Cambridge University Press 1999) you will find the Czech consonant written as r̝. *Dvořák* is now ˈdvor̝aːk.

Some people say they regret this decision, and I am half inclined to agree with them, though it does seem an unnecessary luxury to have a special symbol needed only for one language. (But compare Swedish ɧ.)

The fricative trill also occurs voiceless, though only as a positional allophone after voiceless consonants (*tři* 'three') and word-finally (*pekař* 'baker'). Both with the old symbol and with the new one there is a problem about transcribing this variant (if you feel you need to). There's no room for a voiceless diacritic underneath, so it has to go on top: r̝̊.

Bill Lee's *Teach Yourself Czech* (English Universities Press 1964) offers excellent pronunciation advice to the learner. See also the *Handbook of the IPA*.

7.10   all the speech sounds in the world

The emails I receive about phonetics range from the very naïve to the very sophisticated. Sometimes it is difficult to know which is which. One correspondent writes:

> I am particularly keen to know where I could find a single list that would include all the sounds found in all the languages. Does such a list exist?

Is my correspondent a beginner who should be advised to consult a textbook of general phonetics, e.g. Peter Ladefoged's *Vowels and Consonants* (Blackwell 2001), or, even better, to enrol for a course in general phonetics?

Or is this a serious question for which a serious answer might be sought in Maddieson and Ladefoged, *Sounds of the World's Languages* (Blackwell 1996)?

I replied, I hope helpfully, that an obvious starting point would be the International Phonetic Alphabet.

But I think a qualified phonetician would not have asked the question in this way unless putting on an act of being naïve. There is a difficulty not always appreciated by non-specialists: you can't enumerate 'sounds'. This is because there is no real way to say whether sounds are 'the same' or 'different' except with reference to a specific language or dialect. For example, English /t/ is by default a voiceless aspirated alveolar plosive, Dutch /t/ is ditto but unaspirated, Swedish /t/ is aspirated but dental and French /t/ is both unaspirated and dental. So depending on language /t/ may by default be aspirated or unaspirated, alveolar or dental.

Once we start to add in allophonic variation within a language, the difficulty is multiplied. Sometimes English /t/ is not voiceless, sometimes it is not aspirated, sometimes it is not alveolar (in certain positions it can be dental or glottal), and sometimes it is not even plosive.

So how many 'sounds' are we dealing with here? For everyday purposes, they are all transcribed with the same **t** symbol, because we apply a principle of transcriptional simplicity. But in a sense they are all different.

The English **l** phoneme comprises two sounds (two allophones), as we know. The clear **l** is clear (= has a palatal resonance, sort of), but not as clear as the German **l** and nothing like as clear as the Russian 'soft' **lʲ**; the place is alveolar, i.e. retracted from what we might think of as the cardinal dental position, but not as retracted as that of the Korean **l**. Factor in the various l-sounds of thousands of other languages: how many l-sounds are there altogether?

Even if you start with a list of the 109 alphabetic IPA symbols plus 33 stress, length and tone marks or thereabouts, there are still 32 diacritics that can be applied to the alphabetic characters to symbolize secondary articulations and various other attributes. Sometimes more than one diacritic can be applied to the same base. The combinatorial explosion makes it unrealistic to attempt to count the resulting 'sounds'. And we haven't even started on voiced or nasalized clicks, double articulations, affricates and diphthongs, all of which can be represented in IPA by combining two alphabetic symbols with a tie bar, but are arguably single 'sounds'.

7.11   WALS

If you want to follow up the question of the range of vowels and consonants to be found in the world's languages, you can now access WALS (the *World Atlas of Language Structures*) online at wals.info. You can read the entire text of each chapter and look at all the maps. The size of the consonant inventory in a language is revealed as ranging from 6 to 122, the record holder being !Xóõ, a Southern Khoisan language of Botswana, which has 122 consonants, mainly because it has a very large number of different click sounds with which a word may begin. Most languages, though, have 20–25. Vowel inventories range from 2 to 14, with an average of 5 or 6. The record holder here is German. That's among the languages included in the WALS sample, and using its criteria for analysis. (There are difficulties in deciding how to treat long vowels and diphthongs when determining how many 'vowels' a language has; after all, for EFL purposes we usually consider 'British English' to have 20 or so.)

7.12   IPA in a logo

The city of Szczecin in Poland got itself a snazzy new logo incorporating an IPA transcription of the name as ʃʃʃɛˈʧin.

This provoked the local paper to ask *Czy nasze miasto nazywamy SzczeCIN?* (Do we call our city SzczeCIN?)

Answer: no, you don't. You call it *SZCZEcin*. Like almost all other Polish words this name is stressed on the penultimate.

This could be a delicate matter, since before the Second World War the city was in Germany and called by the German name *Stettin* ʃtɛˈtiːn, which is indeed stressed on the last syllable. But now it's part of Poland, and is called by its Polish name, which is stressed on the penultimate.

It was a nice idea to use eye-catching IPA symbols as the main content of the logo, with the usual orthographic form written very small underneath. But what a funny transcription!

I have touched elsewhere (3.20 above) on the question of the Polish *sz, cz, ś, ć* and how to transcribe them. (The letter *c* before *i*, as in *Szczecin*, is pronounced like *ć*.) Pretty well everybody agrees on writing the latter two, the alveolopalatals, as ɕ, tɕ. The former two, postalveolars, are usually written simply as ʃ, tʃ, though you could argue for ʂ, tʂ.

What I have never seen before is the use of diacritics for apical and palatalized applied to the basic palatoalveolar symbols. I don't think they are needed here.

We can argue about whether the first vowel is best written with the simple symbol e or the comparative symbol ɛ. We can argue about whether or not we ought to use tie bars with the affricates to show that they're not plosive-fricative sequences. We can agree that the stress mark ought to be in the right place, showing initial stress.

Me? I would write the simple ˈʃtʃetɕin. That's if I wanted to transcribe the Polish pronunciation. The nearest we can get in English is ˈʃtʃetʃiːn.

7.13   frozen in Italian

Pronouncing Italian words is fairly straightforward, as long as you know where the stress goes.

All too often, the classical music commercial radio announcers don't.

More than once I have heard them say *Che gelida manina* with the stress in *gelida* on the -*li*- instead of on the *ge*-.

If you watch or listen to this aria being sung (try YouTube), you can hear the correct stress. It's **ke ˈdʒelida maˈnina**. It has the same rhythm as its English version *your ˈtiny hand is ˈfrozen*. Duh!

In Latin we have adjectives *ˈacidus, ˈgelidus, ˈrapidus, ˈsolidus*. The suffix *-id-* has a short vowel, therefore stress goes on the antepenultimate. Correspondingly, in Italian (and also in Spanish) it's *ácido, gélido, rápido, sólido*; in English *acid, gelid, rapid, solid* **ˈæsɪd, ˈdʒelɪd, ˈræpɪd, ˈsɒlɪd**. I could go on: it's just the same for the Latin and Italian words corresponding to English *avid, horrid, liquid, rigid, splendid, valid* and many others. Where's the problem? Why would anyone suppose that the stress fell on a different vowel in Italian?

Perhaps the French that we British learn at school is to blame. Although French *acide, rapide, solide*, etc. in theory have no word stress, in practice we treat them as having final stress: **aˈsid, raˈpid, sɔˈlid**. Taken over into Italian, this could be the source of the announcer's mistake. (The actual item **gelide* seems to have been lost in French: they say *gelé*.)

And by the way it's *Plácido* Domingo.

7.14   ugh!

All good students of phonetics learn to recognize and perform a close back unrounded vowel, **ɯ**.

But because it is perceived by most of them as a very strange and exotic sound they tend to overarticulate it: tense jaw muscles, tensely spread lips, extra length, grimace.

Those in whose language it occurs, on the other hand, naturally treat it as a perfectly ordinary and everyday sound. They pronounce it in quite a relaxed way.

As far as the languages I have come into contact with are concerned, that means speakers of Korean or of Scottish Gaelic. In both of these languages it contrasts with a close back rounded **u**.

The Korean word for 'writing, a piece of writing' exemplifies this vowel: it is 글 **kɯl** (or you might prefer to show the initial consonant as a devoiced g̊). Of the two competing romanizations of Korean, one represents the word as *geul*, the other as *kŭl*.

You usually get something similar for the close back vowel of Japanese. But that's not so good for demonstration purposes, since Japanese has no contrast of rounding.

In Scottish Gaelic both long and short **ɯ** occur, in contrast (7.1 above). Thus for the long vowel we have, for example:

caol **kɯːɫ** (narrow)
saor **sɯːr** (free)
laogh **ɬɯːɣ** (calf)
aois **ɯːʃ** (age)
faoin **fɯːɲ** (silly)

and for the short:

uisge ɯʃɡ̊ɪ (water – the etymon of *whisky*)
uiseag ɯʃaɡ̊ (lark).

7.15   Icelandic

Iceland's financial difficulties brought the name *Kaupthing* to our television screens and newspapers. Its Icelandic spelling is however *Kaupþing*, which includes the special letter *þ* (thorn). None of our newspapers attempts to reproduce this character. Even the bank itself writes its name with *th* outside Iceland: *KAUPÞING* at home, *KAUPTHING* abroad.

The sound corresponding to *þ* is a voiceless dental fricative, θ. Icelandic orthography also has *ð*, with the same sound as in IPA, ð. I believe that these are in complementary distribution, with the letter *þ* used morpheme-initially and *ð* elsewhere, and the two sounds likewise (except that phrase-medial function words can have initial ð, spelt *þ*).

It is remarkably difficult to find a good account of Icelandic phonetics in English. I have a book-length description in Icelandic, *Hljóðfræði*, by Árni Böðvarsson (Reykjavík: Ísafoldarprentsmiðja 1979), which the author, now dead, gave me on the occasion of my visit to his country in 1988, but I can't say that I can actually read it. Fortunately he also gave me his Esperanto booklet *Islanda lingvo* (Reykjavík: Islanda Esperanto-Asocio 1977), which furnishes the most comprehensive account that I can understand.

When we did Icelandic in my informant class at UCL the sounds that people found most interesting were the nasals and liquids devoiced (i) before voiceless consonants, as in *verk* 'work' with r̥, and (ii) in final position after a consonant, as in *vatn* 'water' with n̥ and *fugl* 'bird' with l̥. Another tricky consonant is the laterally released voiceless alveolar affricate tɬ spelt *ll*, as in *fjall* 'mountain'.

7.16   wie war das?

As I finished checking in to my Berlin hotel, the receptionist asked me *Möchten Sie* ˈveːlan? 'Would you like [something not understood]?'

The nearest word that I could think of here was *wählen* ˈvɛːlən 'to choose', but that didn't seem to make much sense.

It turns out what she had said was *W-LAN*, the German for Wi-Fi, the facility for connecting a laptop to the internet wirelessly. So having sorted that out I said yes, please.

Wi-Fi is one of those computery words that I expected, evidently wrongly, to be international, borrowed by every language you come across; but it isn't. I gather that it is actually a proprietary trade name. According to the German

Wikipedia, it doesn't stand for 'wireless fidelity', as you might think. It is a name (a *Kunstbegriff*) invented merely for marketing purposes.

I also discovered that the Germans believe their terms *Handy* and *USB stick* to be (i) English and (ii) international. But the first is what we Brits call a mobile and the Americans a cellphone. The second is normally known, in Britain at any rate, as a memory stick or a memory key or a flash drive or a thumb drive: we can't agree on just what to call it, but 'USB stick' is not one of the options.

7.17   simplicity

We normally transcribe the English word *red* as **red**.

But there are two things here that worry some people. First, they argue, the initial consonant is a voiced postalveolar approximant and should therefore be written ɹ. Second, the vowel is lax (short) and should therefore be written ɛ.

Let us take first the question of how to transcribe the initial consonant. It can indeed be narrowly represented as ɹ. That would be an appropriate 'impressionistic' transcription.

However, in the old IPA *Principles* booklet (1949) we read:

> 27. (a) ... it is desirable to substitute more familiar consonant letters for less familiar ones ...

> (e) The letter **r** may, when convenient, replace ɹ, ʀ or ʁ in the transcription of a language containing one of these sounds but not a rolled lingual **r** ...

[Note to the young: until quite recently, to substitute A for B always meant to use A instead of B, not the other way round.]

This idea was put most clearly by David Abercrombie in his *English Phonetic Texts* (Faber 1964, pp. 17–18).

> A simple phonemic transcription uses letters of the simplest possible shapes. This is a typographical principle: the simplest shapes are the most familiar, the most typographically satisfactory.

He goes on to say that ŋ ʒ ɯ ʌ are less simple, because less 'romanic', more exotic, than the traditional letters of the alphabet.

> The conventions and traditions of the IPA often allow, for the representation of a particular sound, a choice between two or more different letters. In these cases where such a choice exists, one of the letters will usually be found to be more romanic ... than the alternative.

Somehow this principle of simplicity seems to have got dropped from the current *IPA Handbook*, but I believe it is still valid. It immediately justifies the use of **r** rather than ɹ and **e** rather than ɛ for English.

In the case of the vowel, there is the further point that, as the *IPA Handbook* itself mentions (p. 30):

the vowel phoneme of *get* in Standard Southern British English has allophones, according to phonetic environment, which mostly lie between the
cardinal vowels [e] and [ɛ], some realizations being close to one and some
to the other. It is therefore permissible to choose either symbol as the one to
represent the phoneme.

Since the DRESS vowel can be unambiguously written **e**, an English transcription
with the symbol **e** is simpler than one with **ɛ**. The same applies in those languages
that have just five vowels (or just five peripheral vowels), such as Modern Greek,
Serbian, Polish, Czech and Japanese. In these languages the mid front vowel is
best, and most simply, written **e**. Whether its quality is closer to that of cardinal
2 [e] or cardinal 3 [ɛ] is irrelevant. On the other hand, in languages that have a
close-mid front vowel in contrast to an open-mid one (e.g. French, German, a
Scottish accent of English), the two symbols **e** and **ɛ** must both be used; and
that means **ɛ** for French *même*, German *Bett* and Scottish *dress*.

There is not some great phoneme system in the sky from which particular
languages select their phonemes, with one IPA symbol always standing for the
same thing. Languages differ. We use the symbol **t** for the aspirated alveolar
plosive of English and the unaspirated dental plosive of Russian because it is
simpler to do so. We use the same symbol **l** for the clear alveolar lateral of
German, the variably coloured alveolar lateral of English, and the retracted
postalveolar lateral of Korean, because it is simpler to do that than to festoon
the transcription with diacritics. It is better to state such information in the
conventions that accompany a phonetic transcription rather than in the transcription itself. In a language that distinguishes dental and alveolar (or postalveolar)
plosives, we obviously need to symbolize their place of articulation explicitly,
by distinguishing plain **t** from **t̪** and/or **ʈ**. In a language that doesn't, we don't.

Nevertheless, people do quite often query the convention whereby I (and
various other phoneticians) write the DRESS vowel as **e**.

7.18   Calon lân

Some of the emails that come to me out of the blue are difficult to
know how to reply to. One correspondent asked simply 'Have you any idea
where I can obtain a phonetic version of the Welsh song *calon lan* please?'

I should explain that *Calon lân* ('A pure heart') is a well-known Welsh
hymn, often sung for example at international rugby matches. Unlike, say,
Cwm Rhondda, which is often sung in English under similar circumstances
('Guide me, O thou great Jehovah'), *Calon lân* is always sung in Welsh, even
in the non-Welsh-speaking parts of Wales, perhaps because it has no established
English translation.

Welsh spelling is extremely regular. If you know the spelling-to-sound correspondences, you can just read a written Welsh text out, sound by sound, with only
very occasional uncertainties or exceptions.

My correspondent probably didn't know this, or didn't know what the spelling-to-sound correspondences are. Otherwise he wouldn't have been asking for a transcription of a particular text.

It's also possible that he was not familiar with phonetic symbols, either. If he were he would probably not have asked for a phonetic *version* but a phonetic *transcription*. (People sometimes ask for a phonetic *translation*, which is even more confused.)

It may be, then, that what he wants is a guide to the pronunciation using English spelling conventions. Since Welsh contains both consonants and vowels unknown in English, this is not a satisfactory way of proceeding. I suppose it might begin *need oo-in govin buh-wid moythis*, but already we are up against the problem of how to represent the Welsh stressed schwa in an open syllable. The second line, perhaps *ire uh beed nye behr-lye mahn*, brings us up against the problem of how to write **aj** (**ai**) unambiguously, and how to show **er** in a way that won't be read as **ɜ:**.

So here is the first verse in orthography and in IPA.

> *Nid wy'n gofyn bywyd moethus,*
> *Aur y byd na'i berlau mân;*
> *Gofyn rwyf am galon hapus,*
> *Calon onest, calon lân.*
> *Calon lân yn llawn daioni,*
> *Tecach yw na'r lili dlos;*
> *Dim ond calon lân all ganu,*
> *Canu'r dydd a chanu'r nos.*

> **nid ujn govin bəwid mojθis**
> **air ə bid naj berlaj maːn**
> **govin rujv am galon hapis**
> **kalon onest kalon laːn**
> **kalon laːn ən ɫawn dajoni**
> **tekax iw nar lili dlos**
> **dim ond kalon laːn aɫ gaːni**
> **kaːnir dið a xaːnir nos**

There are several excellent recorded versions of this hymn available. Take your pick of Kathryn Jenkins, the Welsh rugby team, Bryn Terfel and others. There are occasional minor differences in the wording (e.g. Bryn Terfel sings *Does ond* rather than *Dim ond*) and various phonetic differences reflecting local pronunciation (e.g. Kathryn Jenkins pronounces *rwyf* as if spelt *royf*, cf. *llwyd* becoming the English name *Lloyd*).

In the refrain, it is interesting to note the successive mutations of the word for 'sing', which appears not only as *canu* (its basic form), but also as *ganu* (soft mutation) and as *chanu* (so-called aspirate mutation, i.e. with its initial plosive changed to a fricative).

7.19   Ystrad Mynach

There's a village near Caerphilly in south Wales called Ystrad Mynach. In a national news bulletin, I heard BBC announcers call it ˌʌstrəd ˈmʌnəx, as recommended by the BBC Pronunciation Unit.

Phonetically, the name is an interesting mixture of English and Welsh. In standard Welsh it would be ˌəstrad ˈmənax, with strong vowels in the final syllable of each word. In Welsh, vowels do not get weakened as in English, and in particular you never get schwa in the final syllable of a content word. You do, however, frequently get schwa in stressed syllables.

So the anglicization involves weakening of the final vowels, as well as the usual mapping of Welsh stressed schwa onto the STRUT vowel (which in south Wales English is pretty schwa-like anyhow). But it does not extend to the replacement of **x** by an English consonant.

Outsiders, though, would surely change **x** to **k**. And outsiders wouldn't know how to treat the Welsh spelling *y* (which in proclitics and non-final syllables stands for schwa). They would probably say something like ˌɪstrəd ˈmɪnək. So due credit to the BBC announcers for getting it right.

Ystrad, by the way, is the Welsh equivalent of the Gaelic *srath* that we know from Scottish place names such as *Strathclyde* (*Srath Chluaidh*, Welsh *Ystrad Clud*). *Mynach* means 'monk' (< Latin *monachus*): so on the face of it the whole name means Monk's Vale. However, there appears to be no former monastery nearby, and experts tell us that the name may actually be derived from some lost personal name.

Postscript

Where did my interest in phonetics come from?

I have always been interested in languages, and particularly in pronunciation. I started French at school at about eight years of age, then Latin from age nine and Ancient Greek from age twelve. For my twelfth birthday I asked my parents to give me an Italian-English dictionary, since I had started to teach myself a little Italian. I passed my O level exams in French, Latin and Greek at age fourteen, and my A levels in Latin and Greek at age sixteen. That same year, once my exams were out of the way, I decided to teach myself Esperanto, which soon became my best language after English.

Seeing my interest in languages, my parents made the far-sighted decision when I left school at eighteen to arrange an exchange with a German family. I stayed in Kiel with the family for six weeks, followed by six weeks for their son with us in England. I was determined to make good use of this, my first trip abroad, learning German ab initio by total immersion. My exchange partner, Klaus, took very seriously the task of ensuring that by the time I came back to England I could speak fluent German. I can see in hindsight that I also picked up excellent German pronunciation habits.

So by the time I became an undergraduate at Trinity College Cambridge I had a thorough knowledge of Latin and Greek, reasonable ability in French, and good though non-literary fluency in German – oh, and fluency in Esperanto.

For the last year of the Classical Tripos at Cambridge I chose to specialize in language. This meant comparative philology, plus some general linguistics and (optionally) an introduction to phonetics. The phonetics teacher was John Trim. He taught us to recognize and produce most of the sounds represented on the IPA chart, together with their articulatory classification. We learnt to transcribe English and to make ejectives, implosives, clicks and cardinal vowels. I was hooked.

In summer 1960, aged twenty-one, I was fortunate enough to win a travel grant, which enabled me to visit Greece and see the antiquities in Athens, Delphi, Mycenae, Delos, Knossos and elsewhere. The grant covered my return ticket to Piraeus by train and boat, but little else. I toured around in Greece, living very simply and of course doing my best to speak and understand Modern Greek. I stayed in youth hostels and in private rooms, hitch-hiking and island-hopping by ferry. (This was before the days of mass tourism in Greece. At the time very few Greeks spoke English.)

The next academic year, following Trim's advice, I moved to University College London to pursue a master's degree in general linguistics and phonetics. Among my teachers were A.C. Gimson, J.D. O'Connor, Dennis Fry and Adrian Fourcin. I did a course in French phonetics, taught in French by Hélène Coustenoble and Marguérite Chapallaz, and visited SOAS for linguistics with R.H. Robins. I could not have asked for better teachers. At the end of the two-year master's course UCL offered me the post of Assistant Lecturer in Phonetics. I jumped at the offer, and was accordingly able to spend my entire career teaching phonetics at UCL, doing the subject I loved.

I took my PhD in 1971, exploring the phonetic adjustments Jamaican immigrants in London made to their English pronunciation in response to their new circumstances. At UCL I also frequented the English department, benefiting from the teaching of Randolph Quirk, and the linguistics department, under Michael Halliday.

Later on I enrolled for an Introduction to Zulu course at SOAS. (But it was not until 2013 that I actually visited South Africa for the first time and could try out as much as I remembered of what I had learnt of that phonetically very interesting language.) I also enrolled for courses in Modern Greek and Welsh at City Lit in central London. Meanwhile, Esperanto had taken me to many different countries in Europe, where I regularly tried to find out about the pronunciation of the local language – Polish, Dutch, Swedish or whatever.

One of the courses I most enjoyed teaching at UCL was a practical class working on ten or twelve different languages each year, using a native speaker to demonstrate words and phrases which the students and I would then analyse phonetically, transcribe and reproduce. This gave me a good knowledge of the phonetics (if not much else) of languages as varied as Modern Standard Chinese, Japanese, Korean, Arabic, Polish, Spanish, Portuguese, Danish and Icelandic.

The only language I learnt thoroughly in adulthood was Welsh, which I continued to study in evening classes in London up to A level standard.

It was marvellous being in a university department along with half a dozen or more other phoneticians, with whom one could always argue about phonetics and discuss this or that problem. Teaching students phonetics was always a pleasure, too – particularly postgraduate (research) students whose dissertations I had to supervise. We also had many excellent academic visitors over the years, a stimulus for new directions in my own research.

You can perhaps see why when I retired in 2006 I felt the lack of regular phonetic discussions with students and colleagues. That is the reason I started my phonetic blog, in which I could discuss phonetics with the world and conduct a dialogue with the many followers who commented on what I had written. This volume, as I mentioned in the Preface, is based on some of my postings there.

Index of words

affect, 55
albatross, 68
Alcester, 8
amiodarone, 13
analogous, 147
angrily, 57
Antigua, 7, 167
apostate, 34
artisanal, 3
athlete, 44
aubergine, 160
Audi, 19

balcony, 68
bandied, 54
Beijing, 37, 150
Berlins, 29
bevy, bevvy, 151
Birmingham, 83
Blaengwrach, 27
bleeding, 118
Bournemouth, 67
Braun, 19
Burgh, 8

C. diff, 4
calendar, 176
Campbell, 23
cannot, 49
cervical, 7
Chagos, 11
character, 176
Charon, 10
chorizo, 189
Christmas, 69
code-share, 74
crazies, 53
Cretan, Cretian, 26
Cymru, 16

data processing, 70
definitely, 155
deity, 11
diaspora, 48
digoxin, 147
diocese, 6

diplodocus, 48
diploma, 47
divorce, 72
doh, d'oh, duh, 25
Dominica, 8
Dvořák, 192

-ed, 56
elevator, 66
England, 44
entombment, 49
Entwistle, 36
escalator, 2
etc., 83

feng shui, 16
fiesta, 45
following, 44
Freixenet, 19
Friern Barnet, 28

gaol, 147
Gauguin, 13
genuine, 42
glorious, 42
gonna, 73
good deal, 49
goodbye, 106
Gwaun-cae-Gurwen, 27

Hamburg, 88
Hamish, 184
Haut de la Garenne, 28
Hawai'i, 145
hello, 31, 105
Hokkaidō, 90
holey, 167
Honshū, 90
horrorshow, 66
hypernymy, 12
Hyundai, 18

i.e., 83
imma, 73
incidence, 71

jaguar, 7
Judea, 11

Kyocera, 18
Kyoto, 45

Lagos, 21
Leatherhead, 23
liege, 21
linguolabial, 140
Llantwit Major, 34
Lloyd, 27
Llwynywormwood, 14
London, 88
Lucida, 32

Machynlleth, 187
Málaga, 88
mange-tout, 160
margarine, 147
marm, 65
Mbabane, 17
meningococcal, 147
meta-analysis, 39
mine, 76
money, 88
mores, 161
Myanmar, 64
Mynd, 27
Mynydd Bach, 27
Mytholmroyd, 31

Nestlé, 19
Newcastle, 31
Nicaragua, 7
Novi Sad, 88
nuclear, 2

omega, 5

Penwortham, 30
percolator, 2
pizza, 189
Placerville, 9
plenty, 63
plethora, 5
Polyfilla, 65
Pontypool, 27
porpoise, 20
Poznań, 88
precede, 12
proceed, 12
prostate, 24
prostrate, 24
pukka, 15
Punjab, 15
purgative, 147
pwn, 35

quantitative, 51

remembrance, 45
repertory, 30
Richter, 15
Rotherhithe, 22
Rothersthorpe, 22
royal, 39

Salida, 8
Sarkozy, 29
sarnie, 65
scarper, 65
schnitzel, 2
sentence, 180
settee, 72
Sexwale, 19
shar pei, 65
shih tzu, 4
silicon, silicone, 24
sloth, 1
some, 58
sphygmomanometer, 51
St John's wort, 148
Sydney, 87
syringa, 147
Szczecin, 194

tart, 94
tattoo, 72
terrorist, 74
thrombolysis, 13
tinnitus, 25
torte, 94
tortoise, 20
trial, 39
twenty, 63

um, 77
unchartered, 55

veg, 147
veterinary, 29
volcano, 86

wanted, 63
Whiskas, 65
wind, 75
Winstanley, 31
wintry, 45
Wolverhampton, 23
wort, 148

Xhosa, 19, 190

ylang-ylang, 16
your, you're, 171

Zheng Jie, 36

General index

abbreviation, 83
accentuation, 115–16, 127
affricate, 143
alveolopalatals, 98, 152
apostrophe, 158
Arabic, 150, 202
Armstrong, Eric, 65, 93
Ashby, Patricia, 149
assimilation, 38
Australian English, 174
Azeri, 144

Bantu, 19
Barry, Martin, 76
Bengali, 178
Bergman, Christopher, 120
Berry, Cecily, 65
Bible, 26, 77, 132
Bigelow, Charles, 33
brand names, 18
Brazil, David, 104
Brown, Gillian, 50
Brown, Gordon, 67
Bulgarian, 46
Burgess, Anthony, 65
Burma, 64

Cantonese, 135
capital letters, 139
cardinal vowels, 83
Caribbean English, 176
Cassidy, Fred, 165
Cauldwell, Richard, 76
Chatterji, Suniti Kumar, 141
Chinese, 36, 65, 88, 202
Chomsky, Noam, 12, 47, 147
Chung, Karen, 95
chunking, 103
clicks, 138, 190
cockney, 70, 178
compound stress, 75, 83
compounds, 70
compression, 39–40
consonant doubling, 151
contrastive stress, 125

counterpresuppositionals, 111
Cowan, John, 74
Cruttenden, Alan, 111
CURE, 171
cynghanedd, 186

Danish, 202
Davidsen-Nielsen, Niels, 73
decompression, 44
degemination, 49
Deterding, David, 68
devoicing, 90
dictation, 82
Dutch, 149, 193, 202

Edwards, Ernest, 97
elision, 90
empty words, 109
English as a lingua franca, 94
epiglottals, 84
Esperanto, 155, 201
Estuary English, 173, 178
eszett, 163
ezh, 150

fall-rise, 108, 171
Figueroa-Clark, Martha, 187
fillers, 77
French, 13, 95, 98, 201
fronting, 69

gemination, 48
German, 13, 19, 75, 88, 114, 120, 122, 128, 188,
   193, 201
Gimson, A.C., 39, 73, 202
glottal stop, 146, 177
GOAT, 44–5, 85, 171
Grand Turk, 176
Greek, 35, 39, 47, 201

Halliday, Michael, 104, 202
Hannisdal, Bente, 171
haplology, 51
happY, 52–3, 56
Hausa, 151

Hawai'ian, 90
hesitation, 77
Hindi, 15
Hirst, Daniel, 135
homographs, 75
Hungarian, 30
Hymns, 56
hyphen, 139

Icelandic, 202
idioms, 120
insists, 112
intonation, 31, 103
intonation phrase (IP), 103, 107, 134
intrusive r, 38
IPA Chart, 83, 201
Irish, 23
Irish English, 169
Italian, 194, 201

Jamaican Creole, 178, 202
Japanese, 45, 66, 202
Jenkins, Jennifer, 154
Jersey, 28
Johnson, Samuel, 156
Jones, Daniel, 44, 143

k-backing, 179
Kera, 139
Kerswill, Paul, 178
Kjellin, Olle, 84
Korean, 193, 202
Kotercová, Zuzana, 161

labiodental flap, 136
Latin, 10, 35, 47, 133, 150, 156, 161, 201
lenition, 169
lexical stress, 62
lexicographers, 156
LPD, 29, 159

Murphy, Lynne, 74
macron, 152
malapropisms, 24
Mandarin, 16, 84
Montserrat, 86, 170, 183–4
mora, 90

Nadsat, 65
Nama, 138, 190
neutralization, 53, 55
New Zealand, 68, 101
Nguni, 17
non-rhotic, 170
nt reduction, 64
nucleus, 103–4
numerals, 33

O'Connor, J.D., 104, 202
ogonek, 169
Omnish, 94

palatalization, 153
Panglish, 154
Panjabi, 15
Papiamento, 190
pharyngeals, 84
Phillips, Zara, 168
phrasal verbs, 123
Polish, 84, 88, 98, 188, 194, 202
politeness, 107
Portuguese, 154, 202
postalveolars, 98
prefixes, 56
Prince Harry, 169
pronoun, 130
prosodic marks, 145
pseudo-elision, 72

Quirk, Randolph, 39, 202

R sandhi, 172
reading rules, 85
reduction, 50
respelling, 157
retraction, 142
retroflex sounds, 142
Romanian, 46
Rösel, Petr, 70, 100
RP, 171
rule of three, 126
Russian, 55, 66, 88

San Serriffe, 140
schwa, 46, 54, 143
Scots, 150
Scottish Gaelic, 23, 150
Seidlhofer, Barbara, 155
Self, Will, 174
Serbian, 88, 188
Shockey, Linda, 50
sibilants, 159
siSwati, 17
Slovak, 189
smoothing, 40
Southern British English, 68
Spanish, 21, 45, 202
spelling, 161
Spelling Society, 149, 165
St Martin, 189
St Thomas, 190
Stoller, Amy, 187
stranding, 58
stress, 60
stress shift, 32, 125

STRUT, 60
Swedish, 84, 120, 202
syllabic consonants, 41, 180
syllabification, 36, 143
syllable structure, 89
system, 106

T voicing, 171
Taiwan, 95
Teutonic Rule, 18, 60
TH fronting, 23
THOUGHT, 85
tonality, 103, 107, 119
tone, 103–4
Tongan, 146
tonicity, 106–7, 121, 131
transcription, 82
Trim, John, 201
Tswana, 152
Turkish, 189

Ulster, 101
unaspirated consonants, 88

Unicode, 104, 136, 139, 141, 150,
    152–3, 163
Upton, Clive, 46
Urdu, 15

velar softening, 147
Venda, 19

Wales, 93
Ward, Dennis, 152
weakening, 52–3
Welsh, 5, 13–14, 16, 27, 184, 186–7,
    202
Wesley, Charles, 41
Williams Parry, R., 186
Windsor Lewis, Jack, 41, 50, 149,
    187
word boundaries, 42

yod coalescence, 172
yogh, 150

Zulu, 138, 188, 190, 202